A deep and thought-provoking invitation to truly experience beauty as a way of life. *The Beauty Chasers* gives permission and direction to seek the beauty we long for. This book will forever change your perspective on the vital role of beauty in your everyday life, just like it did in mine.

MYQUILLYN SMITH, *New York Times*
bestselling author of *Welcome Home*

Timothy Willard is a writer's writer. If this book doesn't light your fire, your wood is wet.

SEAN DIETRICH, "Sean of the South," author
of *Will the Circle Be Unbroken*

Tim is my go-to source to learn what God calls beautiful. Not only has he studied beauty, but he writes beautifully. This book captures the imagination while guiding the reader along a journey of spiritual discovery and renewal. If you're like me, always on the lookout for books that will inspire while also giving you time to catch my breath before God, then you will love *The Beauty Chasers*.

ESTHER FLEECE ALLEN, bestselling author of
No More Faking Fine and *Your New Name*

The Beauty Chasers is Tim Willard in book form. Though it falls into the category of spiritual formation, *The Beauty Chasers* is something entirely new—a book I think we all need as we move through the world today and seek out beauty in the midst of suffering, violence, and our everyday problems and stresses. A guidebook of sorts, *The Beauty Chasers* inspires me to find the beauty that's already present around me. It's not a beauty that's skin deep or found on our phones; instead, this kind of true beauty is an overflow of our relationship with God. Seeking it out is a challenge I'm excited to continue in my own life, and I thank Tim for giving me the tools I didn't know I needed in order to find beauty, not just on vacation or special occasions, but on the most average of Mondays.

ADAM WEBER, lead pastor of Embrace Church, author of
Love has a Name and host of *The Conversation Podcast*

Tim is an expert for our times. Even before the world became more aware of its need to be awakened out of media-induced malaise, Tim was a student of beauty and its power to revive the human soul. The message in these pages is not one I can merely read but have to share: there is hope for even these days. With rich storytelling and prose, Tim gives us the guide to recapture the wonder we all need right now.

SARA HAGERTY, bestselling author of *Unseen*,
ADORE, and *Every Bitter Thing Is Sweet*

This book is a whimsical, meandering journey into a vast and (mostly) unexplored geography: the world of beauty. What is it? Why are we drawn to it? What are the ramifications for us as a society if we misrepresent or squander it? Tim Willard, willing and eager, ushers us into this vast expanse with stories and conversations and exposition, leaving us finally with the belief that there is so much more to the world than the material things we can see—and this is good.

SHAWN SMUCKER, award-winning author of *The Weight of Memory*

Tim's book is a radiant invitation not just to learn about beauty, but to live it; to taste and be transformed by God's loveliness in a radical and restorative way. Tim is a kind and experienced guide who offers his readers the vision they need to undergo a transformative journey, to read the signs and understand the times, but he's also a friend who comes along, helping them step-by-step into a wide and wondrous way of living. This book is a gift.

SARAH CLARKSON, author of *This Beautiful Truth*

Tim writes with rare beauty and soul, like the great ones before him. C. S. Lewis. Frederick Buechner. Eugene Peterson. His new book, *The Beauty Chasers*, calls us away from shallow distractions and to a deeper life.

JOHN SOWERS, author of *Say All the Unspoken Things*

I'm obsessed with Tim's way of seeing the world. It convicts me and nourishes me all at the same time. We've never needed a book as much as we need this book right now. I'm sitting down and I'm listening. This book is helping me "see when the world goes blind." Thank you, Tim, for nudging us a little closer home.

DR. EDIE WADSWORTH, author of *All the Pretty Things*

Tim Willard has invited us into a thrilling exploration of a long-neglected aspect of God's glory. Often, God is gazed upon from one dimension, a dimension that can seem distant. Willard exposes the reality of God's majesty and places us in a multi-dimensional world of his beautiful creation, where his voice rings closer, clearer, and more personal. It's not a page-turner, it's a page-stopper. You will find yourself pausing to ponder, reflect, and smile at the insightful message *The Beauty Chasers* calls us to. *The Beauty Chasers* journeys us to adoration, thankfulness, wonder, and awe. It leads to worship!

JASON ELAM, NFL placekicker 1993–2009, author of the
Riley Covington Series, and special ambassador to the
Bible Translation illumiNations Global Movement

If you think beauty is something extra or optional, if you think it's the cherry on top of life or a gift reserved only for those with more money or more time than you, you must read Timothy Willard's inspiring book. I love the folksy cadence of his storytelling. I love the surprising theological insights. I love how he weaves in the voices of so many philosophers and artists. *The Beauty Chasers* will open the eyes of your heart, soul, and mind until you become exactly what it describes: a fully alive human being chasing beauty with everything you've got.

CHRISTIE PURIFOY, author of *Placemaker* and *Garden Maker*

Wrestling to communicate the transcendent beauty within my darkest memories was where I met Timothy Willard. Thank God that Tim wrote *The Beauty Chasers* in such distracted and despairing times, to share his own heavenly joy and revive our tired souls. This book will remind you to be in awe and wonder, to laugh and cry over the transforming song of beauty all around you.

LACEY STURM, cofounder of the platinum-selling rock band
Flyleaf, solo rock artist, and author of *The Return*

The Beauty Chasers is the book our souls need right now. It's one to linger over and return to, so keep it close. The power of these pages is that the life painted within them isn't just for the writer, the poet, or the naturally creative; it's for all of us. You'll be led into a place of spiritual gratitude, awe, and insight through Tim's stories from his days in Oxford, conversations between the likes of Moses and C. S. Lewis, and his accessible theological teaching. I feel nourished, uplifted, challenged, and led into a world I've been living in but can finally see.

LEAH BODEN, author of *Modern Miss Mason*

Looking up from the heads-down busyness of life can be tough for me, so I am always looking for ways to refocus. *The Beauty Chasers* is just the type of book to help, and Tim Willard is the perfect guide. He takes us on a slow path towards finding God in new and imaginative ways. Along the way, Willard encourages us to let the pressures of the world fall away and to accept God's invitation to a life-changing adventure in chasing beauty.

JASON LOCY, designer and coauthor of *Veneer*

With a subject that may be perceived as trite or tired, Timothy Willard masterfully guides us to reexamine beauty with fresh perspective and imagination. Drawing upon Scripture and classic literature, Willard opens a window to our spirit, sharpening our lens for beauty as we receive the adventurous invitation of a loving God. *The Beauty Chasers* is a balm for weary and despairing hearts; it is also an astute call to our attention in daily living.

BETHANY DOUGLASS, writer and home educator, creator of *Cloistered Away*

Beauty is not something to look at; beauty is a life. That is the message in Tim Willard's new book. *The Beauty Chasers* is the guidebook we all need to embark on the journey that will lead to a life where beauty is the air we breathe and the food that sustains us.

ROBERTA GREEN AHMANSON, writer, art curator, explorer

The Beauty Chasers draws us back to a recognized beauty lost, then reminds us of beauty's name, so we may know why we are drawn.

ROGER W. THOMPSON, fisherman, surfer, and author of *My Best Friend's Funeral*, *Losing My Voice to Find It*, and *We Stood Upon Stars*

THE BEAUTY CHASERS

THE
BEAUTY
CHASERS

RECAPTURING THE
WONDER OF THE DIVINE

TIMOTHY D. WILLARD

ZONDERVAN
REFLECTIVE

ZONDERVAN REFLECTIVE

The Beauty Chasers
Copyright © 2022 by Timothy Willard

Requests for information should be addressed to:
Zondervan, *3900 Sparks Dr. SE, Grand Rapids, Michigan 49546*

Zondervan titles may be purchased in bulk for educational, business, fundraising, or sales promotional use. For information, please email SpecialMarkets@Zondervan.com.

ISBN 978-0-310-12221-0 (hardcover)
ISBN 978-0-310-12316-3 (audio)
ISBN 978-0-310-12315-6 (ebook)

Author is represented by The Christopher Ferebee Agency, www.christopherferebee.com.

Cover design: FiveStone.com
Cover art: © helga_helga / Envato Elements
Interior design: Denise Froehlich

Printed in the United States of America

22 23 24 25 26 27 28 29 30 31   /LSC/   15 14 13 12 11 10 9 8 7 6 5 4 3 2 1

For Phyllis, my mother and friend.
Your laughter taught me joy.

CONTENTS

Part 2: Footpaths of the Park
Beauty Desires Your Participation

Part 3: Footpaths of the Hills
Understanding the Mysterious Side of Beauty

PART 4: FOOTPATHS OF MOUNTAINS
Joy, the Life-Giving Mark of Beauty

A Note for the Curious

Beauty can change you if you let it. That's what the path of life has taught me so far. Beauty changed me. It still does.

But don't worry. This isn't a book about sitting on beaches or mountain roads watching the sunset or meditating in art galleries—although I have done (and still do) these things.

This idea of chasing beauty is about pursuing a lifestyle that goes against the cultural grain of busyness, loudness, and naked ambition—you know, the kind of ambition we're told we must have in order to find success in this cutthroat world.

My relatively short life has taught me that Beauty Chasers are thinkers and listeners. They see when the world goes blind. They embody quietness when all the world wants to do is scream. They promote the good of others when the world says to promote yourself. They give life to others when the world seems hell-bent on killing. Beauty Chasers live their lives to a different cadence. They walk the path less traveled.

If you're interested in these things, and you're willing to risk change, then read on, my friend.

Timothy D. Willard
Waxhaw, North Carolina, 2021

PART 1

SOMETHING STIRRING IN THE DEEP

Uncovering the Story of Beauty

CHAPTER 1

THE WINDOW

A Secret Passageway to a Place Called Love

There's an old tale that goes something like this: Two terminally ill men shared a hospital room. Over time, they became close friends. Every day, they spoke for hours on end about their lives. They discussed their families, their children, their vacations, their high times and low times, their favorite times, and their times of service in the military.

One man's illness forced him to lie on his back all the time. Let's call him Sam. The other man, whose bed sat near the only window in the room, was allowed to sit up each day to take his medication. We'll call him George. Each day, when George took his medication, he looked out the window and described what he saw to Sam.

The window happened to overlook a grand park, full of trees and pathways. People walked here and there and around the large pond at the center of the park. Ducks and geese swam in the pond. Great, old oak trees rose from the landscape and towered over the other trees and shrubbery.

"It's such a wonderful park," said George.

"Indeed, it is," replied Sam. "Tell me more about it."

"Well, just beyond the pond, the foothills of the mountains etch across the horizon, and if you look really hard, you can see the giant peaks rising into the distant clouds."

"Wonderful," said Sam, half whispering as he imagined the awe-inspiring view.

Each day, George described what he saw in great detail. Sam yearned for this hour to arrive. One autumn afternoon, George described a small parade as it passed through the park.

"I see families walking together and laughing. And oh, look, here comes a band marching through the park with floats and clowns and all kinds of merriment trailing behind it."

Though Sam could not hear the parade, he could see it in his mind's eye. *What joy*, he thought to himself.

On another occasion, George described a young couple reclining on a blanket near the pond. The young man played the guitar and sang, then stopped, leaned in, and kissed the young woman. Though neither George nor Sam could hear the serenade, they spoke about the moment in hushed excitement that night before they fell asleep.

One morning when the nurse came to give George his medicine, she found him lying lifeless in his bed. He had died in the night. She walked over to Sam, who was still sleeping, woke him gently, and told him about his friend. After a few moments of shared grief, the nurse called for the hospital attendants to remove George's body.

For two days, Sam did not eat for the weight of his sorrow.

On the third day, the nurse visited him with a light lunch and urged him to eat. Sam obliged, and as he took a sip of his tea, he asked the nurse if she would move his bed in front of the window, where George's bed used to be.

"I'd be happy to," she said.

She moved his bed beneath the window, tidied his things, and left the room.

Though his heart was heavy, Sam brimmed with excitement and anticipation. If he could somehow pull himself up to the window, he could catch a glimpse of the park George had described to him every day. He knew he'd have to endure severe pain, but he had to prop himself up—he *had* to see.

After several pain-filled moments, struggling to raise his body high enough to see out the window, Sam was able to strain his neck and peer outside. To his utter shock, the window faced a brick wall. He fell back onto his bed, racked with pain and disappointment.

Confused, Sam called for the nurse. When she arrived, he explained to her how every day, when George sat up to take his medicine, he described the beautiful park, and everything that was happening inside of it. He told her how they often spoke for hours about what lay beyond the window, remembering their lives before their illnesses and their desire to return to the world they knew and loved. He explained how he had looked forward to the time each day when she'd bring George's medicine and how those short moments had awakened hope in him once again.

"What compelled George to describe such beauty and joy to me every day?" Sam asked the nurse. "Why would he do such a thing?"

As the nurse listened, a gentle smile spread across her face. "I don't know, Sam," she said, emotion filling her throat. "George was blind."[1]

HAVE WE FORGOTTEN ABOUT THE POWER OF BEAUTY?

What does this old story teach us about beauty? Think about the way you felt as you read about George describing everything he saw outside. We empathize with Sam, who could not sit up and see it for himself. We *want* him to see the park, and we're delighted that his good friend George took the time to describe its beauty to him. Now he, too, can participate in the natural wonder that lies beyond the windowpane. Now he, too, can revel in the simple, beautiful things that make life what it is.

As I read the story, I was reminded of my own life and thought to myself how I, like Sam, would have desired to be reconnected with the outside world so filled with the qualities I loved and missed. In recent years, like so many of you, I'm sure, I experienced uncommon valleys of despair as a global pandemic raged. I lost work and income and struggled with feelings of isolation and failure. I found myself in a sickbed of alienation longing for the park, hills, and mountains. It was a longing to feel human again. I relate to this story because it reveals the truth that when we strip life down to the bare necessities, we're left with the things that matter most. *And beauty belongs to them all.*

Beauty jumps out of this story with the power to inspire Sam, to encourage his despairing heart. The beauty of the landscape invited his imagination to fire images in his own mind from years past—images that combined to form a nostalgic scene in his mind's eye. *Beauty reminds.*

After George passes, it is beauty that moves Sam in his desire to see for himself the lovely park and hills and mountain peaks. He decides that his own pain is worth the vision awaiting him on the outside. And so he suffers through the act of propping himself up, urged on by the lure of what lies beyond the window. He wants to see for himself, to fulfill his longing. His desire infects him with an overwhelming need to return to the place he loves. *Beauty inspires.*

And what about his good friend, George, who died? What does his act show us?

It shows us that blindness cannot thwart beauty, and that each person possesses a deeper sight of the heart.

It shows us *the power of the imagination* to bring to life a world bursting with nostalgia and wonder.

It shows us that *beauty possesses the power to sustain a life, perhaps even save it.*

It shows us how *beauty, when viewed as a gift, shapes the giver with humility and infuses the willing recipient with joy.*

It shows us how *beauty transcends the ill circumstances life throws at us*; that even in a state of illness and near-death, something out there, beyond us calls to us, and offers hope.

Perhaps most importantly, this story reminds us of our own lives and how, when we stop and think—I mean really *think* about it—we realize how filled with beauty our lives really are.

I can't help but think now of Sam. What if he was cured and could leave the confines of his hospital room? With a new lease on life, and a renewed love for beauty, how would he live differently? How would he approach each day? What would he do with his time?

I can see him walking out of the hospital doors, wide-eyed and laughing. Walking at first, then skipping, then running into the world, full of delight, and seeing everything again for the first time. I can imagine his whole body feeling like it did when he was just a boy—his heart beating out of his chest, his mouth forming a constant smile.

How would his renewed sense of beauty influence the way he talked to his family, I wonder? What would conversations with his friends sound like now, with beauty and joy ever on his heart and mind? Would beauty affect the way he spent his leisure time and the time he spent working?

How would his life take on new meaning now that beauty played a more central role; would it look different?

Would yours?

Would mine?

IS THERE MORE TO LIFE THAN MUCK?

God speaks to us through the everydayness of life. But God's words sometimes come to us veiled and hard to understand. That's because they are, as the writer Frederick Buechner puts it, "incarnate words," spoken during the act of living. Each person must "ferret out" the meaning of those words. Every day, Buechner says, is another opportunity to listen and hear what God is saying. And not just what he is saying to the world at large, but to you, and to me personally.[2] Living is how you and I make sense of this world. Living is a kind of active language, and if we're not paying attention, we'll miss the meaning.

When I review my life, I can see how I spent my twenties largely on the road, living from college to college, from tour to tour—I toured in a band for several years—from one adventure to another. In my thirties, I found myself embroiled in another layer of life, trying to figure out how to live not on the road but with a wife, then with children, working at a "real" job, and then in academics.

I was trying to make sense of everything, just like you. My life wasn't some gleaming romantic ideal. The everyday road on which I found myself was littered with the pains of growing up, of loving and failing to love, of peace and discord. I hurt people. I saw people crushed by the loss of loved ones due to cancer and suicide. I was betrayed by friends, and I betrayed friends myself. I fought my way through feelings of rage and lust.

What was God saying through all of this to me? Where were his "incarnate words?" All I saw was the muck of life. But then it hit me.

The Secret Passage behind the Bookshelf

One night, several years ago—May something; I can't remember—I sat on the floor of my study, combing through some of my favorite books by C. S. Lewis. I thumbed my tattered copy of one of Lewis's essay collections, reread the sermon "The Weight of Glory," and noticed something.

While Lewis wrote about the term *beauty*, the word he used to communicate an accurate biblical understanding of the word was *love*. But he didn't use the word *beauty* to only describe objects we find pleasing to the eye (aesthetics). Instead, he described beauty as a staging point for something far bigger than mere aesthetic pleasure. Not the image of the galloping stallion but the quality of his movement. Not the "dappled dawn drawn falcon"[3] but the edge of love we feel when we witness its flight.

For Lewis, beauty possesses a kind of magic that charges objects with visible delight. It also possesses a mysterious quality that invites the viewer to take up a quest.

But a quest for what?

The quest intrigued me. Was it a quest for something beyond the muck of life? Had I missed this magical something because I was too busy trying to keep pace with the world?

What unfolded that night in my study was the truth that God speaks to us through beauty. But in order to hear the words, we must slow down and listen with our hearts. Think about it. What would happen if you and I slowed down and looked at the world and our lives with new eyes, like Sam?

I didn't find a hidden portal into a snowy realm behind my bookshelf that night in my study. A faun with an umbrella didn't tell me grand tales of wonder. But I did discover a secret passageway that led beyond the muck of life. Was a lion waiting inside to lead the way to Sam's distant mountains? Well, I'm not telling.

CHAPTER 2

CURIOUSER AND CURIOUSER

Beauty Defies Definition

I grew up and still live in a Christian world that commonly says, "True beauty comes from within." But my experience in the world tells me this is not the whole story. Yes, we encounter the intimate kind of personal or spiritual beauty found in the soul of a person (beauty within). But what about beautiful things, beautiful experiences, physically beautiful people, beautiful talk, beautiful acts, beautiful art, beautiful math, beautiful science, beautiful feelings, beautiful work, beautiful religion, beautiful aliveness? You and I experience beauty through four primary categories: nature, art, the human form, and the everyday charm of life.[1]

Did Sam sense a kind of beauty we might associate with a person's spirit alone?[2] Or did his mind's eye connect memory with reality, experience with wonder, the goodness of life with hope? When we reduce beauty to an overly spiritualized idea, we diminish its potential to change us by drawing us closer to God.

We reduce things because we are modern. The Hebrews did not understand such a limited idea of beauty. Beauty was a given in their world because they related it to life with God and saw it reflected in his created order. It's fashionable to rail on the Platonic idea of forms, but Plato was on to something. He understood how meaning was communicated through the cosmic order. We call this *mimesis*. The Hebrews might not have had representational or abstract artwork like we moderns, but they possessed a different worldview. God and his qualities were imprinted everywhere they looked.

"Eh, but Tim," you say. "Isn't that a paradox? Doesn't beauty need to be a spiritual idea if it's to connect us to God?"

"Ah, yes," I reply. "I see how it sounds paradoxical, but I hope you'll let this little adventure of a book unfold how, when we set beauty free, we can grasp the clarity and purity of its character. In God's creation, nothing needs to be spiritualized by humans because it was created sacred already. Reducing ideas like beauty and wonder marginalizes them. Like canning fruit, we scoop it up into its jar and set it aside on a dusty shelf. It's there if we need it, but it's not part of our daily diet."

This "true beauty within" notion limits beauty to one dimension, shallowing it, like filling the sea with concrete to make it more manageable. My experience has shown me a beauty rich with passion, holiness, even a sense of dread—a sense of something beyond myself. A far-reaching beauty, touching every aspect of life. A beauty tuned to the observation found in Gerard Manley Hopkins' line, "The world is charged with the grandeur of God."[3]

Beauty feels like a staging point for something grander than feelings or my inner self or aesthetic pleasure. Beauty rises. Beauty moves me from my spot, as it did Sam, and invites me to explore beyond those boundaries, out in the edges of life.

I want to discover what lies behind the mysterious and glorious of this world. Don't you?

Things like the eerie wonder of the first snowfall. The feeling of a jubilant "YAWP"[4] after conquering a trail on my mountain bike. The breath-halting mystery of the birth of my children. The gulping ecstasy of the marriage bed. The gentle kiss of my daughters. The joyful satisfaction gained from my work. Uncontrollable laughter.

Autumn bonfires with friends and relatives. The quiet sobs of grief. The holiness of healing. The mountaintop screams of forgiveness.

Because I am a lover of the wildness of nature, adventure, and deep relationships, an expanded view of beauty resonates with the movement of my passions—passions engraved into my soul by God. As a student of theology and literature, a creative (whatever that means), a hack musician, a husband, father, brother, and worker, casting a broader net for beauty makes sense to me, as it draws on the weight of my every experience.[5]

The beauty I touch, feel, and perceive daily feels colossal yet intimate at the same time, like how the sun floods the sky with residual light even when it has set, or how dew shimmers on the skin of my tomatoes on a spring morning. I'm reminded of John O'Donohue's words: "Beauty is so quietly woven through our ordinary days that we hardly notice it."[6] C. S. Lewis was one of those who needed help to see that beauty wasn't just wrapped up in the grandeur of landscape but was also found in our common everyday experiences. In his spiritual memoir, *Surprised by Joy*, he recounts how his friend, Arthur Greeves, taught him to appreciate "homeliness."[7] To Arthur, homeliness was the charm found in a vegetable garden, moonlight on a puddle, the opening line of *Jane Eyre*, the weather, food set on the table, or the goodness found in family. My experience of the world makes me feel like I am living in an unfurling corner of some great wonder—grand, yet cozy. And when I slow down and attend to the weaving of beauty's invitation to me, I feel like the newly born calf, kicking as I run, at home in a world I do not fully know, yet joyfully skipping for the wonder of it all.

Do you experience beauty like this, from the marvelous to the tender, from the wonder-filled to the delicate? Have you ever thought about what such beauty teaches us about God and our relationship to him?

If we fail to open our eyes and hearts to beauty's full significance in this world, we will rob ourselves of God's voice in our lives. Relegating beauty to the spirit of a person removes its profound touch from our daily experience; it quiets its voice so much so that we will soon forget what the voice of beauty sounds like.

Beauty unfurls itself in the natural world in a dynamic dance, rousing our applause, inciting our pursuit, our love, and our own attempts to copy what we see, feel, and experience through craft, art, and our way of life.

Beauty alive is, itself, enlivening. It is that "indescribable something"[8] echoing in our daily moments of wonder and charm. That instance when you, like Sam, sense that something or someone stirs behind the veil of reality. We sense it and yet fail to define it.

"Nay," writes C. S. Lewis, "the very beauty of [a beautiful thing] lay in the certainty that it was a copy, like and not the same, an echo, a rhyme, an exquisite reverberation of the uncreated music prolonged in a created medium."[9] Lewis gives us lyrics *about* beauty more than he defines it. And we don't mind because we love talking about beauty.

BROADENING OUR VIEW OF BEAUTY

In all of this, we've merely scratched the surface of *describing* beauty. Perhaps that's all any of us can do. It is, however, the attempt to grasp beauty's meaning, through language unique to our experience of beauty, that aids our understanding of what beauty is and how it works in our daily lives.

Theologian and philosopher Patrick Sherry also believes we should cultivate a broader perspective of beauty. He reminds us that beauty, as understood by Plato and early Christian writers of the church like St. Cyril of Alexandria, was multifaceted.[10] Beauty is related to the spiritual and the divine, to the physical and to the arts.[11] So, there is moral, spiritual, and intellectual beauty and the beauty of the divine. Beauty touches so many aspects of our lived experience that by limiting it to, say, "beauty within," we not only restrict its significance, but we promote a kind of dualism that emphasizes the inner life over the physical life. This perspective does not work in the Christian worldview.

If we can broaden our view of beauty, we empower our senses, both physical and spiritual, to gain a richer and fuller understanding of God.

"But Tim," you say, "how can this be true? Don't we run the risk of reducing the meaning of beauty if we broaden our view of it? If beauty can mean anything, doesn't it mean nothing?"

"Ah, yes," I reply. "It's a good question. But what if we broaden our view of beauty not so we can let it mean whatever we want it to mean, but so that we can take in the wonder of God? What if thinking this way about beauty did more than making us more aware of all the pretty little things in life? What if reflecting on *beauty itself* made us more like Christ?"

If you and I can keep this in mind as we look further into the passageway behind the bookshelf, we'll discover that the contemplation of beauty keeps us human, with souls aflame.

GOOD LUCK DEFINING BEAUTY

Our modern sensibilities push us for definitions. We enjoy precision when discussing subjects we can't quite get our heads around. The words "transcendence" and "immanence" are prime examples. These terms rose to prominence during the Age of Reason so we could describe God more precisely. For centuries, it was exactly God's mystery that prompted theologians and philosophers to refer to God as *other*—totally unexplainable, incomprehensible, and unique. The Latin term *sui generis* (pronounced 'soo-ee jeneris') was used to describe God. It means, *of its own kind, unique.* But that won't do for us in the modern age, will it? We want to understand. Knowledge is power. Knowledge about something makes us feel more in control.

The concept of beauty falls into this trap, too. I know scholars who refer to beauty as a "slippery idea" or "problematic." We moderns have replaced the term "beauty" with the more sophisticated "aesthetics." In true Enlightenment fashion, Alexander Baumgarten (1735) broke down our experience of beauty into a science called *aesthetics*. His aim was to psychologically detail how the human psyche responds to objects of art and the concept of the beautiful. Baumgarten's lectures were the first crack in the dam, so to speak. Once he introduced the idea of detailing our perception of beauty, others contributed.[12] It was the moderns who diced up beauty using terms like "the sublime," "transcendence," and "aesthetics." The supernatural nature of beauty faded. A new model of beauty emerged, rooted in our feelings rather than something beyond ourselves.[13]

Even though we've done our best to lasso beauty, taming it for our sophisticated sensibilities, we've come no closer to defining it.

If we sat down for a cup of tea, and you asked me to define beauty, I'd tell you a story. If you pressed me for something more concrete, I'd pour you more tea and tell you another story. So, it only seems fitting that I should embark upon another tale through which we might discover a usable definition of beauty for our excursion into the secret passageway behind my shelves.

Come with me to a not-so-secret gathering of dead prophets, poets, and philosophers. Let's listen in, shall we?

A CONVERSATION THAT SHOULD HAVE HAPPENED

Moses walked into a quiet spot by the River Cherwell. The river is a stone's throw from Christ Church College, Oxford, where he met Jack, the famous British writer of children's stories who taught at Oxford and Cambridge. Jack is what his friends called him. You might know him as C. S. Lewis. Jack was seated on a large boulder near the water packing his pipe, entrenched in a conversation with Plato, the Athenian philosopher, who listened intently as he paced back and forth along the water's edge. Moses, the Old Testament prophet, stood nearby listening while leaning on his staff. Lewis had invited Plato and Moses to the riverbank hoping they might help stir his imagination. He was outlining a portrait of beauty for a story he was writing.

"You see, Jack," said Plato, "everything we see with our physical eyes in this world is a copy of the original. You and I see a field of poppies and proclaim it as beautiful. But the beauty in the field of poppies is only an echo of the true and objective Beauty—an eternal Beauty."[14]

"Ah yes, I see," said Jack. "But if we look at all of life like we do at the poppies, don't we create a divide between the real, in our case here the field of poppies, and the spiritual?"

"Possibly, but doesn't our very life experience whisper to us that there is something *else*, something beyond this physical world?"

"It does," agreed Lewis, who couldn't seem to get his pipe lit. "But perhaps instead of viewing the beauty of the poppies in our physical world as merely an echo of the *real* beauty that lies somewhere in the beyond, we might see it as an invitation from the origin of all beauty, even Beauty itself."

"I say," said Moses as he leaned on his staff and stroked his beard, "all this talk about two beauties sounds confusing to me, Plato. My people, the Israelites, might draw you a different picture for your story, Jack," said Moses.

"How so?"

"Your English word 'beauty' did not exist in our language in the way that it does in your modern tongue. Our Hebrew language uses seven word groupings to describe your 'beauty.'"[15]

"Fascinating," said Plato.

"Yes, quite," said Jack. "Do go on Moses. Though I was hoping the others might have arrived by now."

"You've invited others?" said Plato.

"Yes, and I do think you both will find them agreeable."

Jack hardly uttered the words when a modern-looking woman wearing spectacles and smoking a hand-rolled cigarette, stepped into the glade in a quiet discussion with an African man wearing fourth-century attire.[16]

"Simone! You made it!" exclaimed Jack, puffing on his pipe as he blurted out his welcome.

"Yes Jack, and I was able to wrangle Augustine away from the Bodleian Library so that we might all benefit from his wisdom."

"Brilliant. Moses was about to explain to us how his native Hebrew language paints the idea of beauty using multiple word groupings."

"Oh, I thought everyone knew that," said Augustine nonchalantly.

"See," said Simone. "This is going to be fun."

"Plato, Moses, I give you the French philosopher Simone Weil (pronounced 'sea-moan vay') and Augustine of Hippo—both are admirers of your thought, Plato. Perhaps the three of you can get on after our discussion for a pint and further discussion at The Turf."[17]

The five exchanged brief greetings. Simone sat on the bench under the oak tree beside Jack and his rock, while Augustine squatted next to the water's edge beside Plato. Moses, now in the center of the group and leaning on his staff, continued his explanation.

"To stand in the presence of YHWH, well, this was central to our understanding of the beautiful. Who else is clothed in majesty and glory like our Father?[18] My apologies, Plato. I realize and appreciate that you might be undecided on what or who this origin of beauty is. Perhaps our discussion might sway you. And, of course, my first-hand experience of standing in his presence."

"Not to worry, Moses. I thank you for your kindness. I'm eager to hear about your experience."

"I remember how it was God's presence that kept me alive, attentive, and strong enough to hear his voice while I was on the mountain; a voice that sounds like the crushing sound of thunder.[19] His presence sustained me, physically and spiritually—is there a difference between the two from heaven's perspective?

"But how can I explain the depth of his presence? His sustaining power reminds me that his presence is life itself."

"I understand the beauty in our world to be an Incarnation of God, his presence," said Simone.[20] "But I have not thought about how his presence, the beauty in the world, sustains me."

"Yes," continued Moses, "the weight of YHWH's presence was more satisfying than any pleasure this world offers. When I stood within it on the mountain, all I wanted to do was worship him. I felt whole. And I don't even know what I mean by that, only that I didn't feel fragmented in my spirit or broken in any way.

"You see, Jack, even as I think about the different words we use for *beauty*, already I'm reminded that there are other words that also relate to it. For example, on the mountain, I was enveloped in the glory and majesty, or what we call the *weight* of his splendor. This is an idea I think most of you have written about in some form or another."

Augustine, Plato, and Jack all nodded in agreement.

"And what about what God saw after he created the heavens and the earth?" continued Moses. "Your translators like to use the word *good*; as in 'God saw all that he had created, and he said it was good.' But the word is closer to *beautiful*.[21] Think what it would sound like to say that God created every living thing, the heavens and the earth, light and darkness, and human beings and he looked upon all of it and called it *beautiful*.

"This first grouping we'll call *honor-beauty*, as it relates to heads of state and nations.[22] The second we'll call *beautify-beauty*. Strange sounding, I know, but it refers to the act of beautifying or turning something into an object of adoration. YHWH does this to us as his children. Third is *desirous-beauty*. Imagine God delighting in you, the way you and I delight in the things he's made. Imagine his intention of obtaining you as his own. I admit to feeling this kind of beauty upon the mountain; a weighty—what is your word for it, ah yes—*holy* affection and desirous love.

"But this word grouping can mean both proper desire as well as lust. This idea of desire falls in line with greed and covetousness. When we covet, we desire something that does not belong to us. This kind of desire gives birth to a lust that devours. But remember, this is the *bentness* of the word, to use one of your favorite words from your cosmic writings, Jack."

"Ah yes, so you've read them?" said Jack as he folded his arms and puffed on his pipe, pleased with himself.

"I do believe Jack appropriated the idea of *bentness* from my writings on sin,"[23] said Augustine, chiding Lewis with obvious joy.

"Quite right," said Jack. "Nothing new under the sun you know. Blast it all, I should have invited King Solomon!"

And the two scholars shared a boisterous laugh.

"The fourth grouping describes something we all know well," continued Moses. "*Physical-beauty*. The Scriptures mention others known for their physical beauty. Sara, Rachel, Esther, Joseph, David, Abigail, all lovely to look at. But, like all physical beauty, it can become a snare of lust and pride. Because of God's favor, my own people, the Israelites became known as lovely to the surrounding nations. But her beauty led her into harlotry as a nation.

"But what many don't understand is that this word also refers to YHWH himself. He dazzles. 'Out of Zion,' writes the Hebrew poet, 'the perfection of beauty, God shines forth.'[24] This *physical-beauty* can also characterize God's presence, as well as God's people. There's a mysterious and even haunting nature to this kind of beauty.

"It makes sense, then, just as this dazzling God of ours is himself Beauty, what he creates reflects that beauty. Plato, perhaps this notion of beauty relates to your own work."

"It is interesting, Moses, how so much of the different viewpoints of beauty can be gobbled up in this ancient understanding of the word," said Plato.

"I believe this sentiment is captured in Solomon's passage in chapter three of Ecclesiastes."

"You see, again! I knew I should have invited him," said Lewis, laughing once more with Augustine.

"Yes, Jack," said Moses, now also laughing a bit, "it appears Solomon possesses a good bit of wisdom."

At this remark, the whole party laughed for some time.

"I've wondered about that passage in Ecclesiastes," said Augustine after regaining his composure. "God made everything *beautiful* in its season. Later, he says that we possess eternity in our hearts. By this he means we sense the divine because we are icons of God, created in his image. We still possess pieces of that Edenic wholeness, and yet we cannot fully grasp the eternity within us due to our bentness. I hint at this idea in my memoir, *Confessions*, when I wrote how our hearts are restless until they find their home in God."[25]

"Yes," said Moses, "a beautiful work of devotion. I'll hurry along here and wrap up. Let's call the fifth sense *fitting-beauty*. Our field of poppies *looks* lovely to our eyes, but God's temple, or even the cathedrals from your own time, Jack and Simone, fit their designed purpose. It is fitting that God be worshipped in such a place that reflects the goodness of the created order.

"*Moral-beauty* relates to character rather than appearance. We writers of the Old Testament use this idea to refer to God's Word. God's words are good, pure, beautiful.

"Finally, there is *glory-beauty*. It's almost as if this word was meant just for YHWH himself. It means to honor or glorify. We use this word to describe people only when they reflect this godly quality. The idea of glory-beauty communicates a sense of weightiness in the glory—and this is unique to God."

"Moses," said Jack, finally able to keep his pipe going. "Thank you for this wonderful tutorial on beauty from an age well before our time. This Old Testament beauty presents all of us with a way of looking at the entire world. This otherworldly kind of beauty considered objects, people, relationships, art, events as contributing to the meaning of God's created order. I see it like this: beauty rises from within and shines from the surface, mixing the temporal with the infinite. It is within, yes. But it is also on the outside, catching our eyes, intoxicating our experience, and frightening us with a holy resonance."

CAN'T WE SIMPLIFY THE MEANING OF BEAUTY?

Yes, we can. When we go back even further than the classical thinkers like Plato, we find a beauty that startles us even as it draws us to it. We find a beauty that reminds us we are seen by God. We find a beauty that matters.

Beauty matters because it connects us with the heart of God. It's a connection that cuts to the core of who we are as human beings.

Beauty teaches. A beauty as deep as love involves more than our senses. It engages our knowledge. It inspires our sense of meaning. It exposes a world ripe with value. It reminds us that plurality and diversity shape its contours.

Beauty stirs our imaginations and sends us exploring. And not just exploring the world we see with our eyes, but the world we feel inside—our souls. It is not a dualist enterprise; it is all-consuming. It connects our desire to examine and express ourselves to our natural desire to pursue the good life.

Beauty acts as a prompt and a goal for us. It prompts us, making us "aware of being ourselves and being in the world."[26] It's our goal, linking our sense of identity and our quest for self-understanding and self-explanation. Beauty prompts our desire to do good and becomes our common goal—politician, activist, philosopher, artist, or whomever. The prompt and goal work together and produce beautiful deeds like those of Martin Luther King Jr.; the culture-shaping contemplation of the eternal by the likes of Plato, Simone Weil, or Charles Taylor; and the capture of light on canvas by luminaries like William Turner.

Such a prompt, such a goal is for us the rallying cry of significance and hope. How else are we to bear the weight of this world, its calamities and contusions on our souls, without the reviving quality of hope propelling us toward that eerie fullness when we sense redemption and holiness all around us, and are, in a moment of climax, able to whisper words of wonder and astonishment in the beautiful moment? It is beauty that flies in the face of disappointment and continued failure, and it does so arm-in-arm with hope. "You must honestly confront your shattered dream," writes Martin Luther King Jr. "Place your failure at the forefront of your mind and stare daringly at it." Do our eyes not well up with fervent tears at his words because we know the beauty of their weight? It is she whose mind lives awash in beauty who sees through the dirge of the moment into the beautiful hope of redemption: "The cross which was willed by wicked men, was woven by God into the tapestry of world redemption."[27]

Beauty nourishes. It becomes the goal of our affections and molds us into people of gentle hearts,[28] for it points beyond us. It reminds us that our desire for happiness cannot be filled by echoes, but only by the resounding source: beauty itself. We must press on in our quest for the source of beauty. That is where we are to drink—the fountainhead of beauty. "The whole man," writes Lewis, "is to drink joy from the fountain of joy."

"Oh, Tim," you say, "can we please go to that place beyond the classical thinkers and dense descriptions of beauty? Can we visit the event of beauty you're describing?"

"Ah, yes," I reply. "It'd be my pleasure to walk with you along that path. It's my favorite place to go. The path does go back quite a ways. But if you're up for it, so am I."

Beauty confounds us in all the right ways. Don't you agree? But let's not allow its indescribability to frustrate our modern minds. Instead, let's press on to that place beyond the classic thinkers, even early civilization; that place Sam and George sensed even as they were isolated from it. And let's put this working definition of beauty in our pocket: *beauty is an event.* But as we wend our way along the footpath, let's allow that definition to breathe. If we dare venture forward, I'm confident we'll not only find a simple definition of beauty, but we'll discover the pathway to beauty itself.

CHAPTER 3

WHERE BEAUTY BEGINS

Stumbling upon the Deep Words of God

For thirty-six hours, I stared at the mist gathering in the valley and discussed the world and heaven with two close friends. It was midsummer. The Black Mountains of western North Carolina rise to the clouds. A spur of the Appalachian Range, they contain six of the Eastern United States' highest peaks. Mount Mitchell gathers its summit at 6,684 feet—the highest of all. The Blacks range for fifteen miles and get their name from the dark fir and spruce trees that coat their heights. The boreal evergreens look black in winter as they contrast with the deciduous hardwoods upon the slopes.

Our cabin sat at 3,100 feet and jutted out, like a manmade promontory, into the steep river valley south of the spur. The first night, thunderstorms raged through the mountain basin, and we watched the ominous clouds gather overhead. They unleashed. The sounds of the storm took over. Lightning and rain and claps of thunder pelted and shook the cabin. Then, as quickly as it had gathered, the storm dispersed, vanishing over the ridge.

A cluster of stars peeked from behind the indigo veil and dripped their light into the valley that had just been ravished by the beauty of the summer storm. With the heat of the day gone, we lit the fire and laughed beneath the stars, writing haikus about the storm and trees and the smell of pine and whatever caught our fancy.

The next morning, we departed, filled up by camaraderie and joy. I let the joy guide me to a more scenic route home. Instead of barreling back to Charlotte on the highway, I wound my way to the Blue Ridge Parkway and drove toward the summit of Mount Mitchell. With the windows down and Gipsy Kings blaring in my speakers, I let my hand hang in the mountain air as the temperature cooled.

A thousand feet, then a thousand more; 85 degrees, then 75, then 65. The mountain air poured into my truck, sweet with mint and bergamot and pine and fir.

Wild bee balm lined the parkway with a crimson thread; their joyous red heads stood tall and confident, showing off their stunning glory. Beside them, the spindly rudbeckia beamed, their yellow petals a parade of color.

I drove with a permanent grin, as if I'd happened upon a secret meeting of angels who'd left a trail of heaven in their wake. I could almost smell the celestial goodness in the air. The summit waited for me with its height and range and glory. Perhaps I'd find the angels and listen in on their meeting.

When I turned up the steep road, I heard distant thunder and found that for which my heart yearned: thunder-filled storm clouds marching toward the peak, while a great blue expanse spread out to the south: the meeting of the heavens.

I took in the view and thought how God greeted me with a billion joys, for that is all that can fit into the Black Mountains: countless trees, branches, leaves, flowers, clouds, deer, bear, bobcat, mist and storm, sky and sunshine, the intoxicating elements of it all working together. Yet my eyes could only drink in so much, leaving me wanting more.

"But Tim," you say, "why didn't you invite me on your mountain escapade? For I, too, long to see the joys of God on the mountaintops. This world of ours makes me want to stop everything and return to the remote places, if only to restore my sanity."

"Ah, yes," I reply. "I do apologize for the oversight. I only share this story to inspire you to head out on your own mountain escapade. When you ascend to the places of wonder, keep it in mind to let go of the world's pace. If you're really daring, sit and stare at a view for an uncomfortable amount of time. Let the sights and sounds bend in on you. I'm sure you, too, will find an angels' meeting of your own."

GOD INVITES US INTO HIS BEAUTY

The bounty of wonder you and I discover in this world is no accident. God created the world with deep intention, care, and love. He created with an irresistible flair to draw us to himself.

When the apostle Paul stood before the stoics at the Areopagus, he noted their deep religious beliefs, ignorant and blind as they were, and invited the philosophers to *see* the billions upon billions of joys.[1] For the seeker, the one groping for God, he said, these joys reveal the invisible qualities of his eternal power and divinity. And yet the beauty of natural wonder is not sufficient for spiritual salvation. Beauty unconnected to God leads humans into pagan idolatry. God himself says he will destroy all beauty not rooted in him (Isa. 28:1–4).[2]

For the disciple of Jesus, the one groping for deeper intimacy with God, the revelation of these joys—of God's power and divine nature—remind of his unlimited grace and care. But even more than that, they remind one of the lover who leaves flowers on his beloved's doorstep. The flowers signal his loyalty and tenderness, but they also impart something of his heart concerning his beloved. The flowers say, "You remind me of this bouquet—full of life, bursting with color, alive with fragrance, a bounty snatched from the mountains." The bouquet is a symbol of Christian love.[3]

In the half-light of heaven, blowing through the incandescent clouds descending upon Mount Mitchell, I discovered the meeting of angels. They told me the story of the light that came so long ago, before humans walked the earth, and how it filled the cosmos with wisdom. The angels reminded me of the ancient philosophy that used to rule the earth, the one that predated our modern materialism (that is, the belief that the world is composed only of matter and the supernatural does not exist, as opposed to the love of material possessions).

It was basic and true, not because it was simple, but because it was so deep, full of paradox and the spectacle of wonder. It was a knowledge—a Word—bound up in the Artist's mind behind the flower that blows in the mountain air, whose bend and bob can give "thoughts that do often lie too deep for tears."4

As I pondered this ancient philosophy from the angel's story, I remembered that we journey through this world, stumbling upon the deep words of God at every turn, if only we have ears to hear them. Such a glorious paradox it was, that day at Mt. Mitchell, to hear the deep words of heaven with my *eyes* and tastes their fragrance with my *nose*. They smell like bergamot, and behold, they are good.

We eulogize spaces that possess an "otherness" quality like I just have in marking the top of Mt. Mitchell as a place where angels gather. Places like this mountaintop burn into our memories. Why?

Because God's creative touch fills the world. He imbues our world with physical and spiritual beauty. Perhaps this is why we all, from Plato to C. S. Lewis, can only grasp at the concept of beauty with adjectives and analogies. We see the wonder of the heavens and sense they are calling to us with an ancient tongue, a heavenly language. We rush to explain the phenomenon of wonder with our words, all the while the fire of holiness burns our souls.

On my Mt. Mitchell drive, the closer I came to the peak, the more I sensed this heavenly language. Joy attended, but also a healthy fear. The heights do that, don't they?

"Something stirs in the deep," I thought to myself. "The unfolding of a cosmic story. What kind of story is it, I wonder? It feels too wondrous to be a tragedy. And yet too sad to be a comedy. Perhaps it is a hero story."

It turns out that it *is* a hero story, and it's also a comedy and tragedy. It's all of these rolled up into a love story. This is the story I found behind the bookshelf that night in my room when I ventured into the secret passageway. It's the story of how beauty begins with God because God *is* beauty.

I LOVE YOU LIKE THE OCEAN

One day, far into the future, God sat down with a woman and a man, who looked very much like you and me, and he told them the story of the world.

"What was it like, *before*?" the woman asked. "Before the light came, and the rivers, and the oceans, and the lands and the mountains and the trees covered the earth? What was it like before humans walked on the earth?"

We humans love to ask questions. We're curious creatures. And God knows this, so he didn't mind the woman's inquiries. In fact, he loves being asked questions.

"It was different," God said. "Before the light and all that you've mentioned, there was the heights, or what you know to be heaven. The heights are my home, my abode. And there was nothing before heaven, and nothing after."

"The light. Tell us about the light," said the man.

"Before the light came into your eyes, it was a whisper," said God. "It was the whisper after a thought, one of my most precious thoughts."

"Why was it so precious?" the man asked.

"That won't be easy to describe to you, but I'll try," said God. "It was precious because it was a thought that formed upon ringing notes of life, or joy, as you know it. And there was nothing like it ever before because the whisper-thought was about *you*. From that whisper-thought came intentions, potential, wonders, and mysteries. Thunder came, too; from the heavens it came, full of fury and density. You understand thunder and lightning to be related to the tumult of nature. In the heights, however, thunder and lightning are simply the sparks of my power and beauty.

"But as great as those potentials came to be in your world, they were not the most precious part of the whisper-thought. And I loved that thought. I loved *you*, even before there was a you.

"The light was for you, and everything after the light was for you: the skies and mountains and rivers and sun and moon and each other. It was all part of the plan to create a place in which you'd thrive; a place you'd love, a place where we could be together, a place where everything dripped with my presence, with wholeness."

"I think I understand," said the woman. "It is a little hard to think about being loved even before I existed. I'm not sure I can comprehend a love like that."

"Yes, that's why I said it will be difficult to explain in a way you can understand. But if you reach deep inside your heart, like Job did when I questioned him, you can gather the strength to comprehend all that I'm saying. I know because I made you. But it will be hard. Truth and beauty are always hard because they come from the heights.

"It's difficult to explain 'before time' to you, because you were born in the realm of time, nourished on light, and loved with whispers that came to you all the way from eternity. How can I explain to you the inside of my heart and how deeply I loved you before time even began? My heart is not a heart like yours, beating red with life. I am not like you in that sense, but at the same time, my heart is like yours because it can connect to your heart in profound ways," God said.

"How does your heart connect to ours?" the woman asked.

"Do you know when you experience something beautiful, charming, or fantastic in your world, and you feel so deeply that words escape you? My heart connects to yours in that space where words escape because I AM the space where your words disappear," God replied.[5]

"I think I see what you're getting at," the woman said.

"Try this," continued God. "Do you know that sensation you get when you fall? It's exhilarating and terrifying. My heart hides in the feeling of your fall."

"So, these feelings like terror and excitement work in me as reminders or even metaphors for you?" asked the woman, puzzled.

"Yes," said God. "How about one more example? Do you know that feeling when you run into the waves of the ocean? You get knocked down but love it. The salt stings your eyes, but you can't get enough. You wade out into deeper water and feel the gigantic pull, and you start to feel frightened that the ocean could, at any moment, consume you. My heart is like the ocean. That feeling you get from the power of the ocean? Our hearts connect there. You cannot fathom the ocean's strength, but something in you loves it for that very reason."

"I know that feeling of being in the ocean," said the man. "I remember it from when I was a kid. And I did love it. It was scary and wonderful at the same time."

"That's how it is when you love someone," said the woman. "It's scary because you have to trust them and wonderful because you can't get enough of them. I think I'm getting a picture of how precious your thought of us really was."

"I am like the ocean," said God, "and from my depths, love comes with all the curling fury of storm-driven waves. Beneath such waves, nothing can live. But through the constant crashing of the waves, the shoreline emerges. Rocks are beaten soft. Earth washed smooth. Air salted clean."

"Is the whisper-thought the reason you created everything to begin with? To love us?" the man asked.

"Yes. I created *for* love and *because of* love. That is who I AM. And I used beauty, through the creative work of the Holy Spirit, to send this truth to you and to give you the choice to love me back.[6] Love requires choice, as you well know. When I spoke to Moses from the burning bush and stormy mountain, I revealed the character of my Divine Name to him and let him experience my glory.[7] Though my Divine Name remains a mystery to humans, you know and sense its qualities; steadfast (*chesed*) and holy. Or, more poetically, love and beauty."

"So the story of the world starts with this whisper-thought of love for us?" the woman asked, getting caught up in the images of love and beauty.

"It does," said God. "With the choice to love came the ocean feeling. With the choice to reject love came the emptiness of despair. The despair came with the lie of the serpent. The ocean, from the shores of heaven."

"Can you tell us about what happened after your whisper-thought and how the serpent brought despair?" the man asked.

"I can. But, unlike the stories you're familiar with that begin with 'Once upon a time,' this story starts *before* the beginning of time."

And so God told them the story that began once before time. You and I like to begin the story of the world in Genesis 1, when God created the universe. But the story of beauty begins much earlier than that. It begins on a cosmic stage before the whisper-thought God described to the man and woman. We get a glimpse of this story in John's prelude to his gospel account of Jesus.

I listened in as God told the man and woman the story that starts before the beginning. I've sketched it for you here so that we can continue down this intriguing footpath that's opened up beyond the secret passageway behind my bookshelf. The story contains hints that unfold God's love and care for us. Think of how Adam and Eve must have felt when they woke in the "Garden of Delight," which is what the word *Eden* means.[8] Certainly, they wanted to know the *why* behind the wonder and intimacy of God's presence, just like you and I do. Imagine their full hearts when they realized their origin story.

THE STORY OF THE FOUNTAIN

Our story does not begin with, "In the beginning." It begins before the beginning. It begins with a word.

"Of course," you might say. "But all stories begin with words."

And you'd be correct. But this story begins with a particular word. This word is more than letters strung together to form a meaning. This word possesses life itself. Think about all the beautiful things that constitute life: dreams, imagination, friendship, a heart beating, love, trees rustling in the spring rain, and I'm sure you can think of many other things. That's what this word contained: the potential to create all those things, even things you and I can't think of.

Imagine, for a moment, this supercharged word existing before anything else, brimming with the creative power of existence. It's where everything we know, see, and love came from.

In our world, creative power begins with an idea that, when put into motion, jumps out of our imaginations and into the world we see with our eyes. Think about how a builder works. She doesn't just start hammering nails; she begins with a plan. That plan comes from an architect. He sets out to sketch a house he can see in his imagination. After he outlines it, he draws it out on special paper with lines, angles, and measurements. His sketch originates in his mind, just an idea. That idea grows into a plan, and then the builder acquires the blueprint and starts to work with her hands and tools to bring the architect's idea to life.

We can go back even further.

Where did the idea of the house come from? Maybe something inspired the architect. Perhaps he saw another house that struck him with its beautiful architectural pattern and wanted to copy it. Or maybe he experienced something special inside a home, and that experience planted the idea in his imagination—like a grand party or an intimate conversation with a friend. Possibly his idea came from a scene in nature, like a meadow or an orchard or an English garden planned just so. Inspiration can come from anywhere. It ignites our minds with ideas.

Have you ever thought about inspiration?

Amazing encounters and experiences *inspire* us. But have you ever thought about where inspiration comes from? Where did the bit of magic that ignited the architect's imagination and inspired him to create something come from? Of course, it isn't magic, but it is something quite like magic would be if magic were real.

That bit of magic is the spark found in this life-filled word. Not a spark caused by two rocks struck together. It is the beginning of all sparks. Philosophers call this life-filled spark a *first cause*.

We like to know what causes things to happen, such as how hurricanes form, or what causes the ocean tides, or what is the source of love. In the field of cosmology, for example, scientists can turn the clock all the way back to one-trillionth of one-trillionth of one-trillionth of a second *before* the spark-moment—the first cause—that ignited the beginning of the universe. The spark-moment, they say, caused a cataclysmic bang, unlike anything humans will ever be able to duplicate. In science, this moment has come to be known as The Big Bang. It takes an extraordinary bit of scientific work to get that far back, almost all the way back to the beginning of everything we know and see. Math and science have given us a picture of a self-contained universe that spans fifteen billion light years, a finely tuned cosmos[9] set up just right for human beings.[10]

Yet the question remains: we get that a bang set the forming of our universe in motion, but what *caused* the bang? No one on earth can answer that question. It remains a mystery.

Mysteries abound in our universe. No physicist, for example, can tell you exactly what energy is, but we harness energy in order to live. No one knows what lies beyond the event horizon of a black hole, but we believe black holes exist. No one knows where gravity comes from, but we enjoy its stabilizing power every second of our lives. Other mysteries hound our imaginations. No one can sufficiently explain why suffering exists in this world.

Where does beauty come from? What is it about the flow of water off the side of a mountain that makes us feel so deeply?

These questions create a thirst in us. We want to know more, even if there's nothing more that can be known. Mystery brings us back to our word. It was there *before* the beginning.

Before the bang, before anything at all, there was the Word.[11]

The ancient Greeks believed in this something called the "Word." Their term for it was *logos*, and it meant reason or wisdom or even science. But there is another Word, another *logos*. It is reason, and it is wisdom, and it is science, and it is so much more. This Word is a person, and it is a deity, and it is the source of all the spark-moments we experience in our imaginations, and it is the source of big bang moments in space before the universe existed. This Word has existed since before the beginning of our world. And this Word is not only *with* God the Father, it *is* God, and this Word *is* with another called the Spirit.

Christians know this Word by another name: Jesus. Together, God the Father, Jesus, and the Holy Spirit form a beautiful tapestry of communion. They are three, and they are also one, another mystery that compels our imaginations. That's what makes the story so intriguing. It does not begin, "Once upon a time." It begins, "Once *before* a time." And not just *a* time but *any* time. We like stories that begin with "Once upon a time," because that phrase places us in some faraway land or in a particular era of world history. It gives us a starting point, and we like starting points.

Imagine the setting. The Spirit, or what the Hebrews called the *ruach*, "covered over" the waters of chaos, like an eagle *covering* her young: protecting, giving life. This language of "covering over" pops up again when God "covered over" the Israelites on the night of the final plague in Egypt. God saved them from the destroyer. This imagery of shelter and care for his children paints a picture of God's beautiful love for you and me. And it is from beneath his caring wings that he breathed life into humanity. The created order ignited beneath the wings of the Spirit when the Word spoke.

The magic of this story is that the starting point takes us to an unimaginable place with a mysterious spiritual being who is about to do something beyond our wildest dreams. It begins *before* the beginning, when the Word spoke into the nothingness and suddenly . . . *light* and *life*.

What misconceptions about beauty and wonder have plagued your thoughts?

I used to fall into the trap of thinking beauty and wonder were merely aesthetic concepts limited to personal experience. But that is not the whole story.

We sense wonder in life not because of a psychological trick, something only related to personal experience, but because the world is charged with a heavenly nobility. Our culture tries to mute this reality. It wants us to think the world revolves around us. This is a lie. Beauty and wonder reflect God's excellent nature. Everything created reaches toward the nobility of heaven. This is why pain and suffering cannot be ends in themselves. Like organic material, they must break down and continue along the rebirth process. Our brokenness stirs with the soil of God's nobility to bring life to the seed.

The cycle of death to life speaks of the overwhelming goodness infused in our world. Death and brokenness are not ends. They are not primary. Death does not possess sustaining power, and so it must give way to the only force that prevails: the strong force, the life sustainingness of heaven, the loving shelter of the covering One.

Beauty is not merely the waving wildflowers upon Mt. Mitchell. It is the abundant heart behind the wind and delicacy. It is not only the brushstroke and the dab but also the virtuous aim of the artist. Beauty is not the vaulted ceiling and stained glass, it is the noble character they seek to express. Beauty is not the math formula, but the rubric of life that science seeks to describe.

I discovered a bouquet of love that day on Mt. Mitchell. It spoke life and light to me—a love note reminding me where beauty begins, a whisper-thought awakening my spirit to these truths:

- God created you for his noble and good purposes.
- Your brokenness will turn to wholeness.
- The delight found in the world is for you.

CHAPTER 4

THE LIFE OF PRACTICAL ROMANCE

Our Need for a Beautiful and Terrible God

L ight and life.

Don't miss the moment of beauty here. Light and life are the building blocks of beauty. If we adjust our perspective and look at the creation with new eyes, we see God's affection in the breath of his creative word. Consider *life*.

What is life?

Something beyond the self, a gift given, a treasure sought? But what *is* it? What gives it meaning?

From the time of the ancients until now, human beings have longed for the *thing* beyond. It quickens the hearts of all. It echoes with the tremors of the truest and purest essence of life. But our hearts betray us in our quest to possess the object of our desire. Veering from the path of true presence with God, we settle for shallow gratification tied to temporal things.

Was this longing present even in Eden, when humans lived in the presence of God without the veil of the cloud to hide God's glory? If so, was it the purest of longings, one ignited by the assuredness each day brought of walking in glory? How differently the first man and woman saw the world, with Godlight suffusing everything they touched and saw. That was life as they knew it: a surging power throughout all things imbued with the movement toward the source.[1]

Think about a seed dropped into the ground. It immediately interacts with its dark, cold surroundings; the moisture from rain, the stream of air moving through the smallest of airways in the soil. The seed awakens, drawn out by the elements, then pushes hard toward the surface, where the sunlight calls to it; a snapshot of the *I-Thou* (you and me to God) relationship: the seed moving toward the energy that gives it life. But it still has some distance to go before it is strong enough to breach the topsoil and emerge into the open air. It reaches beyond itself to survive, toward the life-giving light of the sun.

Once in the open air, the plant continues its relationship with the soil, gathering nutrients with its roots, and utilizes the process of photosynthesis—the converting of light energy into chemical energy—to feed and thrive. It relies upon the sun and soil and water and air to flourish and, eventually, contribute to the food chain. Left alone, however, the seed will not grow. Or, if it does sprout, disease will kill it. Life, then, is not a static endeavor. It teems with effort, requiring the participation of multiple players in order to thrive.

The Christian views God as the giver of all life: "in him we live and move and have our being" (Acts 17:28). He is the sun to our photosynthesis, the soil for our seed, the water for our roots. Jesus reminded his followers to abide in him, the symbiotic relationship of the vine and branches. Nourishment needed for life comes through him. *True life withers away from God.*

We possess this energy called life, and God invites us to be distinct as he is. Thus, the dance of learning to live in God begins, and we spend our whole lives either pursuing him, rejecting him, or ignoring him.

Adam and Eve woke to such an energy; a relationship drenched in an incomprehensible feeling of rest—did they call it peace? The rest of God? But then estrangement entered through Adam and Eve's decision to defy God, to not love him. In a breath, life fractured. Perhaps the light did, too? Maybe we're only seeing the light of the world through a prism bent by sin. Can you imagine what the pure light of God looks like? Or what the energy of pure heavenly life feels like?

Scholars note the drastic difference in language between Genesis 1–3, the story of the creation of the cosmos and human beings, and Genesis 4–6, Adam and Eve's estrangement from God, the withering of life, fratricide, and the first cities of man. Even the Hebrew language ignites in fractures, just as the *I-Thou* relationship does.[2] The energy remains—this thing they understand to be life itself—but the animating source no longer permeates their vision of life. The Beauty Chaser feels this estrangement with keen awareness.

For a moment, let's reflect on the sheer presence of God before Adam and Eve's estrangement and wandering. Let's stay in that moment for which we all yearn: *wholeness*. Adam and Eve experienced a wholeness and a joy incomprehensible in our fractured experience. It was a wholeness marked by joy and the beauty of life. You and I know the story of the fall of humanity from Genesis 2. But let's take our camera lens and focus on a smaller moment, not the eating of the fruit or the deception of the serpent. Instead, let's fix our attention on what the first two humans might have felt being in the indescribable presence of God and then losing that presence.

Take a moment and think about what it would have been like to wake in paradise and live in such proximity to God himself, with his presence permeating your existence. As you read this story, imagining what it would have been like, let these questions wrap around your mind and dive into your spirit:

1. Do you desire God's holy presence in your life? Be honest about what you desire. It's hard but freeing to do so. When the world is falling in on you, as it does all of us in turns, what do you say when you cry out to God?
2. Can you describe the moments in your spiritual journey when

you've felt the most alive? Did you feel as if God covered you? Could you feel a palpable and weighty grace surrounding you? Go ahead and scribble your answers in the margins. That's what they're for.

3. What do you experience when you feel farthest from God and his love and grace? Have you ever felt lost? Have you ever traveled with a group or your family and lost someone—or thought you lost someone? Describe your feelings in one word if you can. How do you think God felt when his children listened to the serpent instead of choosing to love him?

STEP INTO THE STORY OF GOD'S PRESENCE

God is like a rambling man, creating worlds with his words and spinning them with a grizzled grace only he can understand. With childlike whimsy, he speaks. And there you are.

You are Adam—You sit there, next to the lion, next to the salamander; you are being birthed from his crushing thoughts. You are his whimsy. You emerge from his Word. And you are good.

It all happens so quickly, and it all takes forever. But there you are.

You are Eve—You have emerged, too, out of bone and breath. What do you know? Only what is beneath your feet— it is all you *can* know. A presence draws you. It is everywhere and in everything you see. You can even hear it in the wind and in the water—a strange yet familiar tongue, a language you already know, a voice that is life itself.

This voice brings the two of you together. You touch and smile and play in the water. You sleep and wake and eat from the trees. You only know this way of things. The Source, the permeating *presence*, satisfies every need. He walks the evening path, a torrent of wind goes before and follows, but because the torrent of his *presence* is all you know, you feel at ease when it comes. You breathe the torrent deeply into your lungs.

"Ah," you say. "Always what I wanted and needed." And you want the torrent all the time. A voice speaks to you both from the torrent, and you fling your bodies around, dancing to its beauty.

You don't know what hope is, only that when the bright fire wakes you into that time called day, into that space of brilliance, you will find new things that will send your minds racing and hearts pounding. And it will be that sense of anticipation culling your minds to sleep that will, likewise, raise you again, expecting more when you wake. And so the cycle goes. Life unfolds in the liturgical beauty of waking, eating, and sleeping.

Each day you are like children recently born, opening your eyes to a place wholly new. Sometimes you catch the *presence* lifting off both of you in a rush, like the wings of an eagle lifting from her young as she rises up and away, leaving the eaglets to the task of flying. You know the wings covered you, nurturing you while you slept, keeping you safe while you dreamed.

Feelings rise in your gut each day for the first time: laughter, joy, curiosity, eagerness, longing. All the while, the *presence* imbibes you. You know the *presence* as your Origin, the Creator. His name is his existence, and that is all you need. He is the torrent and your breath as well. You talk with him, and he reveals himself more each time the bright light appears in the heavens. The more you see the more you want to know, the deeper the love, the deeper the sense of belonging—of being at peace together.

But you never expected the serpent to speak like the beautiful voice in the air. You never expected to *feel* knowledge. You never expected to fall in love with yourself. As a result, you've lost everything. The torrent returns, but this time the beautiful splendor turns to fury and terror.

Did he change? you think to yourself. *What's happened?*

"Where are you?" booms the voice of the torrent.

Words you'd never expect to hear from the *presence*.

"Doesn't he know everything?" you whisper to your partner.

Then it dawns on you. What if the One isn't really asking for our whereabouts? What if he is trying to send us a warning?

Something's wrong.

The Park, the light; things aren't the same, you think to yourself. *He's calling for me as if he can't find me, but I am the one who feels as though I've lost what is most precious.*

Your stomach aches with that sick feeling you get when you realize your child isn't at the Park Street market anymore. She's lost.

"Everything's backwards," you say to your partner. "He's calling us, and yet I feel desperation."

Your heart rate skyrockets. Your palms sweat. Your breathing becomes erratic. You squint in fear and cry out, "I'm here!"

Your voice cracks like that of a child searching hopelessly for its parents.

"Don't you hear me? Don't you *see* me?" you shout.

Sobs come, heaping despair on you like the light used to heap wonder on you. But the light gave life. This new thing—it drowns you without taking your life. In a final attempt, you shout from the growing shadows.

"Father! Father! I'm *here*!"

The torrent sweeps in around you, so close you can feel it. But the *presence* is gone. It's just wind.

"Oh God—am I lost?"

You and I have been struggling in the shadows ever since that day, striving to regain what was lost. We lost belief. We lost innocence. We miss our Father.

ALIVE WITH THE SUPERNATURAL

Here's the tension in which you and I live and struggle.

We live lost and feel an acute desperation in our lostness while, at the same time, we sense the *presence*. We sense God. The *presence* remains in the world. For millennia, every person felt it and admitted that in some fashion. They did not always admit the *presence* was YHWH, but they knew something was there, covering creation, oozing through the glory and the muck.

Walk with me for a moment down the footpath of ancient history as I sketch the story of how the supernatural was understood in our world before modernity removed it.

History shows us that this kind of mystical experience of nature compelled humans all over the world to not only eulogize spaces but to divinize people. They wanted to identify places, people, and forces that embodied the holy wonder they so desired and feared.

In ancient Sumer, people observed the ebb and flow of nature and concluded that more was at work than the base instincts of animals and their migration to certain areas at the same time every year. They noticed the weather patterns, the profusion of plant life, the seasonal flooding of the Nile and the life produced by the over-abundance of water, the ritual movement of the stars and celestial bodies, as well as many other unexplainable occurrences in nature. They reckoned a supernatural force was behind it all.

For the Sumerians, water possessed deeply mysterious or otherworldly qualities. Water produced life in abundance, and not just one kind of life but many different species. They labeled this mystery an *abzu*. The *abzu* was a mass of water below the surface of the ground; from it came the flood springs of life, and it had a "life and will of its own—a numen [spiritual or divine power]."[3] The Sumerians believed the water itself was *abzu*. It possessed the supernatural qualities necessary to bring forth life.

The *abzu* was a force of life, and it was uncreated—it had always been there. The Sumerians observed this numen in other regions, such as the desert, where thunderstorms formed and watered the arid lands, sustaining grass and trees so the livestock could graze. If you'll excuse my brief detour to the galaxy known for *Star Wars*, the *abzu* was to them what the Force is to Luke Skywalker, but without the ability to guide his lightsaber skills.

Over time, the Sumerian definition of the *abzu* shifted from mysterious life force to a theriomorphic deity, which took the form of an animal that possessed the *abzu*. In time, the view of a theriomorphic deity evolved until the Sumerians believed the *abzu* took the form of a human (anthropomorphic).

Ancient historian H. W. F. Saggs explains this fascinating progression from the belief in a mysterious life force to the belief in a human-like deity clothed in majesty by explaining how reverence worked among humans. In small villages, the male leader was not held in reverence among the people because of economic and social equality. But in larger city-states, where social and economic inequality existed, awe and reverence could more easily form. With the emergence of such emotional responses to their own human rulers, the Sumerians began to identify the *abzu* as "supernatural rulers in human form."[4] The waters, then, did not *possess* a numen. Instead, a human-like deity ruled the domain of the *abzu*. The same was true of the thunderstorm. Human-like deities sprang from natural phenomena that humans could not explain. This explains the rise of nature gods throughout ancient Mesopotamia, like Marduk (the precursor to the Greeks' Zeus and the Romans' Jupiter), god of creation, or Baal, god of thunder.

It is only in the last five hundred years that humanity has abandoned the gods. For the better part of world history, human thought and its reflective culture lived, breathed, and existed beneath the shadow of the supernatural. The earliest known civilizations did not ask the mechanistic question, "How did all this (creation) happen?" Instead, they observed their natural world as possessing *numinous* (having a sense of the divine) qualities. They took for granted that mysteries abounded in the created world with no explanation other than that something divine existed beyond their own physical reality.

EMPTYING THE SKIES OF WONDER

The modern consciousness, however, divorces the supernatural, or the "invisible qualities," from the experience of beauty, awe, and reverence. Instead, it begins its analysis of beauty with the physical object or person and how that experience of beauty makes a person feel (aesthetics). It skips over the metaphysical (existing beyond the physical realm) and ontological (questions about being) elements of beauty that, for millennia, left people awed.

In 1902, William James, in his landmark book, *The Varieties of Religious Experience*, said, "Religion . . . shall mean for us the feelings, acts, and experiences of individual men in their solitude, so far as they apprehend themselves to stand in relation to whatever they may consider divine."[5] When a civilization gives individuals permission to decide what the divine is for themselves, as James encourages, the wonder and distinctness of true religion empties from the collective consciousness.

What is left? Man, without God.

In this vacuum, you and I stand free to gaze at the brokenness of the world, and to revel in the imperfections we see and experience daily.

To make religion more utilitarian, we must denude it of the holy, making it altogether unadventurous. Our modern thirst for redefining language takes the word "religion" and transmogrifies it into something safer, something more inclusive.

The Pulitzer Prize–winning author Annie Dillard once lamented how the world drones on in a kind of suppressed silence. This silence, she says, is the hum of the world: birdsong, the trees waving in wind, all the things that happen whether I am there to watch or hear them happen or not. All this is silence because we have removed the holiness from it.[6] We've muted everything that used to be sacred and full of language. God used to speak to humans from the thundercloud, says Dillard, but the Israelites feared him (Ex. 32) and sent Moses to the mountain. So God talked only to Moses and told the Israelites to go into their tents. God stopped talking to us, says Dillard.

But did he, really?

I agree that we've muted the holy with our self-centered and isolated lifestyles, but it is not God who decided to stop talking. It is us. *We* walked away from the conversation.

When Moses trekked up the mountain, the impatience of the Israelites boiled over and, in their haste to have a religion they could control and feel safe in, they transgressed the holy and built their own pagan idol. This pattern of idol-making marks us still.

And yet, even though we've seemed to empty the skies of glory, we bemoan the lack of holiness we experience in the world by blaming God. Does this sound familiar to the rhetoric of the modern West? We cast God out of politics, education, arts and entertainment, business, even the church, and then complain about the decadence and despair of our culture, when in fact, it is the existence of religion within any culture that gives it an ethical center. And central to the ethical center of culture is the pursuit and expression of wonder and beauty.[7]

Beginning with the early civilizations of the ancient Near East (3000 BC), people perceived the world through a supernatural lens.[8] Whether that lens was pagan idolatry or the worship of YHWH by the Hebrews, people recognized that their natural place in this world was touched with the fullness of divine presence. Prior to the great casting off of the sacred, the sense of the supernatural was consistent in all societies, both pagan and monotheistic.

WE NEED A BEAUTIFUL AND TERRIBLE GOD

The force of life pulls us each morning out of our beds.

We shuffle across the kitchen floor, sip our morning beverage, and try, for a few moments, to take in the morning.

Is it meaning we grasp for in these quiet moments?

Is it meaning we reach for in the chaos unfurling in the day?

Is it meaning we cry out for when sickness, death, and war rake across the *presence*?

Is there a force strong enough to *cover over* the chaos and pull us to the mountains? Does the beauty we love in the world possess both the wonder and the power to crush the darkness?

It *is* meaning.

Like Sam, in our moments of isolation, pain, and loss, we long for what lies beyond the window, not only because we want to go there physically, but because we *know* that somewhere, beyond this material world, God waits for us, full of meaning and purpose. For life is more than food and the body more than clothes. Jesus pointed to the splendor of the flowers as an example of God's tenderness and love toward the most fleeting of life forms. Beauty reminds us of God's care in the fleeting times, the times of seeming waste and anxiety. Meaning, says Jesus, is found in seeking (Matt. 6:23–34).

"Seek the kingdom. Wait with me," he says.

"Wait *in* me," he reminds. "For I am the Strong Force, and I have overcome."

We need a God who is more than an icon we remember at certain times of the year. We need more than a high-five Jesus. We need the terrible and beautiful God of the universe. When C. S. Lewis was about eighteen years old, he created a word to encapsulate this kind of awful splendor. He called it *terreauty*.[9] Without a terreautiful God, our worship will fall flat and disappear. And worship is the *why* of our existence.

G. K. Chesterton also saw the need for an existence balanced with safety and strangeness. "We need this life of practical romance; the combination of something that is strange with something that is secure," he writes. "We need so to view the world as to combine an idea of wonder and an idea of welcome. We need to be happy in this wonderland without once being merely comfortable."[10]

But we've drifted far from the whisper-thought that dazzled the cosmos with instant wonders. Do you feel the drift? In your own spiritual life, does the strangeness of wonder and beauty counterbalance the pragmatic? Do you live with an *abzu*-like sense of the divine in your life?

And what about the Christian church? Do our worship gatherings express the worship of a terreautiful God, or do they express our own lust for emotional satisfaction at any cost?

We've boxed up wonder for consumption and have left beauty on the canning jar shelf. The church is complicit with the greater culture in this dimming of beauty. Our meeting places resemble malls instead of sanctuaries for the worship of our *terreautiful* God, places where we can experience the hush of holiness and the power of his glory. How did we get to this point where our world no longer appreciates beauty?

CHAPTER 5

BEWARE OF THE PLASTIC PEOPLE

Why the World Hates Beauty

My seven-year-old daughter crawled up beside me, her slight frame a twig against the trunk of my body. Then, as Zion is prone to do, she slipped up and over my leg and onto my lap. She burrowed her head into my chest as if she could somehow get inside me, her hair a tangle of gold and spring sunshine.

"What are you doing?" she asked as she emerged from the hole she was burrowing into my chest.

"Oh, I'm just sitting here, listening."

"To what?"

"Listen. Do you hear it?"

She squirmed over, her back on my belly. I closed my arms around her, and we sat for what felt like her lifetime.

"Oh, the wind," she said after she'd grown up in my arms.

"Yes, you stinker. The wind. Look, look there—that one tree. See it swaying back and forth?"

"Uh-huh. And all the other trees aren't swaying. Just leafing."

I smiled. "Yes, just leafing. Look at how far it sways. And it's so big."

"Daddy?"

"Yes, my love?"

"I love how wind feels on my skin, so soft and light, and how it's strong enough to move trees."

I looked down at her and smiled in disbelief at the magical power of *seeing* she possessed. Zion held her arms out to the tree line and moved her left hand over her right arm, acting like the wind was gently passing over her rosy skin. Then she pointed both hands toward the tree line and, with fingers spread, made a grabbing motion, acting out the other side of the wind.

Suddenly, a gale pushed through our woods—violent, clacking limbs and trunks.

She squirmed around and burrowed back into the hole in my chest, then fell asleep.

The mystery and strength of wind; that's what Zion observed. The mind of a child sees wind for what it is: magical and full of beauty and terror. When a child reads the words of Jesus to Nicodemus, they think, "What if I *am* born of the wind? Can I move the trees in the backyard? Can I make the leaves dance?"

> "The wind blows wherever it pleases. You hear its sound, but
> you cannot tell where it comes from or where it is going. So,
> it is with everyone born of the Spirit." (John 3:8)

I told Zion she was born of the wind. But she already seemed to know.

KILLERS OF BEAUTY

Beware of the Plastic People. They can't hear the wind. They don't take time to watch the trees bend in the breeze. They annihilate space with speed and noise. They're plastic because they kill beauty.

They've bought into the modern way of thinking about the world.

The Plastic People have figured everything out with formulas and predetermined GPS coordinates for life. They've shaped our world into a land of bottom-line thinking, pragmatic living, and market-driven achieving. Because, of course, the best way to measure success is whether we can scale something.

Whatever happened to the dreamers, the pioneers, the explorers, the people running to the frontiers of life? What happened to the people who viewed the world not as something to be conquered but as something to be experienced in all its terrifying, mysterious wonder? What happened to the people who do not follow the Plastic People's coordinates?

How desperate we are for these people. How incomplete our world would be without them.

Without you.

The Plastic People see nature as a material reality, rather than a gift from God. They view the world through a utilitarian lens; they want to know what it *does* for them rather than looking at it as an opportunity to participate with God through the created order.[1] It's a crucial shift.

We've stopped reading the book of nature.

Now, nature is the consumer item pinned to the backgrounds of our social media posts. We forget that God intended nature to factor into our daily lives. I'm not suggesting everyone needs to become a farmer, though I won't stop you from doing so. I *am* suggesting, however, that we open our eyes to the world God created, and *see* it again, for the first time.

I'm suggesting that, like generations before us, we do our utmost to learn from the created order. I believe that, as Hans Boersma writes, "our attitude toward creation should be as toward the Eucharist, to which we show much attention and care, so that no minuscule crumb will fall and be trampled upon."[2] Cultivating a eucharistic mindset invites enchantment. We see a world touched by God, full of his glory, and singing his praises. In contrast, cultivating a utility mindset invites disenchantment into our lives, a stale way of seeing the world, and a diminishing of spiritual realities in our lives, a dimming of beauty.

In Psalm 19, King David connects the inaudible language of creation (general revelation) with the eternal language of Logos—the Law of God. One directs us to the other. The diurnal grandeur of the celestial bodies speaks not with words but with movement, a dance of light and shadow. It is a language dripping with wonder, testifying to the craft of the artist, for the heavens "proclaim the work of his hands." This silent language speaks wherever the tongues of man reside. No person can escape the language of God's beauty seen daily in the sky.

And yet we do our best to keep it at bay through distraction, an unsustainable pace of living, and the constant feed of digital devices that we allow to supplant God's grandeur with a hollow world of fakery.

We're All a Little Plastic

I think we all have a bit of plastic in us. It's just that some of us choose to remain in the plastic world, while others happen upon a way out of it. Once we squeeze through the portal, we find the whole world staring us in the face.

"What do I do with it?" we ask.

"How do I understand it?" we puzzle.

I find the best way to understand something or someone is to explore it. I suppose, in this age, we think there's a set of directions on the browser we call "life."

"Just check the manual. Ask Google. Or call the help desk."

This won't do. We must listen to the voice buried deep inside of us and take the first step into exploration.

Even the famed atheist Richard Dawkins concedes our need to wake up and break out of the *anaesthetic* of life brought on by familiarity and the so-called ordinariness of the day. He wants us to break free from the humdrum, the sedative of ordinariness, and see the world afresh. We need to look for ways to break out of our plastic hell and reignite our imaginations. But Dawkins' god is science, so we are not surprised when he turns to examples found in biology, cosmology, and chemistry as a means to lift the anaesthetic of existence.[3] He praises the need for wonder in life but shuns the more *numinous* elements of existence found primarily in the humanities and religion.

Dawkins' approach to wonder, as is typical of mature deconstructive thinkers, regards culture with an authoritarian skepticism. He wants to strip the religion from culture, because he knows a culture devoid of religion dissolves into a monochrome civilization, where people live by the education of the powerful and elite rather than by the education of their curiosity and wonder. What Dawkins does not understand is that religion acts as the primary cog in any culture.[4] Culture without religion is like a sky with no sun.

Escaping the plastic world is a feat in and of itself, but it is only the beginning. Once out, we must learn to live in this gigantic, organic world of floating white rain bubbles (otherwise known as clouds); ever-moving celestial orbs (or planets); heaving bodies of tumultuous, wind-driven water (that would be the oceans); unwieldy jagged-topped rock formations (mountains!); and strange, two-legged creatures called human beings.

Learning to live does not require our complete understanding. Learning to live only requires our participation with the divine, and perhaps a cup of Earl Grey with some honey and a splash of whole milk (organic, of course).

THE OPPOSITE OF PLASTIC

The opposite of plastic is oak.[5] Think about it with me. A tree is alive, constantly growing, thickening, expanding, reaching for the sky. It sings in the breeze, howls in the wind, and creaks in the night just to make us uneasy. It is *alive*.

I trace the idea of living to the giant ninety-five-foot poplar that lived in our backyard for over a hundred years, until its roots rotted.

That old poplar did just what trees do, until it lost the strength provided by its roots.

"God, if you could just give me the strength," I whisper to myself more times than I can remember.

How many times has that prayer fallen from my lips into blank air? Still, how many times has wonder found me, renewing me, feeding me, just when I thought God was away on a walkabout? Perhaps he was—and that was the point.

"Come out here, Tim. Find me. Look. *See*. Be *oaken*. Explore this gift I've given you, and *live*."

The words of William Least Heat-Moon come to mind: "Maybe all a man gets is strength to wander for a while. Maybe the only gift is a chance to inquire, to know nothing for certain. An inheritance of wonder and nothing more."[6]

How did the world become plastic? How did we lose our oaken hearts? Why did we surrender our inheritance of wonder, ransoming it for bottom-line living?

TRAPPED IN A DARKENED ROOM

Let's look at the story of Sam and George from a different angle. Though their story communicates a few immediate insights into the nature of beauty in our world, if we press further into it, we can also draw cultural insights by way of analogy. Like Sam, we (as a culture) live trapped in a room, but not because of a physical illness. Our sickness affects our souls; we live trapped in a darkened room, sick with isolation and despair, with our participation and delight in the created world a fading memory. Indeed, despair and uncertainty mark us, and hope is a luxury we cannot afford.[7]

Our ailments, in many ways, are self-inflicted. Our collective isolation, brought on by the hyper-use of digital devices and the advent of social media, continues to plague us with feelings of inadequacy. We lie on our backs, unable to pull ourselves up and see beyond the walls of the reality we've created for ourselves.

What is this reality? We live alienated from each other and the natural world, severed from a concrete understanding of meaning and value. We believe knowledge and understanding of our world can only be achieved by reducing things, events, and humans to their simplest form.[8] This is what is known as reductive materialism, the philosophical idea that "the world is entirely composed of matter,"[9] and nothing else. Nothing in the beyond. What you see is what you get. If you want meaning, find it yourself, within yourself.

We believe technological innovation empowers us when, in truth, it enslaves us to those Nietzschean few who seek control.[10]

We find ourselves speeding into the Fourth Industrial Revolution, a time when the human body itself will see unprecedented change in the form of biological augmentation; at least, that's what some experts believe will happen. Soon, we will struggle to distinguish real from artificial human life. Will we create superhumans, extend life forevermore, and join our natural brains with computers? These questions do not come to us from science fiction anymore. This is our real world.[11] The Fourth Industrial Revolution will challenge what it means to be human.[12] It is a dark irony that at the height of our human powers to create and know, we will create something that will make it more difficult to know *ourselves*.

Our cultural affliction extends further than isolation and confusion about what it means to be a person in this world. It reaches into the very heart of beauty itself. For Sam and George, beauty existed outside of the self and worked as an instrument of hope and daily joy. Beauty was something they remembered as present not only in art but in nature and relationships as well, and it drew them out into the beyond, hinting at a source greater than any one person.[13]

Roger Scruton calls the loss of beauty in our culture the "postmodern desecration."[14] Scruton chooses his word, "desecration," carefully.

It is a religious word that implies the spoiling of what is sacred. Our culture is sick yet seeking, fraught with despair yet straining for something else, something more.

LOSING THE AIM OF ART

Art reflects the philosophical and anthropological values of a culture. We can see how deeply people think about beauty and religion by walking through a museum or watching a popular film or listening to music. Artistic expressions reveal the heart, intellect, and soul of a people; they also reveal the aim of such work. When the provocative art critic Dave Hickey views modern art as devolving into a "predictable, safe, formulaic money-driven enterprise,"[15] he's leveling a judgment upon an American culture that has shoved beauty into a box since the 1960s. He's decrying the banishment of beauty from one of our culture's major arteries: the world of art.

It is not that in order to understand beauty, one needs to understand art criticism or theory, the ballet or any of the fine arts, or even philosophy of art—whatever that is. These areas of artistic endeavor serve as our cultural witnesses; they act as portals into how we value beauty and religion and how they shape our culture. Beauty was pushed off a cliff shortly after the Renaissance. There was no water below. Just a death on the jagged rocks below.

Before the Enlightenment, artists considered beauty sacred, and it served as the goal of their work. But beauty lost its sacred position for the artist and became definable by the individual person. Scruton highlights *Piss Christ*, created by Andres Serrano in 1987, as a primary example of the desecration of the sacred. The photograph shows a small plastic crucifix submerged in urine. Serrano explains the work as indicative of his Christian faith and what it means for him to reflect upon the brutality of crucifixion. The aim of the piece is pure self-expression, even transgression.[16]

But we can go back further than *Piss Christ*. Picasso's program embodies the modern consciousness and even the postmodern mind, putting his transgressive eroticism and egomaniacal work into a world thirsty for art devoid of the supernatural. Picasso once said of his paintings, "To displace . . . to put eyes between legs, or Sex organs on the face. To contradict . . . Nature does many things the way I do, but she hides them! My painting is a series of cock-and-bull stories."[17]

In 1926, Picasso had an affair with a seventeen-year-old woman he picked up outside the Galeries Lafayette department store in Paris. Her name was Marie-Thérèse Walter. Picasso, forty-six at the time, used his desire for her body as inspiration for a series of his paintings. Picasso's style was rough. He wanted to "seize, penetrate, and immerse himself in the objects of his attention."[18] His paintings reform the young woman's body into "a series of orifices, looped together."[19]

Scruton describes our contemporary modern times as existing between two forms of sacrilege: on one side, there are the sugary dreams of *kitsch* (art with no message of its own),[20] and on the other, the savage fantasies of postmodernist desecration, as evidenced by *Piss Christ* and the erotic work of Picasso. Both reject the higher life of beauty, along with its values.[21] Scruton suggests the remedy to both kitsch and desecration is found in the relational notion of sacrifice. It is "when sacrifice is present and respected, life redeems itself; it becomes an object of contemplation, something that 'bears looking at,' and which attracts our admiration and our love."[22]

There is, however, one great obstacle to this remedy. It lies in the reality that kitsch and desecration exist because we are not *attentive* to the values of beauty. We live as if beauty does not matter.[23] This statement hurts our modern sensibilities.

"Of course, we care about beauty," we say, indignant as we rummage through our not-so-distant memories for an example of how we participated in something beautiful or produced something beautiful or appreciated something beautiful.

But Scruton's evaluation is cultural, not personal. And as confusing as that may sound, it makes sense even for those among us with strong affinities for modern art or who possess strong modern aesthetics. Scruton's critique observes the loss of the beautiful as the loss of a major value or virtue in our society that governs other aspects of life, like our rhetoric (the way we talk to one another in public), our judgment (what we deem worthy of esteem), or our ecology (the way we view nature).

It can be too easy to brush the art world aside. "It's fringe," we say. "It doesn't affect our day-to-day lives." But it does. The world of art connects to the entertainment industry. The entertainment industry feeds on the philosophies handed down from universities and colleges. Desecration of the beautiful begins in the classroom. And once students receive the amoral edicts from the ivory tower, the floodgates of cultural sacrilege open wide.

The Desecration of the Beautiful

In our culture, we are free to follow our desires almost without consequence. Today, artists and entertainers value self-expression over beauty as an end goal.[24] I'm reminded of what the popular philosopher (and musician) Taylor Swift once said, while shooting a cosmetic commercial: "Unique and different was the new generation of beautiful."[25] Beauty, for Swift, begins with the self.

I'm not suggesting that one's unique identity cannot be discussed as part of something beautiful. Nor am I indicting Swift's music. We've enjoyed many a family baking session with our daughters to the soundtrack of Swift's music. I just want to show the subtle slide of beauty in something as common as the world of cosmetics. For Swift and most of our modern culture, beauty has turned inward; *we* define it because we believe it originates with us, it's something we produce, something we define.[26] Discussions of beauty now devolve into discussions of aesthetics, focusing on how something looks and how its appearance makes us feel instead of dealing with the nature or essence of a person.

"Eh, but Tim," you say. "I thought you said earlier that we should expand our view of beauty in the world. And that it was okay to 'feel' beauty."

"Ah yes," I reply. "Indeed. I did encourage us to expand our view of beauty in the world. And I do hope you'll afford me this slight nuance. There is a difference between expanding our view of beauty, allowing it to encompass inner beauty and natural beauty, and resigning beauty to the pleasure of appearance and how that pleasure makes us feel. The subtle shift now has you and me defining beauty in any way we see fit, rather than understanding beauty as something greater than us—something out there in the beyond."

Let's continue with pop culture examples of beauty's downward spiral, because the examples are endless, right? Beauty's fall from something out there beyond the self to something found within the subjective opinions of human beings goes beyond mere self-expression. Modern artists relish transgression. They view themselves as outsiders, and provocation defines their work, so anything that shocks an audience or pushes beyond moral norms is art.

In the world of film, director Quentin Tarantino (*Pulp Fiction*, *Kill Bill*, *The Hateful Eight*) is the poster child for postmodern desecration. Tarantino uses extreme violence to transgress the moral norm and entertain his audience. Speaking at the British Academy of Film and Television, Tarantino said, "I feel like a conductor, and the audience's feelings are my instruments. I will be like, 'Laugh, laugh, now be horrified.' When someone does that to me, I've had a good time at the movies."[27] Tarantino justifies his self-expression by the end goal of amusement. The shallowness of Tarantino's artistic goal reveals his lack of emotional sensitivities. Meaningless violence operates as the tool of shock that desecrates the sacred. In this case, that which is sacred is life itself.

What are we to do with the dissonance we perceive between our perception of beauty in the world and the constant grating of modern society?

I am reminded of Iris Murdoch's stinging cultural critique. She said, "We no longer see man against a background of values, of realities which transcend him. We picture man as a brave naked will surrounded by an easily comprehended empirical world."[28] Ours is an unprecedented time of technological progress, moral bankruptcy, and loss of the sacred. The world is in desperate need of a George: someone to paint a picture of hope, someone to point the way to beauty.

LOSING OUR MORAL FIELD

What precipitated the desecration of beauty and elevation of the self above the sacred? We could spend the next several chapters discussing all the historical events and movements of thought that contributed to the desecration of beauty. Or we can summarize the last five hundred (or so) years with a couple of key figures. I've chosen the latter, but let's keep it in our pockets that cultural movements don't just spring up out of nowhere. An event, or person, or government shift, or war precipitates them. Nuance and time work their magic over the years, and it is impossible to ferret out all that has occurred throughout history. But we can point to tremors and the rumblings of movements of thought that give us clues to what brought us to our current situation in the modern world.

We can, for example, look all the way back to a figure like Dante (1265–1321) who, some say, was the first writer with a modern worldview.[29] Or we could go back even further, to the fourth century, and observe the abrupt end to the visual language of the ancient Greek pantheon of gods, which occurred when Constantine gave Christianity near-imperial status.[30] Perhaps we can put it this way: from the fourth century until now, human culture has endured a massive shift away from the ancient way of viewing the cosmos, which viewed reality as infused with the divine and the good as related to the supernatural (this viewpoint is called "cosmic piety"), to a modern perspective where the elevation of the "self" was the primary way to achieve the good.[31] And now, here we are, reading the cultural critique of Iris Murdoch and curious about the thought that got us here.

We see this movement of thought in the writings of David Hume, for example. In 1757, the Scottish philosopher wrote an essay titled, "Of the Standard of Taste," from which we get the axiom, "Beauty is in the eye of the beholder." Hume writes:

> Beauty is not a quality in things themselves: it exists merely in the mind which contemplates them; and each mind perceives a different beauty.
>
> One person may even perceive deformity, where another is sensible to beauty; and every individual ought to acquiesce in his own sentiment, without pretending to regulate those of others.[32]

Hume's thought is emblematic of a time in history when philosophy was changing right along with science and industry. It's popular to look at the birth of the machine and point to it as the icon of the demise of Romanticism. But with our growing understanding in science came the call for complete freedom of thought as well. "Freedom" was the cry of the Enlightenment.

A few decades after Hume, we find the German philosopher Immanuel Kant, who wrote several tedious books, setting out the intellectual (and moral) parameters of the Age of Enlightenment. In 1784, Kant wrote an article for the *Berlin Monthly* titled, "What Is Enlightenment?" The manifesto touts enlightenment as the process of growing up; to stop relying on the masters of old to dictate what we are to feel, think, love, and believe. Kant urged people to think for themselves. "Dare to know!" was the rallying cry, taken from the Latin axiom *Sapere aude*. "The public use of one's reason," wrote Kant, "must be free at all times, and this alone can bring enlightenment to mankind." A cry for intellectual freedom does not pose an existential threat at face value. But as with so many things in our world, when taken to the extreme, great harm can ensue. In this case, we find the mixture of the subjectivity of Hume mixed with the cry for intellectual freedom from Kant and are left with what we recognize as the modern cultural mind.

The turning points[33] in history orient our theological gaze and remind us that the cultural sickness in which we find ourselves in the twenty-first century is part of a progression of thought that leads away from the divine. Think about the ramifications of a world that throws off the shackles of authority in its quest for intellectual freedom. Icons of authority are treated with contempt, and along with them, God and his church. Just as artists turned inward and defined beauty for themselves, philosophers championed human will over God's sovereign will.

The British ethicist Oliver O'Donovan describes this shift as a time in history where "the structure of the creation with its variety, order and reflection of the Creator's glory no longer served to shape love and action." Our moral field was lost, and the "will became the exclusive giver of practical meaning."[34] That is to say, as long as a will finds satisfaction within itself, that is enough; the will of a person is its own end. We see this movement away from admiration of the Creator and his created order, and toward sacrilege in art and the dimming of beauty.

It's easy to talk about moral relativism in general terms regarding its impact on truth, but we seldom reflect on the destruction of love and admiration of the beautiful and the good, and the impact that has on a person and a society. Through self-assertion and self-expression, we've turned our backs on the beauty of the infinite and invited despair.

FIGHTING MAGIC WITH A DEEPER MAGIC

In the summer of 1941, C. S. Lewis preached a sermon at University Church of St Mary the Virgin in downtown Oxford, England. Students packed the chapel to hear the always dynamic Lewis give his address.

We now know this address as, "The Weight of Glory." Lewis's rhetoric soared as he exhorted the audience of undergraduates to beware of the magical charm that had subtly bewitched society. "Do you think I am trying to weave a spell?" writes Lewis. "Perhaps I am; but remember your fairy tales. Spells are used for breaking enchantments as well as inducing them. And you and I have need of the strongest spell that can be found to wake us from the evil enchantment of worldliness."[35] Lewis wants to fight magic with a *deeper* magic.

Considering the desecration and isolation embraced by the modern West, a loss of the spiritual shape of life,[36] and a vision of the world that dims and reduces,[37] Lewis's words come to us now as prophetic of our own time. Indeed, who will stand up and be George to the world?

Chesterton said it is the great paradox of history that each generation is converted by the saint who contradicts it the most. Chesterton believed that when a generation becomes too worldly, it is up to the saint, or the church, to rebuke it.[38] He says, however, that each generation chooses its saint by instinct. The saint is not what the world wants, but what it needs. A saint, writes Chesterton, is *someone who runs incongruous with the modern world*, like that weird uncle of yours who lives on a farm and seems a little off because he doesn't use the internet (I may or may not be that uncle).

If you are a Christian, then you are a saint. But it's not that you and I should come off as the weird internet-less uncle *per se*. It's that Christ himself called Christians to follow him. Such a spiritual pursuit gives the saint new eyes; she sees the world through the lens of heaven. Christians, asserts Chesterton, are the "permanently incongruous and incompatible people,"[39] the salt of the earth. And when the world leans too much in one direction, the Christian must offer a course correction.

The world needs an *incongruent people* who stand not against the world but outside of it, calling it to something *other*. If isolation and desecration spiral the world toward despair, what Søren Kierkegaard described as the impotent consumption of the self,[40] then the world needs saints who walk the path of enchantment, who speak in songs, who live in wonder with their eyes fixed upon heaven.

Think again of Sam, who finds himself cured and bursting back into the wonderful world outside his hospital room. What if he found George's vision of life beyond the hospital doors waiting for him? Can you picture it? I can see him meandering through the park, eyeing the hills beyond, smiling at the thought of somehow making it to those distant peaks. I can see him happening upon an incongruous person—a Beauty Chaser—who shows him the path toward the source of beauty.

Will that person be you? Will it be me?

A RETURN TO WONDER

What can heal us of the malady? It is only through a return to the wonder of the divine. But how do we do this?

The pathway to understanding the value and meaning of beauty in our world begins with worship. God created mankind to worship him and preserve the beauty of creation (Gen. 2:15). We can, too often, look to the creation account for clues as to how we are to engage with the created order, by being "culture makers," for example. But this view misses the central element in man's relationship with God. For what good is it to create culture if we no longer understand what it means to stand in the presence of God? This central element is *worship*—what some ancient theologians called "the vision of God."[41] The implications of this statement reach far into the nuts and bolts of how we live as Christians in the modern world. We might use the term *ethics* here; a morality lived as a witness to the divine wonder that we believe saturates all of creation.

Some people's eyes glaze over when I try to tell them why beauty matters so much in our modern world. Their indifference, however, shows how well modernity has done its job. It has replaced our sense of wonder with pragmatic, rational, and empty amusements. We treat beauty as novelty and wonder why despair crouches at our door. Or we think beauty is only for the elite in our society—understood by professors and art critiques and pop stars—and wonder why the profane saturates our existence.

We run to psychological answers—the unholy plane of Jung and Freud—because we no longer believe that the world of the spiritual provides sufficient answers. We say we believe in God but reduce his Word to a self-help guide. We retreat into our woundedness to find healing, because the mountain of God proves too rugged for our taste. This is what modernity does. It reduces and replaces the sacred with the profane. It casts doubt upon the unknown and mysterious while asking us to venture down a nihilistic path to nowhere.

Sam and George found themselves cast off, in the sick room of isolation. What about us? What was it that put us in that room with them? Perhaps we need a blind guide to help us escape. Or perhaps the guide has already come, and we are the blind ones.

When I held Zion that day and watched the wind toss the trees back and forth, I was teaching her to be oaken. And she was teaching me the same. We need constant reminders, alarms that keep us from falling asleep and returning to the world of the Plastic People.

One way to remain oaken is to take up the rugged path to Sinai. Not the real Sinai, of course, but a metaphorical one. It is the path of worship. But this worship doesn't occur in a sanctuary built by human hands. It begins in the sanctuary we call life. And the path to the mountain is cut with the *terreautiful* sword of God's holy splendor.

CHAPTER 6

WALKING THE PATH

How Chasing Beauty Can Transform Our Lives

I pulled up to the tiny airfield at 10:30 P.M. It was a cloudy Alaskan summer day in Anchorage.

My friend Jason had said, "Just get to the airfield, and I'll have someone pick you up."

That someone was Seth. I'd never met him. And I was about to hitch a ride in his plane, which was so small that I wondered if it was a remote-controlled toy. Our destination? Lake Clark. Where is Lake Clark, you ask? In the middle of nowhere, or what those who live there refer to as "the Alaskan Bush."

No big deal. Just a dark ride in a miniature plane with no lights into the Alaskan wilderness with a complete stranger over remote mountain passes and glaciers. I was completely calm.

"Tim?"

"Yeah; you Seth?"

"Yep. This is my daughter, Ashlynn."

"Hi Ashlynn."

She said nothing, just shot me a shy, if not wary, eight-year-old glance.

"Whelp, we gotta get moving so we can make it out to Lake Clark before it gets too dark," said Seth.

"Right, let's go."

I hopped into the back seat, which wasn't a seat at all—more like a sling topped with a Therm-a-Rest cushion. Seth handed me a headset and showed me where the lap belt was located. He murmured some numbers and said "Niner" at least once, taxied us out to the runway, and took off.

We climbed to one thousand feet and set a course for Lake Clark Pass, a high mountain passage that leads to Lake Clark National Park and Preserve and Port Alsworth, our destination. Jason had invited me to his cabin in the remote Alaskan wilderness for rest and retreat. We continued to climb as we passed Cook Inlet, a splinter of the Pacific Ocean.

"Hey Tim," said Seth, "I think we're going to take a little detour so we can beat these clouds."

Single propeller planes can't fly in clouds, a fact I only learned *after* our journey. We took a right over the Blockade Glacier. As we approached the glacier, Seth shouted into the headset, "Look! A bear!"

Fifteen-hundred feet below us, a brown bear was running across the open plain that swept up to the glacier. Seth whipped the plane around and dove down. My stomach shot up into my throat. My heart pounded. My mouth stretched ear to ear. We gave the bear a flyby, banked back toward Blockade, and continued our ascent into the mountains.

The glacier spread out in front of us like the uncoiled tail of a sleeping dragon. It wedged itself between the peaks; its color spiraled within itself—greens, blues, aqua, gray from the fissures, with white covering all. I waited for it to wake up.

We neared Lake Clark Pass. The clouds gathered around the ridge like a phantom gate, closing off the pass.

"We're just going to peek into that hole in the clouds there. If we get through that and down into the pass, we're good. If not, we'll have to turn back."

"Sounds good." What else was I supposed to say?

The clouds covered the surrounding mountains. The snowy gray mountain-scape disappeared slowly. Our hole was closing. We were close. I could see into the hole.

"We're going for it!" said Seth. He wasn't kidding.

Up and over, and, then—*whoosh!*—down we went under the canopy of clouds. In a moment, we descended from the dimming gray of overcast Alaskan twilight into the world beneath the clouds. The white pushed down on all sides, the mountains shooting up into the invisible while a streak of glacial blue ribboned beneath us, cutting its way through the valley.

We made it.

Beneath the clouds and into the pass we flew. A deep green covered the base of the mountains like a Christmas tree apron, but without the annoying tinsel.

My head swiveled as I tried to take in the rifling grandeur of the mountains, snow, rivers, waterfalls, and the massive lake that covered the valley floor for forty-five miles. This was a land of giants, of gods, of magic. This was where the great myths came to life. Eagles and angels ruled here, patrolling the skies with noble intent. Great Dall sheep silently guarded the craggy heights, while moose and bear scouted the outer reaches of the valley floor. I felt as if we'd flown into a parallel dimension, allowed to observe as long as we left the place the way we found it.

Finally, we approached the gravel runway. The light was weak, but Seth landed the Stinson with ease.

"Welcome to Port Alsworth," he said.

I exited the little plane and greeted my friends, who waited on ATVs along the runway. The night was still awake, but barely. The smell of pine blew into me faster than I could breathe. The mountains darkened, and the clouds drifted low, almost to the lake. I'd arrived in that quiet land, and all I could do was smile. No words came. It felt wrong to talk.

Something Lurking behind the Wonder

Think of one of your own experiences with beauty. Perhaps it was a profound and new experience, like mine in the Alaskan bush, that left you speechless; or maybe it's the memory of a quiet moment spent taking in the simple charms of life. We can all think of such moments, and not only for nostalgia, though that is certainly part of the joy. A story like the one of my flight over the glacier reminds me of three important keys I want us to keep in our pockets as we continue our adventure.

First, there is more to the world than material reality. Something lurks beyond moments of wonder. And though it gives us pleasure to experience it with our senses, the richness of the vision compounds when we contemplate and learn from it. This requires patience and time, two things in short supply in our raging world of hurry. My hope is that our discussion here will provide you with some tools to quit the hurry and find your contemplative sweet spot.

Second, we cannot manufacture beauty or mass-produce it. It travels like lightning across time and space and into our lives as a gift. It is precisely when we attempt to bottle beauty in quaint doodads that we lose the gift.

"Eh, but Tim," you say, "certainly you don't mean to say that we can't buy beautiful things."

"Ah, yes," I reply. "You are correct. I'm not suggesting that. Beauty creates in us the desire to replicate it through art, craft, music, dance, and whatever else we can think of. My comment here relates to our tendency as modern people to kill beauty by plasticizing it. Modern art suffers from this exact sickness. Find something cool and popular, mass-produce it, make a killing. But when we travel up the holy mountain and experience the fountain of beauty, we realize the beautiful in our world and in our private lives takes time. Producing something beautiful is hard; it takes toil and mastery. The rugged beauty of the Lake Clark Pass testifies to the care and ability of the Master Artisan."

Finally, our intuition tells us that beauty reaches beyond our

senses and inspires us to chase the Source. Remember, it was beauty that inspired Sam to pull himself through pain to see what lay beyond the window. The Beauty Chaser cannot be stopped—not by despair, not by pain, not by disappointment. The Beauty Chaser fights through it all to bring the hope she sees in her mind's eye. The Beauty Chaser lives as a beacon of joy.

Let's get chasing.

Sketching George and Sam's Park

The path of this book takes us beyond George and Sam's park and up to the peaks, to God himself. This is where we will rediscover true life. This is where beauty begins: with God himself. And when we discover the Source, we discover the *why* of beauty.

I want to take a walk with you, if you don't mind. I like walks. The slow kind wherein we ramble up hills and wind into glens. The rest of this book will be such a walk.

As I considered the story of George and Sam, the thought struck me: George's vision of the park, the hills, and the mountains looks like my own life. My own journey moves back and forth, from parks to hills, back to parks, and every so often, to the mountains. I mean this both literally and metaphorically.

Think about it. People gather in parks. They sit and relax. They take in the day. They walk around and try to free their minds from the rigors of life that push in hard against their spirits. People connect with other people in parks. They sit and talk. They play chess. They throw frisbees. They laugh. They cry. Parks, to me, look like giant puzzle boards in which all the edges of people's lives butt up against each other, connecting and forming a mosaic.

There are other places that serve as parks in our lives— metaphorically speaking, of course—places where we convene and love and worship and drink and eat. These are park-type places. Places of solitude, rest, and escape.

What about hills and moutains? Do we experience those metaphorically in our lives? I'm sure we do. We use "mountains" and "hills" as metaphors for challenges in life, yes. For me, however, the hills and the mountains that George described, and which Sam saw with his mind's eye, are very real. They are out there—beyond our gathering places. The hills and mountains draw us to them, but they also frighten us. They are not tame places most of the time. I feel like we must go to them, especially in this post-industrial age of ours. Then, after we've ventured out, I do believe we will have a metaphor to discuss. But not before.

The hills roll out toward the mountains, are cut by rivers and streams, are stretched by open fields and blotted by woods. Deer run in the hills. Foxes hunt. Coyotes, too. Pheasants nest. Rabbits hop. Owls stand watch. Hawks circle. Turtles waddle across the leaves in the afternoon sunlight. Hills act as thresholds to the wilderness of the mountains. Thresholds are always mysterious. And mystery, as we all know, can possess its fair share of dread, excitement, and beauty.

Mountains intimidate. Their heights lure us. They are dangerous, brutal, and solemn. At least, that's the typical view we have as we stand far off, looking at them. When approaching the base of a mountain, I feel a sense of awe—its ominous presence works on my mind and heart, for it is both awful and wonderful. But something incredible happens when I finally stand *in* the mountains, atop a rocky lookout or on a bald. I no longer feel the ominous presence of the mountains, as I did when I stood miles away, just looking at them. Rather, I feel joy. I stand giddy. Ah, the mountains—what a surprise.

Now, this walk I want to take you on will take us to very real places I have experienced—real parks, real hills, and real mountains. When I considered George and Sam's story and thought about how beauty inspired Sam, giving him new life, I was flooded with memory. For as long as I can remember, the outside world, with its natural wonders, has spoken to me through its beauty, and all the different elements associated with it—delight, joy, awe, dread, longing, hope—are the virtues of beauty I hope to uncover on our walk.

FOLLOWING A TRACK

To learn means "to walk a path." In the field of spiritual formation (in French, the word for "formation" means "training"), we like to use words like *practices, disciplines, rhythms,* or *cadences.* I've adopted these over the years, like many of you. In our family, for example, we use the phrase "Our Oxford Rhythm." It was during our time living abroad in Oxford that we learned what it meant to slow down, live simply, and focus on one thing at a time. Our rhythm of life changed from an anxiety-inducing existence in Atlanta, Georgia to one with a gentle pace in Oxford. By *rhythm,* I mean our daily routine, or habits, changed. But it was the footpaths of learning that confronted me with lasting heart transformation. There's no doubt that we *are* what we habitually *do.* We become what we love.

As in any kind of liturgical setting, the rhythm of existence can turn into a cold, rote way of life. Just as we can repeat real spiritual liturgies, such as catechisms, without the joy of their truth shaping us, we can also fall into an existence in which we might change our daily rhythms but our hearts, instead of growing in love for the spirit behind the life change, grow cold. Think of it like the "whitewash tombs" criticism Jesus leveled at the Pharisees. Or liken it to working out daily and eating healthy food but filling your mind and heart with junk entertainment. You are body-strong but soul-weak.

Let me explain more about what I mean by "footpaths of learning."

In his book *The Old Ways,* Robert Macfarlane, a British writer and fellow of Emmanuel College at Cambridge, reminds us how footpaths cut into the landscape over centuries serve a greater purpose than getting us from point A to point B. *The act of walking teaches us.*

The phrase "to learn" (Old English *leornian*), he says, falls to us through etymology that means "to follow or find a track." In this way, a footpath stretches out before us and invites us to learn with each footfall. Think about your favorite walk or hike. The path takes you to a place. But if you pay attention as you walk, you will realize each step leads you to a deeper knowledge of your surroundings.

I want to apply this idea to our spiritual adventure in this book. I want to show you the different footpaths that continue to teach me about beauty. In some cases, I will literally take you on a walk along a path in a dark wood, in the wilderness, or through a town. We'll observe the landscape, the light, the flora and fauna, the people walking the streets, and see what truths we can uncover. But I will also use the metaphor of the footpath as a structure. Every person walks their own path in life. Our journeys take different routes, but we all arrive in the same place: before God. What will our footpaths teach us? Where will they take us spiritually? What footpaths are we carving out for ourselves throughout life?

TOGETHER INTO HOLY WAYFINDING

Now that we're drawn together into this community of Beauty Chasers, let's get our bearings for the path ahead.

Let's pretend you and I are navigators. Not just the run-of-the-mill navigators, but old-world celestial navigators who rely on the stars and planets to guide our vessel to safe shores. Think of our little interaction here as an exercise in what I like to call "holy wayfinding." It is a cosmic anthropology of sorts, in which I attempt to sketch a map for the countercultural among us; namely, *you*.

A Wayfinder is an expert navigator. He uses the tools around him to navigate the mountains, the oceans, the secluded paths that lead to who knows where. When we find ourselves on the far side of the world, in waters seemingly too rough for safe passage, we have no choice but to look to the stars to find our bearing, set our course, and ride the dangerous waters home. It is the buffering of the waves and storms that forge our strength. But it is the heavens that turn us into Wayfinders and Beauty Chasers.

In any exploration, the adventurer will mark interesting objects and places along the path called *waypoints*. We'll use our own series of Waypoints as markers of reflection. These pauses are intended to help us find our way through the spiritual adventure of discovering the place "where all the beauty came from."[1] The Waypoints will vary from a list of questions you might choose to use for individual reflection or as a group or a meditative challenge, to a list of suggestions for establishing your own footpath of beauty for your life and home.

FOR THE LOVE

Some years ago, I coached varsity women's volleyball at a private school. I played volleyball in high school and college myself, where I was blessed with wonderful coaches. My coaches were more like mentors of the game than coaches of the game. They did not focus on the strategy or the wins and losses when I was a young player. They were teachers. I soaked it up like a dry sponge caught in a hurricane.

When the opportunity came to coach the junior high team, I jumped at it. Not many people have patience for this age group, for some reason. But I love middle school–age children. They, too, are like sponges. I spent a year coaching those young ladies before I moved to the varsity level. When I sat them down at our first practice, I said, "Listen, my goal for you this year has nothing to do with wins and losses. It has everything to do with your love. I will view this season as a success if, after the last game, you can look back and say, 'Wow, I had so much fun this year. I love my team, and I love volleyball.'"

I'm not one of those coaches who says, "Well, at least we tried, and that's what matters most." I believe winning absolutely matters. Every person needs to understand how to win at something.

But winning is a byproduct of love. If you give me a team that just thinks volleyball is all about right technique and doing all the right things to get a win, I will spend half the season reprogramming that thinking. But if I can take a young team and teach it how to love the game, to have fun playing the game, then I can win with that team in a heartbeat.

This philosophy works! When I moved up to varsity, my eighth graders moved up with me. They understood the stoke I was after. When I say "stoke," I mean a passion and enthusiasm for the game and for each other—players given to challenging one another and standing by one another, come what may. I wanted passionate players who were willing to give everything for each other. I wanted kids who were willing to pour their sweat and blood into a process that was sometimes grueling but always full of stoke. In two years, we won a championship and nearly made it to the state tournament in the public school league. It was an awesome ride. But it began with love.

When you love something, it's nothing to give yourself to it. It's nothing to work hard, stay after practice and hit one hundred balls, serve till your arm falls off, or run the same play again and again and again.

People play sports for all kinds of reasons: status and popularity, dominance and winning, money and fame. But an athlete at any level who can't get enough of the sport, who gives everything in practice, whose attitude is infectious, is a leader whose love for the game will move throughout the locker room and infect everyone. That kind of impact begins with a love of the game.

This same principle applies to our spiritual journeys. In the New Testament, Jesus had to correct the disciples for desiring fame and status in his kingdom, for believing their purpose was political. He had to show them that his kingdom was about love and sacrifice. If you wanted to follow Jesus, you needed to give up everything dear to you and fall in love with Jesus himself and the journey he was undertaking.

So many believe the Christian life is about doing the right things, filling in a moral checklist, or following the rules. But it's not. It is first and foremost about falling in love with Jesus. He wants your heart first. The rest will come in time as your desires form to his heart instead of your bent one.

Stop trying to do the right thing in life and in your spiritual journey. By "right," I don't mean righteous things. I mean the things you think you need to do for success. This is the blurry lie of culture. We are inundated with the "right" ways to get to the Plain of Success. But the problem with this kind of thinking is that it's contrary to the Christian Way.

We need to fall in love first. We need to cultivate intimacy with our Savior. This is the first step of the Christian life. The question that follows naturally is, "Well, how can I fall in love with him?"

Three qualities come to mind.

In the previous chapters, I've sketched a portrait of God's love for us by telling the story of light and life, and the story of the fountain. **First, love for God begins with awareness.** We must do our utmost to cut footpaths in our lives that allow us to journey as participants of his glory, love, and beauty.

Second, love for God begins with clear eyes and a perspective on who he is. When we see God for his goodness and beauty, his power and glory, we feel reverent. His wonder humbles us. This is the beginning of worship. It's a response of clear-eyed love for the Holy One, but also reverent awe.

Finally, love for God begins with a surrendered heart. A surrendered heart does not mean you won't lapse into selfishness or fail morally or spiritually in your life. It means you come under the loving guidance of his Word, the Law and Logos of God.

Remember, a heart and soul that loves something will find it inviting and even easy to submit to the rigors of spiritual disciplines and the training of the soul for worship.

Let's consider these questions as we set off on this adventure of reinvigorating a life lived before God:

1. Does my spiritual life revolve around activism more than contemplation?
2. Has my busyness throttled my prayer life?
3. Does life with Christ invigorate me or frustrate and confuse me?
4. Do I rely on emotional highs to feed my spiritual need for true worship?
5. Do I regularly experience awe and wonder in my experience with the natural world?
6. Do media and screen time dominate my leisure time?
7. Who is God to me: disconnected wise sage somewhere in the cosmos, or wonder-filled Creator?

As you consider these questions, notice how the final one digs into the idea of your spiritual perspective of God. This is important. As you reflect on this, ponder C. S. Lewis's thoughts on how we shape our perspectives.

Lewis once found himself standing in a shed on a sunny morning. A beam of sunlight shot through a crack above the door. He observed the beam, noticing the dust particles floating in the light. The golden beam made the inside of the shed look black. But then he stepped into the beam so that the light fell upon his eyes.

Instantly, the shed vanished. Standing within the beam, his entire world of vision transformed. He no longer saw the beam. Instead, he saw everything else *by* the beam. He saw the leaves outside fluttering, and when he gazed into the light, he squinted into the sun itself, the source of the beam, the fountain of gold that washed everything he saw with wonder.[2]

Lewis wrote about his experience in an essay titled, "Meditation in a Toolshed." In it, he makes the point of cultivating a balanced perspective. Only looking *along*, or only looking *at* the beam will warp our perspective, which will rob us of context and hobble our actions, for our perspectives inform how we live.

PART 2

FOOTPATHS OF THE PARK

Beauty Desires Your Participation

A Fieldnote for Footpaths

The Guiding Principle

God is beauty. And the beauty we encounter in this world directs our hearts not just in God's general direction, but to worship him in his holiness. We affirm his excellence and honor him. This worship posture is reflected in how we live our lives.

Chasing beauty is an act of worship.

A Quick Note for Ramblers

Many of these footpaths were cut centuries ago. Nothing new under the sun, you know. But the age of the path does not determine the relevance of the truth we find along the way.

I offer these footpaths, not as some elaborate map you must follow with rote adherence. No. The beauty of the English footpath is its loose meandering. Footpaths traverse the countryside, inviting free exploration. Adopt these footpaths, but, please, add to them as well. Make them your own.

I continue to learn more about beauty, more about God, as I venture down these footpaths. I pray that as you traverse the trails with me, you will find renewed spiritual adventure and intimacy with the Almighty.

CHAPTER 7

THE ADVENTURE OF HOLY WAYFINDING

The Footpath of a Countryside Ramble

As I sketched out the old story about George and Sam, I pictured the scene for myself. The park I imagined looked as you might expect. A pond, large trees dotting the undulating landscape. A playground, a rose garden, an open field inviting games with balls and kites with tails. The park possessed a familiar beauty—do you know the kind? Like laughter during backyard tire-swing sessions in summer—yes, that kind.

I saw myself walking beneath the old silver oaks and along the pond's edge. I stopped and fed the ducks but did not linger. For just beyond those meandering paths lay the foothills. I could see them from the park. They called to me, with their looming tree lines and mist. And the closer I came to them, the further I was able to see beyond to the mountains rifling up toward the sky. And of course, the vision of the peaks made me want to explore the mountains.

Part of the wonder and charm of the park, I mused, comes from the sense of what lies beyond its edge.

Edges keep us curious, don't they?

Much can be said for edges. You and I live on the edges, where life churns in a kaleidoscope of activity, desires, passions, failures, interests, and relationships; here, the wildness of life meets with the beauty of it. My life connects with my brother's, with my friend's, my colleague's. I often hear people call these connections—or are they collisions?—a beautiful mess.

"Life is messy," we like to say.

But is it? Really? Or are we just saying that because some celebrity said it?

"But, Tim," you say, "surely you must admit life is hard and—well, messy."

"Ah, yes," I reply. "I do realize I am probably the only person on the planet who would say such a thing. But please hear me out. I question this cultural axiom not because I don't see how 'messy' life can get, but because I believe when we say something over and over, to the point that it becomes a cultural trope, the meaning can dig into our perspective of life and even taint it. Our words carry weight. They form our view of the world, each other, and God."

Is life beautiful? Yes. Is it messy? Sure.

But for me, a Christian optimist, what G. K. Chesterton refers to as a "cosmic patriot,"[1] I gravitate toward language that upbuilds, as Søren Kierkegaard liked to say. I don't need to be reminded of the muck of life. I know it's there. I want to champion an outlook that says, "How can we overcome evil with good?" Thank you, St. Paul! So perhaps I can convince you, my dear friends, to look at the explosion of beauty we call life, see it for all its variegated wonder and lift a hallelujah for all the goodness. Like in painting, shadow and light mix to create contrast, contrast works on our eyes to create depth, and in depth we find awe. So, this is me, your friendly neighborhood contrarian, just throwing a curveball at our cultural lexicon and suggesting we reset our gaze on the beauty that our daily connections and collisions bring us.

I like to call these connections "the edges."

I don't see messiness, *per se*.

I don't see chaos—well, not in a primordial way.

I see a collision of worlds, diverse, unique, filled with mystery, touched with delight, and tinged with sadness. Like you, I spend my entire life trying to get beyond these edges and into the lives of the people I love. I call this "getting to know someone," or "building friendships," or "falling in love." Is that what you call it, too? I feel an unmistakable force that pulls me out of my comfortable places and into the worlds of other human beings. I love the edges, even as I suffer through them.

Let's make a mental note, shall we?

Edges are good, and the more we walk to the edges, into the edges, and beyond the edges, the more of this beautiful life we'll experience, understand, and know.

The Rumblings of an Adventure

Now, back to George and Sam's imaginary park.

Beyond the kite field, where the tree line shadow lurks, the deep part of a great river slows. There begins the foothills trail.

It opens, as all trailheads do, like a shadowy green portal into another place. I see the first few feet of the trail, then it disappears. It is a vanishing I love, for it draws me to it. It's a pleasant walk for a mile or so, then the path steepens. Up it climbs, over rocks and roots as the leafy giants give way to evergreen soldiers guarding the heights.

The further I look, beyond the hills and toward the mountains, the more I realize this is no ordinary walk in the park. Taken as a whole, the natural beauty of the landscape unfolding before my eyes in joyful beauty, the wonderful collisions of people walking about, entangled in one another's lives, creates a longing within me. I desire to collide with the people in the park. I also want to head out into the hills and see what lies beyond. And suddenly, I realize that this little imaginary scene I've created looks suspiciously like the beginning of an adventure.

"Adventure? Well, Tim, I have no time for an adventure," you might say.

I seem to remember Bilbo telling Gandalf nearly the same thing:

"We are plain quiet folk and have no use for adventures. Nasty disturbing uncomfortable things! Make you late for dinner. I can't think what anybody sees in them."[2]

But I must insist, like good ol' Gandalf, that this adventure requires my presence and yours. It's one I believe we won't soon forget.

Adventures, from my experience and from my knowledge of the childhood stories that I love, always begin in the comfort and safety of the familiar. I think of Bilbo entertaining the merry band of dwarves—eating cakes, drinking ale, and singing songs in his grand hobbit hole. At one point, as he sat and listened to the dwarves sing, Bilbo's heart leapt at the thought of hearing pine trees and waterfalls, of seeing mountains, of exploring caves and wearing a sword. For a moment, Bilbo thought of his own potential—of what might be if only he'd take up the adventure.

Beginnings are like that. They tease with visions of grandeur, then turn into something not-so-familiar. Eventually, the adventurer looks back and notices that the park, or hobbit hole, has disappeared. The path, no longer familiar, stretches on into the unknown, and the landscape changes. This can be frightening, but also invigorating. If you happen upon an old hobbit named Bilbo, just ask him.

My favorite adventures take me to new places, perhaps not dragons' lairs, but to places and things just as wonderful, just as terrifying.

When I was twelve, the Lancaster County cornfield that butted up against our yard represented an entire world in my imagination. When my brother, Jon, and I entered the rows, we disappeared from the land of south-central Pennsylvania and appeared in a new world as soldiers, or warriors, or adventurers looking for new lands. I can remember the sound of the cornfield world.

Shhush, Shhush, Shhush, went the leafy stalks as we passed between the rows, the sound of a childhood adventure. When summer storms came, the stalks danced and sang, ocean-like, to the waves of the wind.

This adventure that you and I are about to embark upon also possesses a unique sound. But it's not necessarily one you can hear with your ears. It's the sound George heard in his mind's eye; it's the sound Sam heard as he remembered the world he loved as described by his blind friend. It sounds like a voice from far off—out there, in the wilderness, beyond the foothills. And it calls.

Do you hear it?

I believe that if we listen closely enough and follow the sound, we just might discover the place for which our hearts yearn.

EXCHANGING OUR WALKING STICKS FOR SWORDS

I want to walk out among people playing chess in the park. I want to hear the wind sway the treetops on the hills. I want the heights to teach me their strength. I want to collect enough moments out in the landscape that I can more fully understand the character of God.

Bilbo, for those fleeting moments when he was lost in the song of dwarves, thought himself an adventurer. He wanted to exchange his walking stick for a sword. But the thought of a dragon swooping in and destroying his village with fire righted his thoughts. Nope, he was happy in the Shire. He needed only his walking stick.

Walking sticks come in handy on familiar trails. They're good for balance and the occasional snake and are quite comfortable to lean on. A walking stick, for my uses here, however, smacks of luxury and convenience and safety—all fine things in and of themselves. But not so fine when they delude us into ransoming our spirits of adventure. And for what?

It's good to exchange our walking sticks for swords for a time. Sometimes, to find ourselves, we need to leave home and listen to the pines and waterfalls. Sure, a dragon might lie close by, but that's what swords are for.

Why We Thirst for Adventure

Why *are* we drawn to the idea of adventure?

What is an adventure? What does the word mean? Is it helpful to view our spiritual engagement with God as an adventure?

Certain words in our culture suffer from overuse, and *adventure* is one of them. Watered down, these overused words become castaways in the lexicon of everyday language; once they carried significance, only to drift into the strange land of ubiquity. *Adventure*, for the modern person, relates to our sensibilities now almost primarily through virtual reality. When we do experience adventure in the physical world, it comes in a controlled environment where safety and knownness dominate the experience. The rise of the novel contributed to our current sanitized relationship with adventure.

Beginning in the nineteenth century, the public engaged with the idea of adventure by way of the novel. Stories like Mary Shelley's *Frankenstein* (1818), Walter Scott's *Ivanhoe* (1820), and James Fenimore Cooper's *The Last of the Mohicans* (1826) captured the imagination of generations of readers who longed to travel, see new parts of the world, and engage with foreigners. The novel, however, lives downstream (so to speak) of the real frontier, of expanding cultures around the world. Fiction springs from experiences in the real world. We hear stories, seek to emulate them, and live them out vicariously through an entertaining medium. But adventure novels do touch something within the human psyche, something profound and on an existential level. We sense a calling to go forth and see for ourselves what lies in the beyond.

If we peer further into history, nearly 700 years ago, we find the world opening to global travel. Ferdinand Magellan (1480–1521), a Portuguese explorer, is credited with organizing the first circumnavigation of the world.[3] Magellan found and named the Pacific Ocean (if it's possible to name such a thing). The story goes that when he and his caravan of ships entered the waters of the Pacific, the ocean was calm. Pacific means "peaceful." But then it took over two months for them to cross the "peaceful" ocean. Many died from starvation and scurvy.

What prompted Magellan's curiosity to plan such a voyage? He set out to discover a way to travel westward to Southeast Asia, where he hoped to find exotic spices and gems. He had only heard of the great ocean that lay *beyond* the Atlantic. He heard the call to, "Come, see, find." To reach his goal, he had to set out into the literal unknown, with only an off-chance of discovering a passage between the Americas. He had to convince 260 men to join his expedition, which required five ships. Adventure always costs us something.

Magellan did not successfully complete the journey. He died searching for gems and spices. Though he planned the expedition, a man from his crew ended up completing the circumnavigation around the world. And yet Magellan left the world a legacy of vision and an example of what it looks like to set out to discover something grand, something beyond us.

Adventure is something that happens *along* the journey. It's what happens to you *during* the expedition. It cannot be planned. It must simply be experienced in the moment.

We Were Born to Explore

Why do human beings risk death for the sake of discovering something new?

Experts in landscape, geography, and navigation remind us that a symbiotic relationship exists between human beings and the world in which we live. There is more to the space around us than location. From birth, human beings exist within and explore space. Even in the womb, we come to know and understand the space in which we exist at a base level. As soon as we enter the world, our minds and emotions churn with an innate curiosity to understand our surroundings.

We make mental maps of everything. The world imprints on us spatially, psychologically, and spiritually (or what some call creaturely awareness).

John Stilgoe, a Harvard landscape historian, bemoans the twenty-first century's trajectory as it careens into the Fourth Industrial Revolution—a time of digital, physical, and biological fusion; a time that will redefine what it means to be human. Stilgoe says living in a world in which everything is mapped out for you, where everything is known and safe, is a disaster for our lived experience. This kind of preplanned and safe world is exactly the kind found in a smartphone. As new generations grow up on portable digital devices from a young age, they will lose their sense of curiosity, wonder, and desire to find their own way in the world. Getting lost, says Stilgoe, is an essential component of the human experience. It forces us to find our way, to explore the landscape, to truly see the world and how to live in it.

Even the way we adventure in our hyper-modern world reflects our inability to *see* the world aright. With the Global Positioning System (GPS) and Google Maps and a plethora of other smartphone apps, we no longer drive to a place reliant upon our experience of it. We listen to the computer. We follow the silly blue dot, when instead, we should be seeing the landscape and what it's doing, how it's shaped, and our place in relation to it.

Since the early Babylonian and Sumerian empires, humans have relied on the landscape—beneath the feet and in the sky—to navigate. Wayfinding was part of what it meant to live and travel. People knew the stars, how they signaled the seasons, and where they moved in relation to their own land. Today, however, if you want to know how to get somewhere, you enter the data in your device and follow the directions. Or worse, you ask the AI app on your phone, in your home, or in your car. Having lost the ability to navigate on our own, having lost our relationship with the physical world, any notion of adventure can only be grasped through a film, a television series, or a novel.

"But Tim," you say, "aren't you being hyperbolic? Adventure

does not need to be a month-long expedition into unknown territory. Besides, haven't we explored everything already? Do we really need adventure in our lives at the level you're suggesting?"

"Ah, yes," I reply. "I agree that we have discovered so much, there seems to be nothing left to uncover. I do, however, wish to point out that adventure is not a consumer commodity. Adventure is our human heritage. The Creator gifted us space on a terrestrial planet and invited you and me to learn and know who we are in relation to it, thus giving us deeper understanding as we relate to him. Adventure, you see, is that, in part, for which we were made."

It's Okay to Wander, Pilgrim Friend

One of Tolkien's most beautiful lines comes from *The Fellowship of the Ring*: "Not all those who wander are lost."[4] Though the line was meant by Gandalf to help Frodo identify Strider (Aragorn), it reminds us of two things. First, *wandering is our natural state*. And second, *navigation isn't always about certainty*.

The ancients used the stars to navigate, and sometimes they even used the planets. Planets, according to Harvard scientist John Edward Huth, are not as reliable as stars for navigation. The word *planet* means "wanderer." The brightest planets (Mars, Jupiter, and Venus), says Huth, can act as "temporary beacons for travelers, but they move against the fixed background of stars."[5] Huth reminds us, however, that planets can still be used for navigation if one understands their motion. The motion of the planetary wanderers reminds us that wandering is a natural state of being. We are planets in motion on the fixed background of the earth. But if we cease moving, we lose our birthright as wanderers.

We've still not defined *adventure*. Adventure comes from Latin and French and means "to arrive," or "what's about to happen." We dub men like Magellan "adventurers" but we do so in hindsight. The moniker comes after the journey has ended in some fashion. Magellan was an explorer. He employed his natural curiosity to discover that for what his heart yearned.

The late literature professor Joseph Campbell, famous for his book *The Hero with a Thousand Faces*, said heroes are called into an adventure. The call might be something tangible, like gems or spices, but there is something else under the surface that calls. As a professor of literature and world religions, Campbell said this call came from the "World Navel," a pagan reference to the source of existence. As a Christian, I call this source the Creator God.

The landscape, or something behind the landscape, stars, and cosmos, calls to us. To answer is to set out on the expedition of human existence. And what happens along the way? Well, that's the adventure!

THE ADVENTURE OF FOLLOWING HARD AFTER CHRIST

Life with God should be adventurous.

The Latin phrase *homo viator* means "man on a quest" or "man as traveler or pilgrim." The concept of human beings as *homo viator* does not indicate hapless wanderings. Quite the opposite. It's the theological idea that we were created to search. There's a lingering sense of incompleteness to life. Even Nietzsche thought of humans as wanderers, only with a nihilistic twist.[6] The fourth-century theologian Augustine of Hippo touched on this idea of *homo viator* when he famously began his timeless work *Confessions* with this reflection: "You stir man to take pleasure in praising you, because you have made us for yourself, and our heart is restless until it rests in you."[7]

Two words stand out to me in Augustine's ponderous statement: *stir* and *restless*. First, let's consider *stir*. What is this act of stirring Augustine sees in his own life? How does God stir us? And with what? Now, let's consider *restless*. Who doesn't feel restless at some point in their life? How many of us fill our lives with things or experiences because we're trying to satisfy the restless hunger in our hearts?

Augustine gets to the bottom of the human condition with this statement, and he spends the rest of his spiritual memoir showing how this restlessness drove him toward pursuits that left him unfulfilled. Augustine was a wanderer, a Wayfinder, and he describes life before and after a person finds God as a journey. Before he found God, he indulged in sexual and philosophical pursuits he thought would satisfy his desires. But it wasn't until he found God, and gave his life completely to him, that he realized all the beautiful things of the world draw us closer to God, and that life itself is a journey into God.

Once, Augustine asked the earth, the sea, the deep, the living creatures, the breezes, the heavens, the sun, moon, and stars, what the object of his love was. But all responded back to him, "It is not us! Nor are we the God whom you seek."

"Tell me about this God," he replied.

"He made us!" they answered.

When Augustine finally realized it was not the beautiful things themselves that he desired, but their Creator, he responded with one of the most beautiful sections of writing you'll ever read:

Late have I loved you, beauty so old and so new: late have I loved you. And see, you were within and I was in the external world and sought you there, and in my unlovely state I plunged into those lovely created things which you made. You were with me, and I was not with you.

The lovely things kept me far from you, though if they did not have their existence in you, they had no existence at all. You called and cried out loud and shattered my deafness. You were radiant and resplendent, you put to flight my blindness.

You were fragrant, and I drew in my breath and now pant after you. I tasted you, and I feel but hunger and thirst for you. You touched me, and I am set on fire to attain the peace which is yours.[8]

It was the beauty of the world that lured Augustine. It was the touch of *beauty* that set him on fire.

Apart from God, beautiful things can become the objects of love and pursuit of the pilgrim. Beautiful things take many forms and provide a level of pleasure. You can spot them easily enough because they find their way into your life as things that delight the senses and often give momentary pleasure. For Augustine, prior to his conversion to Christianity, it was women and parties. For others, it might be status or material possessions. You can spot these beautiful things because they draw you in to the thing itself rather than point you to God.

When the pilgrim lives in communion with God, beauty becomes one of the primary means by which the pilgrim grows in intimacy with the Almighty; it leads her into wonder, and wonder is necessary for worship.[9] Beauty reminds the pilgrim of its Author and Creator. Beauty instructs the pilgrim, guiding her toward its Source, the pilgrim's delight. Perhaps this is what Jonathan Edwards was getting at when he said beauty should be the foundation from which our theology flows, not merely a consolation.

The road to life is our becoming. And there is no one way of becoming. Remember your Wayfinder roots, and keep your eyes peeled, for the glories dance all around us, ready to set us afire.

Am I attempting to lure you into an unfamiliar journey? Perhaps. But whether you are an aged adventurer like Gandalf, a novice like Bilbo, or somewhere in between, we all need to push beyond the comforts of our own spiritual hobbit holes and walk up the mountain, like Moses and Abraham before us. The journey will require some spiritual fortitude, for our well-laid preconceptions of the world, of beauty, of God are not easily undone.

Though we've dipped into the cultural ethos of the modern world and observed the shift from beauty being the aim of expression in the arts to transgression taking center stage, meaningful change does not begin at a macro level. It begins with the individual—not individual-*ism*, mind you, but the heart of the person.

The world may carry on as if beauty possesses no significance, sliding far from the ancient understanding of the created order and its divine origin, but it is the individual—you and me—who can affect immediate change by bearing witness to the foundations of our faith. However, it will not be easy. For there will always be the Plastic People to contend with and convert to Beauty Chasers.

WAYPOINT

Earlier in this chapter, I described the *edges* of life. In the edges, we experience what I like to call "beautiful collisions" with each other. We like to call these beautiful collisions messy, and we refer to our so-called "ordinary" lives as mundane. Remember, I ended the previous chapter with encouragement that we stay vigilant with our perspectives; to look *at* and *along* the beam of light so that we can gain a more balanced perspective of God and beauty. I want us to consider a perspective shift in how we see the messiness of life.

As I mentioned, I don't deny the hard muck of life. It happens, and I can't control it. But I *can* control my reaction to it. I can also control how I view it. The language we consistently use in life influences our moods, perspectives, and understanding. One of the best ways to view our relationship with God as an exciting adventure is to change the way we talk about the journey of life. If everything's always a mess, that's not much of an adventure. But if we view life through the prism of beautiful collisions, that changes things, doesn't it?

Let's reflect on these three ideas related to changing our perspective of the "mundane" in life as we set off on our adventure.

1. The Fury of God's Presence Fills the World with a Spiritual Shape

Before the incarnation and the Communion table, way back, after God crushed the world into existence with his Word, not only did the earth sing with the event of beauty, not only did the world rejoice over having been called out of chaos and into life, but God himself lived among us. This was the beginning of the adventure we call life. Earlier, we observed how God himself spoke beauty into chaos, and how life and light emanate from his presence. It is when we can rest in his presence that the world once again shimmers with the brilliance of that whisper-thought moment.

The point of humankind existing with God in the Garden of Delight was to be in the *presence* of God. The writer of Genesis tells us how God once walked among man in the ancient park, spinning his presence like a hurricane in and throughout the trees. His presence I hear in the wind. It fills even the things I so often hear called mundane with a roundness of spiritual shape.[10]

I find it sad, however, that we now take the modern definition (nineteenth century, from the French) of *mundane* to describe our earthly lives: "lacking interest or excitement." If we used *mundane* to differentiate between this earthly world and the heavenly or spiritual realm, which is the other definition of mundane, then I'd fall for it. But now, I bristle when I hear Christians talk about the "mundane" parts of life. As if this life, our life, breathed into us by God himself, lacks interest or excitement.

2. Rivalry Blinds Us to Glory

My wife and I talk about this often. She thinks people use the word *mundane* to describe daily activities because we live in a culture that loves to compare. Unlike any other time in history, men and women can view the lives of the rich and famous, and of those who are trying to be *like* the rich and famous. We can *see* the events they attend. We can *see* their houses and cars. We can *see* their vacations and their wardrobes. Our lives, in turn, can look bland and without interest.

"Eh, but Tim," you say. "Isn't it natural for us to see the trappings of others and compare ourselves?"

"Ah, yes," I reply. "I think it is natural, to some extent. But I find the act of comparing encroaches upon the spiritual virtues I'm trying to cultivate in my life, and the lives of my family, don't you?"

The Apostle Paul reminded the Corinthian church that comparing yourself to another person can expose a lack of understanding.[11] He also recommended the Galatian church determine from whom they desired approval: man, or God.[12] Our actions expose our desires.

How different does a spirit of comparison look from the Christian virtue of humility?

Paul instructs us not to do anything out of rivalry, conceit, or selfish ambition.[13] But it's difficult to swallow the humility pill. I gain the strength to cultivate humility by reminding myself of Christ's example. Christ, who was in the form of God, took on the form of a servant. He laid aside his glory so that he could become a human being. In considering my spiritual needs, he limited himself. From the God of creation to the servant of man.

Christ's act not only teaches me about humility, but it shows me a pattern in beauty. *Humility is characteristic of beauty.* There's a giving up of self in my pursuit of beauty. If beauty is a goal in my participation with others, then selfish comparison will give way, and humble interaction will prevail.

The same is true of the arts. The goal of beauty with my art or craft will manifest itself in a kind of selflessness. My work will serve something greater than myself. But if transgression or provocation serve as my goals, then my work will serve only me, and self-expression will annihilate beauty. I find the same principle can be applied in other areas of life: my vocation, family relationships, and work relationships.

I do not live in a world in which some things or actions or people matter more than others. Every *thing* and every *one* matter, because everything in the world lives and breathes and has its being through One who moves like a hurricane through the trees to remind us he's there.

3. God's Presence Gives Meaning to the World

God's *presence* gives meaning to my world. Sometimes I feel this through a kind of haunting I sense. One day I sense it in the simple song my daughter, Brielle, plays for me on the piano. One day I feel it in the color of the light spilling into the windows near the fireplace in our family room. How the room feels so filled with morning silence and the increasing light of day.

But another day I sense it in conversation with my friend as he tells me about his work, and then again in the joyful reception as I pick up a longtime friend from the airport.

As we discovered earlier, the ancient Park of Delight contains the secret to my daily purpose: his presence. Practicing being in the presence of God can take the form of whisper prayers, which are daily extemporaneous prayers given up to God throughout our waking hours.

They give a word of thanks or praise.

They call for help.

They express affection.

They express worship.

Practicing being in the presence of God can also involve the discipline of silence and waiting. You can read through the book of Psalms, one each day, and before you read it aloud, pray for the Holy Spirit to speak to you through the Scriptures. And then, wait. Focus your mind on God's majesty, power, and wisdom. And wait for your spirit to resonate with his. This looks or feels like the settling of peace upon your anxious thoughts, a lump of a cry in your throat, goosebumps on your arms, or butterflies in your stomach. If we can practice the presence of God, we can more accurately discern in his presence when he fills us.

Does this sound too "feely"? Maybe.

My encouragement to you? Don't dismiss feelings outright as unreliable. When my daughters come to me after they've heard a new worship song or after they've read a chapter in their Bible and they say, "Daddy, I feel funny in my belly after listening to this song or reading this verse," I tell them that's the Holy Spirit. My daughter Bri often tells me that it's hard for her to read the Bible because she starts crying. I tell her this is the sign of God's presence in her life. Does his presence go deeper than feelings? It does. But we must first understand how to discern his presence before we can step further into it.

But how can I know if my feelings betray me? I like to keep three thoughts in mind when it comes to my emotional experience of the Holy Spirit and beauty.

1. Remember the nature of beauty itself. The beautiful points *outward*, to something beyond. If our feelings bring us to a place of worship, which is a sacred place that looks toward heaven, then we know the power of the Holy Spirit moves within us; it is more than mere feeling. But if our feelings go no further than our own sense of satisfaction, we need to be cautious.

2. Is the vehicle of the emotion in stride with holiness? (1 Thess. 4:7–8; 1 Pet. 1:2) Am I moved toward love and good deeds? Or am I moved toward selfish pride, envy, greed, or malice?
3. Does the experience point me toward the Good? By this I mean, do my feelings point me to truth, the Word of God, and prayer? (Matt. 15:8–9; Prov. 14:30)

His *presence*. If I view the world through the prism of his presence, I don't live in the ordinary, the mundane. No. I live glory to glory.

CHAPTER 8

STOP SPECTATING, START PARTICIPATING

The Footpath of Reverent Participation

et me take you back with me a few years to Oxford, England. I
mentioned earlier that my family was blessed to live there for two
years while I studied beauty. Our way of life changed during those
years. We made the decision *not* to buy a car, and instead relied on
the bus system and footpaths. This small decision created space in our
lives we didn't realize we had.

I want to revisit a few of the many walks I took in the city center
and colleges of Oxford as well as the surrounding countryside. Taking
a walk, though the act might seem elementary, reveals truths that
would otherwise remain hidden.

I find it interesting that Christ walked everywhere; a vagabond
on the road, traveling from city to city, escaping into the Judean
countryside, he used the elements of his walks to teach—fish, a field,
a seed, bandits, the city, mud, cleansing pools, the wilderness. He
used his journey to teach. What does our journey teach us? What
can Christ give us along the way to help us discover new means of
seeing him? Come with me now to Christ Church Meadow for a
walk and a think.

Finding Peace amid the Chaos

Christ Church Meadow is set apart from the speed and sound of the roads and sidewalks of St. Aldates. I walk a few yards down New Walk, choose one of the old trees, and nestle beneath it on the cool grass. The sun feels warm on my face as I stare up into the sky, but the air drifts over me in cool waves.

I lie under the old tree and look up into its gangly limbs. The starlings create an ocean of sound as they take flight and circle the boughs in a murmuration[1]—a phenomenon of instinctual flight.[2] When I close my eyes, I can hear thousands of wings flapping in the late autumn air. The sound mixes with those of a baby crying and women talking and laughing. The joyful noise blends in with the grass and the river, and the smell of cannabis emanates from a huddle of undergraduates beneath their own giant tree. They cackle in mock embarrassment, knowing I can smell their drugs.

As I lie with my eyes closed, I hear walkers reminiscing about a family gathering. Others chat idly as they snap photographs of the Meadow Building, a nineteenth-century structure built for undergraduates of Christ Church College. After what feels like an hour, I rise and walk down New Walk toward the River Thames and look left, out across the sprawling field. The meadow serves the community like any park, and on this cool Sunday afternoon in Oxford, the park spreads out in a blanket of vitality.

I lie beneath the limbs of the great tree and walk the New Path because I am tired of being harried by the noise of the world. I want to find peace amid the chaos. I want to make space for beauty in my life—I want it to touch me through not only my eyes, but through my ears and nose and skin. I want to greet the beauty in the smile of a random walker. So I come to the meadow, my park of choice, to seek out the nourishment my soul desires.

Beauty, a Luxury I Can't Afford

I too often fail to feed myself the food of beauty. Can you relate?

Like my friends and family, and maybe you, too, I ram through my days and weeks and months, forgetting how much my soul longs for the times of limb-gazing and river walks—for a simple walk in the park.

When I take a moment to sit on the grass in a park or walk a nearby path, I find myself battling with the tensions in my life: the necessity of work and my desire to rest, the responsibilities of my role as a father and husband and the longing to soak up moments with my children and wife, the pursuit of a means to live and the craving to live untethered to worldly possessions.

How swiftly I marginalize beauty and rob myself of wonder.

"Luxuries I cannot afford. Time I cannot waste. A commodity with no real-world value," I tell myself.

When I talk to myself like this, too often the pace and pragmatism of this world wins out, and I push through. I leave my longing behind.

I know I am not built to live without the desire for beauty, and yet, I convince myself to do it. What is it that changes in me during the times when I choose to allow the worldly pace of life to take precedence over the opportunities I have to experience true beauty?

Am I knowingly betraying the way God created me? Maybe I've been—or allowed myself to be—rewired by my environment? Maybe my propensity for distraction is simply my cultural programming?

Don't Trade Enchantment
for Distraction

The world grooms me to be a spectator rather than a participant.

I'm encouraged to disentangle myself from the natural world and to attach myself to devices. I'm urged to isolate myself from people and surround myself with virtual reality.[3] I'm asked to trade in the enchantment of my walks for the dim magic of simulation.

I'm not blaming the world for my lack of attentiveness to beauty. In the end, I make the choice to check out. I make the choice to pick up a device rather than interact with people. But I also can't ignore the fact that the world has changed since the time of my youth.

I'm reminded of this fact every time I stop at a red light. Almost without fail, every person in the cars surrounding me picks up a smartphone and begins scrolling. The distraction is mobile now.

Perhaps when I was younger, the distraction was restricted mainly to the living room. The television was the primary (and only) device my parents regulated. I say "only" simply because other devices did not yet exist—except Atari or ColecoVision, and they usually lost out to my siblings and me playing kickball or climbing the oak tree or riding bikes. But now, seven-year-old children carry smartphones, and ten-year-old children whip out tablets. When I was ten, the only things whipped out were my cowboy cap guns. I've watched a young teenager sit through an entire meal at a restaurant with her parents and not once look up from her phone. Lest we think it's all just cute and not a problem, children as young as ten now enter rehab for anxiety attributed to social media and for being addicted to their devices.

Each decision to scroll or view a screen becomes a decision to cultivate a disengaged existence. How we spend our time reveals much about our hearts and what we value, never mind how using devices slowly reprograms the way we think and interact with one another. We now choose online activities over leisure activities with friends and loved ones. When our children ages three to eleven watch 4.5 hours of recorded programming a day, what kind of children do we expect to nurture? Engaged young adults, interested in others, interested in cultivating intimacy in relationships, interested in nurturing the good in themselves and others? Will they hunger for leisure time with the family? Bonding around a bonfire? A thirst for beauty? Or will they grow up shaped by what they value most: noise and distraction?

Since 2012, the average daily time a person spends on social media has increased by a third, from 90 minutes a day to 145 minutes a day.

Adults spend nearly three hours a day watching television or the internet. The average person exercises only seventeen minutes a day, reads nineteen minutes a day, and attends social activities four minutes a day. As a society, we are rewiring our affections. The young, and even the old, believe that scrolling, spectating, and isolating themselves from the real world are acceptable ways to spend their time. Yet it's our heavenly charge to raise Beauty Chasers, not screen scrollers. And it all begins with the willingness to say no to mind-numbing time on a screen and yes to participating with God in this tapestry of wonder called *life*.

CREATED TO PARTICIPATE

Make no mistake about it, shedding our spectator binoculars for a participant's jersey will require a little healthy rebellion on our part. When I think about how I feel when I attend a sporting event or concert, the spectator observation I made earlier makes sense to me.

Here I am, sitting or standing, watching a game or performance unfold. I spectate from the sidelines or from the audience. Here I am, enjoying the concert from a distance. But my mind wanders, and I imagine how the event might feel different if I were to stand onstage while the band or orchestra played. I'm closer to the performers, but I'm still spectating.

It's the same with the sporting event. I imagine myself standing on the sidelines of a football or soccer game. My excitement heightens because I've moved closer to the event itself. I feel a sensational energy. I'm on top of the action, and yet I'm still only a spectator.

Now I imagine myself as a participant.

I can smell the grass and even my opponent. I feel his body move against mine—the force, the sweat, the sound of grass being torn up by cleats. I feel the noise of the crowd rather than making the noise. I sense the thrill of the game like no one else in the stadium because I am playing the game. I'm a participant.

Back at the concert, I hear the music differently because I'm using in-ear monitors. The stage volume sounds much different than the house volume, but I can also hear and feel the venue or "house" sound. It energizes me.

I hear the crowd singing along and screaming and applauding. I see their movements, the light from their smartphones as they raise them, signaling another encore (because, of course, no one uses a lighter anymore). I watch the stage lights casting their beams out into the darkness. I feel the energy of my band mates. And I feel the indescribable magic that comes from performing music, especially my own music.

Despite how the world grooms me, I was created to participate. This much I know, and this I pursue. Participation.

Participating requires more from me. Its requirements cost me. I must work at it—sweat, train, learn, see, listen, respond, move, sacrifice, fail, and begin again. Spectating offers me similar feelings of exhilaration but does not require anything from me. I need only to possess the means to consume.

Convenience joins spectating; sacrifice accompanies participation.

TAKE BACK THE MORNING

How can I participate in the daily fullness God gives us through beauty?

The morning.

Can it be so simple?

The morning offers me a rebirth, a chance to begin fresh in my spirit and in my work and in my relationships.

"Take a chance on the morning," the whisper says. "Change your habit."

So I change.

Instead of immediately filling the morning with work, I slow it down by rising earlier than I'd like to.

That's okay, it'll be worth it, I tell myself as I grumble through the groggy moments of the morning, rubbing my eyes and stretching my stiff body.

And it is.

First, I let the morning breathe. I allow it to be a reverent time of conversation and thought. I find the day goes as the morning goes. If I begin with noise, I will inherit noise throughout the day.

I let prayer enter my mind first. I can pray even while I exercise or find a quiet morning trail on my bike. I let my prayer go out like conversation. I don't overthink it. I talk to God as if he were a friend joining me for a walk or breakfast.

As we talk, I thank him. I find the act of thanksgiving to be an act of life-giving-ness, the same way my friend's eyes brighten when I thank him for letting me borrow a tool; the same way my wife's shoulders relax when I thank her for her help.

When I thank God, it's like turning the key to a magical safe. Once opened, the safe releases new discoveries. The magic of spiritual thanksgiving unleashes reminders of God's faithfulness, blessing, and provision. Specific instances come to my mind: the project I did not think I would get, a house to rent when none seemed available, the timely and unsuspecting gift of a friend as a direct answer to prayer.

These morning moments extend beyond some perfunctory ritual. The act of giving thanks to God eases my anxiety. It does the opposite of what moments on a device do to my mind and spirit.

If you're like me, sometimes you don't know where to begin during times of quiet prayer. Here's how I approach it.

Paul, I recall, does not simply tell me to stop being anxious (Phil. 4:6–7). He tells me how: pray, ask God for help, and thank him for the little things, the big things, the things you forgot to thank him for. How quickly I forget that God delights in me. And that he loves when I thank him.

Simple words whispered in the gathering space of the morning: "Thank you, Lord."

Strangely, I hear the voice of God reply.

"I want you to know something," he says, reminding me like a father reminds his son of important news.

"What is it that you want to tell me?" I ask.

"When you go outside and walk about, when you look over your yard and see the sky coming through the gangly limbs of the trees that surround your property, when you walk on through the trees at the back of your yard and come back to your house, I want you to know that I made all of it for you. The gangly limbs and the sky, the way the light looks by your fireplace as it filters through the windows—I placed you within all of it. You, the man who almost forgot me, I put you there."

"Yes, Lord," I reply. "Thank you. It's quite something."

"Yes, it is," he says. "And something else," he continues.

"Of course, Lord."

"When you're walking around your yard, and you whisper thanks, and when you let your mind settle on things in heaven? It fills my heart with the warmest joy you can imagine. To see you there, in the garden, welcoming my invitation? It makes me feel every inch of eternity."

"Thank you, Lord," I reply. "What I hear you telling me Lord, is that you love me."

"Yes, that's correct. I do. And I can't wait to find you again, in the morning."

With my new and reverent mornings established, I make sure to keep off digital devices. I've found that once on, devices transport my day into their world and all it holds—its constant pull on my attention, its invitation to fill my mind and time with noise and distractions.

Keep it at bay! I tell myself. *Give yourself permission to* see *for a moment.*

I do my best to *see* the day from the solitude of my favorite chair or the back deck or front porch or a walk in the yard. When I say "see," I am referring to my inner sight. This vision lives on my prayerful embrace of the day through thanksgiving.

If I can keep the devices off, even just an extra half hour, I feel the cumulative difference over time. The quiet, reverent mornings stack up, free of distraction, focused on thanksgiving, talking with God, and nourishing my soul with all the beauty morning offers: solitude, quiet, the invitation of nature, the delight of the waking sky.

Almost without knowing it, I'm training my mind and heart to thirst for a different rhythm. How quickly I forget that I form habits through conscious choices I make every day.

It's time to form new habits, I remind myself.

The morning presents a perfect opportunity to turn my focus away from noise and distraction and toward the voice of God—toward a pace that invites reflection, prayer, and conversation with others, a pace that invites me to truly see the world in all its nuance, uniqueness, and splendor.

I love how George Sayer, one of C. S. Lewis's close friends, described how Lewis nurtured his spiritual life with daily Scripture meditation coupled with his "habit of communing with nature."[5] Lewis would walk the garden before breakfast in order to drink in "the beauty of the morning, thanking God for the weather, the roses, the song of the birds, and anything else he could find to enjoy."[6] Often, the men and women we admire the most spiritually use simple practices to nourish their relationship with God. Lewis, a lover of long walks in the countryside and early morning garden strolls of thanksgiving, shows us that we don't need exotic rituals to strengthen our spiritual lives, just the simple discipline of walking the garden with a thankful heart.

WAYPOINT

Participation seems to invite robust activity. But in our culture, participation looks paradoxically different. Earlier, I noted how the world grooms us to spectate, to watch what's going on, whether through a screen or television. Spectating in this context occurs when distraction pulls our attention away from our real lives. Real life contains so much more than simply running to one thing after another. Participating in life requires us to live at a pace that allows us to engage in every aspect of living, including the natural world. And the natural world's pace looks and feels much different from our cultural pace. To suck all the marrow out of life, as Thoreau inspires us to do, we must slow down and engage in life with healthy intentionality and care.

In the summer months, evergreens like pine and spruce grow vigorously. You don't want to plant or replant an evergreen in the summer. You want to give it space and time to grow strong roots. You want to plant evergreens in the cool months of autumn. I've planted some as late as December.

I think of the summer growing time as an opportunity to give myself permission to rediscover practices that help me slow and grow. To dilly-dally on the terrace or by the firepit, to twiddle about in the morning hours with books unfinished and journal entries begging to be written.

I love how, in the New Testament, the gospel writers observe how Jesus often stole away to the mountain before dawn to pray. I love it because it shows Jesus not only taking time to abide with his Father, but that he operated to a different cadence.

What practices help you keep a heaven cadence rather than a world cadence? You don't have to use summer as your growing season. But if you choose to, how will you slow your pace down this summer? The key question in all of this is, *how do you slow down*?

Here are five ways slowing down can help you better participate in the world around you.

1. Slowing down frees us from the world's definition of success, influence, and productivity.

2. Slowing down reminds us how speed breeds distraction, inelegance, irrationality, and ugliness. The grammar of slow, on the other hand, breeds clarity, simplicity, and wholeness.

3. Slowing down allows us to regain our sense of wonder, reverence, and truth in a blurred world of trends and kitsch.

4. Slowing down connects us to the spiritual reality God intended for us. God created us to run on soulish things, not haphazard, thoughtless things. God created us in his image (*imago dei*). When we participate in the beautiful in this world, our souls come alive. When we receive the brutish things of the world into our lives, our souls fall sick. Speed annihilates space while chasing slow expands our view of space and time.

5. Slowing helps us see. And when we see, we notice God.

The digital noise that inundates our daily lives will fade if we let it. It's not a requirement to live life to the fullest. In fact, stepping out of the digital hurricane will contribute to the restoration of everything good within you. You don't need to run off and become a digital monk per se. But a little time under the stars or beside an ocean or on a river or mountain trail will go a long way to helping you feel—well, more like your true self. And who doesn't want that?

CHAPTER 9

SOUL LEADERSHIP

The Footpath of Cultivating Our Affections

Charlotte Mason, the intellectual pioneer behind the modern idea of homeschooling, reminds us that our longing for beauty dies of emptiness when we don't continually present beauty to our senses. "The function of the sense of beauty," writes Mason, "is to open a paradise of pleasure within us . . . It is no small part of education to have seen much beauty, to recognize it when we see it, and to keep ourselves humble in its presence."[1]

For some time now, God has been teaching me along the rugged path of tenderness. I'm a thorny character, brutish yet with a longing for beauty that pushes me into God's glory cloud. But I find that, too often, I cannot stand mid the fire and raging of his holiness.

I need the fragility and tenderness of nature's wonder as much or even more than I need the rugged torrents of its wildness. I find that after I hold a cucumber or rub my hands in the tendrils of my oregano bush, or quietly observe the elegant hovering of the hummingbirds feeding with my arms wrapped around one of my daughters, I unravel.

My thorns turn to blossoms while the brute in me drowns in the delicate touch of God's hand pulling me close, closer until I break in the flood of his purity and grace.

In the years I spent studying beauty, living in the English country-side with my wife and daughters, I discovered more than a high-five Jesus (my way of describing a culturally relevant "Jesus" who wants to be buddies). I stumbled upon the fountainhead of wonder that drew me to its source and away from the cultural artifacts I thought I needed to be cool or relevant. For some time, the fountain bid me stay, listen, learn. For years now, I've waited by the water's edge.

But there is a time to listen and a time to speak. I find myself wanting to speak, but not with words formed of the brutishness that formed me. Instead, I'm leaning into a grammar of joy and holiness.

I speak now, first, to my daughters. We talk of the holiness of imaginations and how God speaks to and forms us through the portals of our eyes and ears. We talk about how the brute also wars against the grammar of heaven seeking to ravage and destroy by tainting our imaginations with the disease of mindlessness and corruption. I tell them they will be among the few if they grow to stand for the pure and lovely.

But they are much stronger than me. For they understand the delicate within the cucumber and the cosmos of wonder in a single blueberry blossom.

And I'm reminded that we need only talk to them and converse of the things of heaven to breathe life into the architecture of their souls.

CULTURAL EDUCATION MATTERS

Our cultural education matters. A young person's aesthetic taste becomes fixed in late adolescence. Cultural education, the discernment of the beautiful, good, and true, is essential, especially for the youngest minds. And yet much of their cultural education today comes from gaming, social media, and YouTube. This is not only a matter of time spent playing games and watching entertainment. Screen time using apps, like Instagram, for young adults (especially young girls) proves extremely harmful to the development of their self-worth. Technology companies are complicit in the harm.

A study from 2021 revealed how Facebook knows that their app, Instagram, is highly addictive for young adults and contributes to mental health issues like despair and depression, disorders related to body issues, and anxiety.[2] Girls and boys as young as ten years old are now entering mental health rehab facilities to deal with these issues, along with addiction to smartphones and social media apps. Most shocking is the complicity and intentionality of the technology companies. They know this information, and they hide it. Why? The simple answer is money and power. The more direct answer is the insidiousness of evil.

How can we combat such a powerful force in the minds and hearts of our most vulnerable? We realize that we all are educators and learners, and we start holding one another accountable for the nourishment of our children. We make hard decisions when it comes to screens and apps we know are harmful to the young, and we offer the beautiful to our children in the form of fine art, literature, music, dance, and outdoor play.

It's not bad to bring high culture to the young or reintroduce it to adults of any age. Beauty nourishes the soul, promotes humility, and refines society. When we empty the skies of wonder, our souls yearn for a holiness we ourselves have removed.

It is our duty as a society to teach and promote ordinate affections—proper loves for the young.[3] The Greeks gave us education. The Romans appropriated it. For the Greeks, education was for the aristocracy. Its aim was to form a young person into a noble person. Rome took a practical approach to education, building on the Greek curriculum.

Our loss of the Greek intention to form the intellect and shape morals feels acute; we've effectively divorced the shaping of the whole person and now shape the minds of people for occupations. The humanities, the philosopher king, the warrior poet, the "man among men"—cultivated and sharp in the ways of goodness *and* the ways of the world—have vanished from state curriculums. We have divorced beauty from the soul and extracted virtue from the heart.[4] But cultural education is for the adult, too. For though most adults no longer attend formal classes, our cultural education continues, fashioned by what we consume via our televisions and digital devices and social media. We are fools to think we do not still attend classes, though they may be of culture rather than arithmetic.

"Eh, but Tim," you say. "The points you make sound good, but what about the Greek influence? Surely you agree, the Greek influence does not fully connect to the biblical perspective on training ourselves culturally."

"Ah, yes," I reply. "You make a good point. I say let's place the two side by side and see if they create a consensus of thought. Shall we?"

Ordinate affections are rightly ordered.[5] When we cultivate ordinate affections, they bring wholeness and health to our lives. We flourish when our affections are ordinate. *Inordinate* affections are out-of-balance and create chaos in our lives. They work in us to establish an idolatrous spirit and idolatrous habits. When we rest our affections upon things inordinately, we bend (corrupt) the things for which we have affection. Bent things promote a spirit of bentness. We find in Scripture a correlation between desiring what is good and the fruit it produces in a person.

In pursuing righteousness, says the writer of Hebrews, God has made your heart glad (Heb. 1:9). The prophet Hosea says, "Sow righteousness for yourselves, reap the fruit of unfailing love" (Hos. 10:12). Seeking YHWH results in showers of righteousness. Thirsting for the good results in blessing (Matt. 5:6). Gladness, love, blessing—these are a holy concoction that produces rich joy. Christian joy is the mark of heaven, for it signals a transcendent vitality. Sad is the person who pursues wickedness; her eyes fail to brighten; her spirit fails to lift even at the warmest light of the sunrise. Goodness and beauty point, then, to something beyond mere objects of taste. Something deeper bubbles up and speaks to our spirits; it echoes with murmuring we find otherworldly. This is the fingertip of beauty touching us, ever so softly.

If we teach the young and ourselves to value noise and distraction, then we will harvest inelegance, irrationality, and ugliness. How can an adult society so bent on distraction and luxury be expected to promote something antithetical to their own favorite thing—time spent on a screen?

In giving a child or a young person a device, the adult effectively programs the imagination out of the child. Perhaps we fear boredom for ourselves and our children or are not comfortable with remaining idle. But boredom ignites the imagination. We should let children—and ourselves—experience times of boredom so that the imagination can stretch.[6]

Cognitive psychologist David Strayer reminds us that our brains are not three-pound machines that can just keep plugging away, consuming the digital world. Our brains, in fact, need time to recalibrate.[7] For Strayer, who is an avid backpacker, brain breaks are best taken in nature. After a few days on the trail or camping, our brains and senses reboot; we smell and see things we'd otherwise miss or pass over.

Our culture will continue to progress in the realm of digital technology. But we cannot abandon *real* life. It is served up away from the noise and distractions and involves things we can touch, see, and smell. Even mountaineer-philosopher John Muir knew the benefits of real life over the machine world. He wrote, "I am losing precious days. I am degenerating into a machine for making money. I am learning nothing in this trivial world of men. I must break away and get out into the mountains to learn the news."[8]

A Child's Cultural Education Begins with Parents and Teachers

Cultural education for the young begins with marshalling our own cultural engagement as adults. How we steward our time matters. How often young people see us on our phones directly influences their own desire to invite distraction via digital devices. Likewise, our lack of guidance in digital stewardship contributes to a young person's notion of digital consumption. Handing a child a device because we're tired or practicing a hands-off approach to the amount of time a teenager sits in a room playing video games are both forms of cultural education. It teaches a young person to choose entertainment over outdoor play, amusement over real experiences.

The psalmist reminds us that children are "a heritage from the LORD . . . a reward from him" (Ps. 127:3). What kind of teachers or parents would we be if we squander these precious rewards from heaven just because we don't want to be the parent or teacher who says, "No, we don't need a device right now." In the New Testament book of Titus, we find the principle of modeling good works while showing integrity and dignity in our teaching. The apostle Paul exhorts all Christians with the Greek axiom, "Whatever is true, whatever is noble, whatever is right, whatever is pure, whatever is lovely, whatever is admirable—if anything is excellent or praiseworthy—think about such things" (Philippians 4:8). Paul was ending his letter to the Philippian Christians with a reminder to aspire to something greater than the cultural baseline.

The word *lovely* here is only found in this verse and is better translated "beautiful." Paul points the early Christians toward filling their minds and hearts with soulish things; things that connect them to the beauty of God. And let's not forget how he closes the list. He uses the word *excellent*. God is beauty because of his excellencies, which are supreme over all creation. This word *arete* in the Greek means "distinct," "majesty," "excellence," "fame with God." Paul sums up his list with a call to contemplate the beauty of God. What better way to guide our cultural education?

Charlotte Mason reminds us that the education of children is the most important work of a society. She asserts that instruction in a school setting is important, but instruction in the home even more so. It is in our homes that we influence young people the most. It is in the home that a child's character forms. When a child grows up and leaves, he or she will draw on the education received at home. This instruction will shape the child's character and determine the kind of adult he or she will become.[9]

Teaching our children what to love, what is beautiful, what is good, what is true determines the fate of present and future society. If we adults live as adolescents in a digital playground, we will teach future adults that they need not aspire to anything beyond the glowing rectangle in their hand. But if we teach children to seek and see the beautiful, we will create heaven culture.

How My Daughters See Me

I attended a sophisticated party some years ago. Beautifully adorned women and smartly dressed men preened along the lodge floor. I sat and observed the wonder of human interaction, how we dip and pirouette in and out of conversations with sighs, laughs, and head curtsies.

I observed one elegant woman sit upon the out-of-the-way leather couch, off to herself, pull out her iPhone, and flip through—well, whatever.

Astounding, I thought. We, the sophisticated, turning from the real to the virtual. Then I thought how most of these beautiful men and women will return home, check their children (if they have them), dress for bed, and sit up, looking back on the evening via news feeds on social media.

I marveled at how we can transition from the delights of fellowship to the gorging of narcissism. This thought sent me reeling. I wondered how *I* looked within the grand context of human interaction. Was I checking my phone whenever I could? Did I return home simply to hop in bed and hop online?

Then I thought, *How do my daughters see me?* They pop into our room during the pre-sleep "I need a snack" time. What's Daddy doing? Scrolling through social media? Binge-watching a show? Playing on the laptop? What legacy am I creating morning, noon, and night?

What am I etching into their hearts via my actions and inaction? Do they see me rush to the virtual world when the physical world demands my attention?

Certainly, digital and social media serves some purpose in our lives. But what struck me was how it has moved from simple augmentation of the real to a weird kind of co-inherence[10] with one another.

So, I scribbled down my manifesto, a declaration of my organic humanity and its relationship to the most important discipleship project I'm a part of: *fathering my daughters.*

My Manifesto

I want my girls to see dirt under my fingernails. Grease in my fingerprints. Grass stains on my jeans.

I want them to see me build a fire. Cook them s'mores. Pitch a tent.

I want them to see me work, hard. And then play, hard.

I want them to be overwhelmed with the wonder and beauty of books. To be humbled, intrigued, and inspired by human thought, because I, myself, respect all humans and their unique and varied thought.

I want them to read poetry, love poetry, write poetry, because I, myself, value poetry and its place in human discourse.

I want them to see me participate in hard conversations, through thoughtful interaction, through rigorous scholarship, and through hard thinking on subjects that demand more than bumper-sticker theology, sound-bite moralism, or blog-deep advocacy.

I want them to see me hold my ground when the whole world shifts toward the popular trends and too-cool ideology sparked by a postmodern narcissism that threatens to reduce sacramental and sacrificial living into a cesspool of self, tagged with the your-best-story-now mantra.

I want them to see me take on adventures. Travels, hikes, bike hikes, day hikes, backyard-capades.

I want them to see me fail. I want them to see me get back up. And try again.

I want them to see me give mercy. I want them to see me accept grace. I want them to see me talking with their mom, in the quiet of the morning on the porch.

I want them to find me playing my guitar when no one is looking or listening. I want them to know how beauty roots in solitude and blooms as an affront to chaos.

I want them to find me talking to God as if he hears and wants to talk back, because he does.

I want them to discover the overwhelming wonder of music, from Bach to Led Zeppelin. I want them to see me drink it in. I want them to see me singing with it, dancing to it, unafraid of the neighbor's surprise visit or what our sophisticated society may think.

I want them to hear my laughter shake the rafters.

I want them to hear my sobs resound in the quietness of my closet.

I want them to find me napping, under a tree, in a hammock.

I want them to find me by the fire just looking at stars, way past midnight when they should be in bed.

I want them to see me heading out on my mountain bike. Cleaning my mountain bike. Fixing my mountain bike. I want them to ask me if they can come along.

I want them to see me bleed.

I want them to hear me tell stories.

I want them to feel free to crawl into my lap, even while I'm working.

I want them never to have to wait until I post something to hear their inquiry.

I want them to be in the world, rather than spending time curating a virtual one.

I want to binge-watch *them*.

WAYPOINT

As a culture, our attentiveness has succumbed to the glam of immediacy. I want my daughters to see me attentive—to them, to our life together, to the moment. I don't want them to see me rushing off to the internet.

I didn't post any pictures from the party. I wanted to keep the images in my memory, private and special. Life events don't have to be posted to be special. In fact, hidden-ness enriches our lives with the value of intimacy.

I offer my manifesto not as something you need to copy per se, but as an encouragement. Take a Saturday morning and write your own. You can use mine as a guide, but make this *your* manifesto. Here are a few questions to consider as you write it.

1. What does your manifesto look like?
2. What things would you include? Why would you include them?
3. Have you thought about how your children see you? If not, why?
4. What habits can you edit? What habits can you include? What new habits do you want to form?
5. How can you bring the beautiful, the honorable, the noble into your manifesto?
6. If you are a home educator, your manifesto might be a philosophy of education. Take a weekend and consider

how you can incorporate Paul's list of virtues into your philosophy.

7. Perhaps you're an empty nester or do not have children, or perhaps you're a grandparent. You are still an educator of the young. Evaluate your cultural life. Are you seeking out the young to mentor? Can you contribute your life experience to your church, youth group, or small group?

CHAPTER 10

GET STOKED

The Footpath of Togetherness

I'm back at the park.

I leave through the gate that leads between Christ Church and Merton College. The pea gravel path crunches underfoot. An empty bottle of champagne stands at attention at the end of the path; a remnant of last night's undergraduate festivities, I assume.

I turn left on Merton Street, wind around Oriel Square, turn left on Bear Lane, and duck into The Bear Pub to meet my friend Matthew for lunch. The pub swims with people as we discuss philosophy and old Norse mythology and suck down our soup and chomp on our bread. We laugh. We challenge each other. We sit in the noisy quiet of the conversation break, each giving and taking. Participating.

I bid Matthew goodbye and scamper out to High Street to catch the 4B bus to Cumnor Hill. The High Street brims with movement and noise; buses, cars, people walking on sidewalks, students crossing the street, tourists gawking at the architectural wonder of Oxford's University Church of St Mary the Virgin. C. S. Lewis preached there once, on a cool evening in June of 1941. Remember, I mentioned his sermon, "The Weight of Glory?" Well, this is where he gave the address. It was one of his wartime addresses, and Lewis spoke of our participation with beauty.

Seeing beautiful things was not enough, he said. "We want something else which can hardly be put into words—to be united with the beauty we see, to pass into it, to receive it into ourselves, to bathe in it, to become part of it."

Full immersion.

Full participation.

Do you want this kind of immersion in your life? Does the beauty of relationships call to you? Has the isolation made you numb to the intricacies and nuances that come with being a participant in life? Have you stopped listening for God in the "daily grind"?

What if we changed our perspective on our daily existence? What if we replaced the word "grind" with "glory"? Might we be tempted to live in the glory instead of being beaten down by the grind? Maybe we've fallen prey to a horrible lie, one designed to keep us brutalized and grinding. What if the particulars of each day jumped out at us as opportunities to participate with God? I wonder what he's up to.

Do you get a sense of what I'm up to? Well, I'm not up to anything, really. It's what footpaths of beauty can do to you. They can change your perspective. Am I trying to get us all to stop referring to life as a mess or a grind on my own? Maybe. But if that's so, it's only because the footpaths, hard as they can be at times, teach me to rest my eyes on the glory instead of the rocky path. They teach me to fix my eyes on the horizon instead of the obstacles in my way along the trail. With my eyes fixed above, obstacles appear less daunting. The rigors of the trail add to the beauty of the experience.

"Eh, but Tim," you say. "How? How do I change my perspective of the grind?"

"Ah, yes," I reply. "Participation plays a big role here. When C. S. Lewis went on walkabouts, either by himself or with friends, he did his best to avoid distractions so he could participate fully with the world around him and with his companions. In fact, he would not smoke his pipe while walking so that the smell of the pipe would not interfere with the smells and sounds of the landscape."

The glory of walking a footpath with a companion like God is his ever-presence. How lovely that some of Jesus's last words were "I am with you always" (Matt. 28:20). You and I can walk by ourselves along the footpath, but we're never alone. And how much sweeter is it to walk the path *with* someone, a friend, a spouse, a family member?

How do you change your perspective on the mess, muck, and grind of life? Remember the *Ever-presence* who never leaves you. And include a walking partner. If nothing else, perhaps your partner can provide you with a match to light your pipe at the next pub.

LEARNING PUB THEOLOGY

"Daddy, it's raining!" she says. "Is that thunder?"

"I'm not sure," I say, in my feeble attempt to keep her mind someplace else.

"But Daddy . . ."

"Here, hop on my back, love. We need to run, or we're going to get drenched."

We run, but it doesn't matter. The storm catches us.

It's our first month in this new place. *Still not used to the weather*, I think to myself.

The first few months in our Oxford village still stick in my brain as I recall the rhythm and harmony we experienced as a family. We've tried our best to preserve it now that we're living back in the States. When we get too harried and busy, too stressed, when we realize we're driving our vehicles far more than spending time walking on paths, we do our best to recalibrate and find that rhythm again.

With Lyric on my back, I run from the small village market, where we'd walked to buy some milk, down the sidewalk to a pub I remember someone mentioning on the bus ride home yesterday.

The Bear & Ragged Staff, yes, that was it.

Lyric pops open a small, black umbrella while mounted on my back, her seven-year-old legs dangling at my sides. I'm running and laughing.

"The rain can't stop us!" I shout, trying to turn the stormy episode into joy.

Lyric laughs and joins in the shouting.

The rain pelts us, heavy and fast. But so does the joy. We run beneath a line of old cedars, and there it is. The ancient stone public house. We duck inside laughing, wet and cold.

We step from the foyer to the bar and order hot chocolate and toast and ask if we can sit in the "old pub" room, because we can see two large fireplaces blazing. It's early fall in England—the perfect time for a rainy-day fire.

We take our seats in front of one of the fireplaces. There's one at each end of the pub. The great hearths face each other, bookends of the old gathering place. The mantels are at least five feet wide and look like splintered relics from an old Viking ship.

Lyric and I hang our jackets on the chair backs to dry and enjoy the crackling fire, reminiscing about the flash storm and our good fortune in finding the pub. After an hour, the storm passes, so we grab our jackets and walk home.

That was the beginning of the pubs teaching me their significance—and their theology. They serve as markers on the map of the city. Pit stops before you arrive at your real destination. Gathering places for intimate discussions, important meetings, creative meanderings, and a general good time.

"I'll meet you at The Bear around five, before Evensong."

"I'll meet you at The Turf—then we'll head to . . ."

"Let's walk the meadow and visit The Perch, where we can really talk."

I soon discovered that pubs in England serve the community like parks: as gathering places, away from the "noise" of life, if you know what I mean. It's an exchange of one kind of noise for another kind of noise. Perhaps Chesterton describes best what I'm getting at:

I know where Men can still be found,

Anger and clamorous accord,
And virtues growing from the ground,
And fellowship of beer and board,
And song, that is a sturdy cord,
And hope, that is a hardy shrub,
And goodness, that is God's last word—
Will someone take me to a pub?[1]

The sounds of the pub are not completely unlike the sounds of the park. The noise of a pub sounds full; it possesses a shape. The closer I listen, the more I understand it's really not noise at all, but a cadence. Something rhythmic catches my ear, and as I close my eyes, I can pick out the natural sounds of men and women speaking, laughing, even singing. Their voices rise and fall, both bolstered and hushed by emotion.

The pub sounds familiar to me, like the Communion table. The banter of life mixed with the commotion of serving and eating and drinking, life touching life, small relational events unfolding around tables and in quiet corners. It's the beauty of human beings participating with one another—one life colliding into another—without the veneer of pretense.

If I use my imagination, I can almost hear the sounds of beauty that rose up around the first Communion table. Can you hear it?

The laughter of Jesus and Peter in the upper room.

The bustle of the table and wine being shared and poured and spilled. I can feel it splashing onto my hand.

I imagine the hush when Jesus started to speak to his followers about eating his body and drinking his blood, then breaking bread and passing the cup, sharing himself with his closest friends. They sat confused, befuddled by his words and actions that night in the upper room.

Did they even think about the gravity of the moment? Or were they too caught up in the politics of the day, still wondering if he was going to deliver them from Rome? Were they too preoccupied with arguing over their own status? Were they *distracted*?

When God came for us, he came eating, drinking, and reposing at the table. He emptied himself, left heaven and gathered around a table to participate with us. The last thing Jesus did with his disciples before he was killed was eat and drink with them. Do you see a pattern being established?

Pubs, like parks, invite.

"Come, sit," they say. "Repose, linger, *be*, and *enjoy being*."

Beauty blossoms in our connections with people as well as with our connections with nature. And the full bloom of togetherness springs from our continual connection with God. Don't let all the progress of society reprogram your innate hunger to gather and participate with the world around you.

Recognizing Beauty's Invitation

Invitation acts upon us as beauty's emissary of communion, hinting at something alive, and even threatening, in the beyond.

Invitation greeted me one wintry evening at The Bear & Ragged Staff, that same four-hundred-year-old pub nestled in our local village. We walked there with new friends in the Oxford dark, sat in deep leather couches and chairs in front of the five-foot fireplace, and talked about our dreams. We laughed and sipped soup, gathered in by the ancient stone and beams, set off by the ageless fire that interjected pops and sparks into our conversation.

We walked and laughed our way back to our house beneath the midnight sky. Then, magic. Half-dollar-sized snowflakes began to fall, blanketing our coats and scarves. We bellowed out Narnia references and unbelieving quips about our good fortune. Then, as we approached our destination, we eyed a tall, messy-haired college student standing at the bus stop, holding a black umbrella.

The jarring sight compelled me to say, "You look like Mr. Tumnus."

To which the young man replied, "Well, I'm not a faun, if that's what you mean."

On that wintry evening, beauty surrounded me the entire night. It came through the pub form, the stones, the hearth, the fire. It drew me in through lived moments of delight.

Invitation.

When we encounter that pub kind of beauty, we *sense* that *something* within the form is inviting us into a quest. This is what we all felt on that pub evening. Beauty itself called out to us, through the fire, wood, and stone. It shot out from our soup, into our conversation, and around our snowy walk home.

The beautiful in this world invites participation. Beauty possesses a cadence, a rhythm. And that rhythm brings life to the eyes. Isn't it true that when we see a beautiful object, we somehow want to possess it? And wonderful moments spent together are beautiful. How many times have you said, "I just want to bottle up this moment for eternity"?

Simone Weil echoed Lewis when she said, "We are drawn to [beauty] without knowing what to ask of it . . . We want to get behind beauty . . . We should like to feed upon it."[2]

Is this not also true of our gathering places, like parks and pubs, churches and homes? Their charm invites us to gather, to sit, to eat and drink, to be together. And we crave these moments.

Are not some of my most beautiful memories the ones layered with the beauty of relationships? I think to myself. *Isn't it brilliant how, again, we find the edges of life in the beauty of togetherness?*

THE GRAMMAR OF TOGETHERNESS

Togetherness.

What does that mean?

It means not letting words go unsaid. It means not living so caught up in ourselves that we forget about the fourteen-year-old girl who steps off the bus each day, walks into her home, shuts her bedroom door behind her and sits on her bed, thinking about how to kill herself.

Together. There's a grammar to this word that has a depth we need in our lives. Let's think about three interesting aspects of this grammar for a moment.

Synonyms

First, let's think of the synonyms associated with it: with each other, side by side, hand in hand, shoulder to shoulder, cheek by jowl, in chorus, of one accord, in unison.

That's how we should live: each day as a song. Not *to* the world—some vague and unrepresented thing, but *to* each other. A song rings out. It carries forth, resonates, reverberates. A song catches our fancy. We hum it under our breath while we work. We sing it in the shower. We can't get away from it. It sears itself into our subconscious. Songs require voices.

And voices carry wherever there is air. In the back alley. In the suburb. Out on the farm. When we breathe, we inhale the voices of the world.

A voice brings magic—powerful magic. Like the voices of a thousand angels singing somewhere on high, a chorus heralds something spectacular coming from somewhere special. And *we* are the chorus. In unison, we sing the notes of life, heralding the beauty of our humanity, proclaiming the wonder of our Creator.

Adverbs

Second, let's consider *together* as an adverb. An adverb expresses a relationship of place, time, circumstance, manner, cause, or degree. *Together* is how we should live during this time and circumstance: a hard time, a slow time, or a blessed time. Or this circumstance, the moment right now, the decision about to be made, a consequence about to be experienced. How do I live it? Apart? Or together?

Together is the way we live in relation to one another. Not apart.

Not alone. Not exiled. Not hidden or lost, but in a way that allows us to touch or combine. Is not life the very picture of a touch, a combination? We kiss, hold hands, embrace, tickle, caress—actions universal to every human being. The ubiquitous language of humanity. Who doesn't understand the words of an embrace? Who doesn't realize the intimate surrender of a kiss?

Do we stand together today? Or do we care more for being on certain sides or within inner rings or shouting our own activism? Do we lock up our souls? Do we cling to our sedatives?

"We need drugs, apparently," writes Wendell Berry, "because we have lost each other."[3] And why? For what, a screen, a binge, a view, an opinion, something *other* than the "you" I'm here on this earth to care for? Sherry Turkle is right. Or is she? "Our networked life allows us to hide from each other, even as we are tethered to each other," she writes. "We'd rather text than talk."[4]

Heritage

Third, let's consider *together* as a heritage of faith.

God is the *together*-One or, put another way, the three-in-one. His power emerges through *togetherness*. He speaks, and the world comes alive. There is sudden abundance and the joy of being alive, together with the Creator.

The holy act of creation was not the act of a solitary god, but the three-in-one God. The Father and the Logos Son, Jesus, take the scene. The Holy Ghost hovers. The first scenes of life erupt with an act of lifegivingness, with Adam naming the living creatures, then finding Eve. He sees her and sings the lyrics of every marriage song forever after: "Bone of my bone, flesh of my flesh." Not only together, but from one another. We fit. And the life chorus of *togetherness* begins, heralding the love and beauty of God. We come from the Holy Community to form our own. Ralph Waldo Emerson writes, "Every man is a quotation from all his ancestors."[5] You and I live as the embodiment of the sayings of the ancients. Imagine it! We are the living quotations of God, the Son, the Holy Ghost. And it is the pursuit of reunion that conquers separation.

When the Christ blistered into this world through the virgin womb, through innocence, through anonymity, through servile means, he gathered us to himself: vagabonds, failures, head strong, loudmouths, swindlers, and zealots. And he continued to gather people, drawing them unto himself through the cross. Such is the beauty of holy pursuit. Such is the wonder of reunion.

Then the Christ whispered for the Ghost to come, and he came; with fire and wonder he came. Hearts came alive and broke at the same time. A new community was formed. It was a *re*creation. They broke bread and gathered, *together*. They sang songs and hymns and spiritual songs, *together*.

The world knew them, but not by their loud words, not by their witty presence on social media, not by their hubris in the public square, not by their "intentional" engagement" or their "influence" with and on culture.

No!

The world knew them by their quiet acts of service. By their absence in the obscene. By their willingness to pass into anonymity. By their willingness to renounce acclaim. By their willingness to burn as garden lights for Nero. By their unnerving existence in the wilderness. The world saw them, out there in the wilderness, and ventured out to them and asked, "What are you doing out here? Why do you help so many, yet ask for so little? Why do you take the jeers and not shout back? How can you invite shame and care not?" And the wilderness glowed bright with the light of the saints. An incongruent people took over the world in the shadows of obscurity.

This is the history of the called-out ones. The cave gatherers. The cross bearers. Do you know them? This is the history of *togetherness*. From Adam to Christ to the church. This is the history of the greatest family love story ever told: a God running, undistinguished, down the road to meet his estranged son and daughter.

Why?

To be *back together.*

When you think of being together, what comes to mind? Perhaps it's the arguments around the table at Thanksgiving. Or maybe it's the peace of the Communion table. Perhaps it's just sitting with your family, watching a movie. God intended for us to experience the joy of togetherness. But the modern "mode" of doing "church" can challenge connecting any deeper than a nod in the halls on the way to picking up the kids or rushing out to find a good place to eat. I think it's time to turn this mode of faux community around. I think it's time to put the stoke back into our corporate gatherings.

THE BEAUTY OF A GOOD STOKE

I've used the word *stoke* for as long as I can remember. After all, it's part of our English colloquial lexicon. A kind of slang.

In the 1950s, "the stoke" became a popular term with surf riders. The stoke is high when you're on the waves. It means to be "overjoyed, ecstatic, thrilled, delighted." You'll also find the word *stoke* attached to town or village names in the United Kingdom. It comes from the Old English term (which is probably rooted even further back in the Old Norse) *stoc*, which means a settlement or farm. So, as a noun, "stoke" can mean a place. But the word *stoke* also has roots in the Germanic language, from which we get "stick." And the German was influenced by the Latin *instigare*, which means "to spur on."

It turns out the German and Latin "stick" and "spur on" root their meanings in the idea of "adding fuel to the fire," or using a stick to push the coals of a fire together—to get the flames up, raging and burning brighter.

We also find this idea of "stoke" in the New Testament. The writer of Hebrews urges his readers to stoke the fires of their faith: "Let us consider how we may spur one another on toward love and good deeds" (10:24). But it's not just about offering fellow Christians a word of encouragement. *The stoke comes from gathering.* It's when we gather that we should be caught up in the act of stoking one another on toward love and good deeds.

Why should we do this?

Because who doesn't need encouragement in their faith? Who doesn't need a time set aside to meet with brothers and sisters of the faith and hear stories of how God is working?

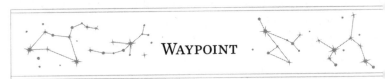

WAYPOINT

Let's consider three aspects related to our discussion about the beauty of togetherness. First, let's think about the personal side of things. Then, let's reflect on why togetherness matters so much for the church, and finally, we'll reflect on how striving for popularity and status in the inner ring ruins togetherness.

The Beauty of Layers

I never understood the significance of a "layer" of anything until I tried my hand at watercolor painting. I believed painting to be reserved for the truly gifted at drawing, and it probably is. I could never draw. Several of my friends paint well, and by "well," I mean they majored in it in college and two of them went on to be professional artists. So I revered painting and still do.

But my reverence for it turned into fear. I grew content to admire it from afar. It wasn't until one day when my daughter, Brielle, asked me to watercolor with her that I shed the fear. I fell in love with the medium.

The first night Brielle and I painted together was rough. I copied what I saw in one of my friend's paintings—a ruggedly wonderful scene of mountains, evergreen trees, and a lake. But even though the finished product was far from good, something clicked in my brain. I could feel it. Maybe it was the brush in my hand, the swishing of the brush in the water, the dabbing of my brush on the paint cakes, or watching the paint run and glide on the paper. *Participation possesses the power of epiphany.* You'll never know unless you try.

We painted way past bedtime.

I woke early the next day, a Saturday, taped down a piece of paper on the kitchen table, and tried to paint the backyard. I painted for four hours. The act entranced me. And it delighted me, even though the painting was, again, not good. But it didn't matter. Something about the stripping away of distractions, something about the deep focus, something about trying lured me further into experimenting with the medium.

I painted with my daughters every day for eight months. In that time, I researched the tools of the watercolorist. I researched technique. I bought new mop brushes for applying heavy washes and fine brushes for detail work. I invested in quality paints and bought packs of cotton paper—cotton paper holds the washes without buckling as much as paper made from wood chips.

One night, I worked on a mountain and forest scene at sunset. I washed in my base colors: a wash for the sky, then for the granite mountain, then for the small forest below. I used a soft red as my wash for the forest, and I didn't know why. But as I let the layers dry and applied more layers of color, as I pulled off some of the edges of the paint with my number seven brush, I noticed the depth of the small, mysterious forest come to life. I could see the very first red leak out around the edges of the forest, while the deep greens and a light yellow made for an interesting, hazy impression of a deep forest.

It was a simple lesson, really. *Layers invite.*

Contrariwise, bold, stark colors blare at the viewer. They contain no depth. They stand alone, and when they are thrown together with other hard edges, they create a visual shout.

I'd forgotten about this togetherness of beauty, this layering effect. I should have remembered Coleridge's idea: *beauty in form gives us pleasure when its many aspects form a unity.* The paint layers worked together to form a unity I found pleasurable.

In life, we can replace the layering of watercolors with the meeting of people, places, and objects that swim in an atmosphere filled with the roundness of God. Seen in this way, life looks like my mysterious reddened forest, inviting me in for a closer look, inviting me to participate in the mystery.

Why do I forget this? Do you? Think about these questions with me.

Is it because I've stopped thinking about my daily existence and the purpose with which I engage in this wonderful world as connected to God?

And what *about* this wonderful world? Why am I engaging with it in the first place?

Does my purpose here merely dissolve into my daily accumulations of money and status? Perhaps so. But if I'm honest, I can't blame distractions and the noise of this world for my lack of vision of God's world. I am to blame. For I have removed myself from the very thing that makes this world so mysteriously wonderful: communion with God. This relationship is the food of my existence, the supernatural food, as Simone Weil puts it. If the bonds between me and God do not strengthen through the act of loving him daily, then the relationship will decay, just as it would with anyone.

What are these bonds that we share? He has made me with a rational mind, has instilled desires into my spirit, has infused me with love, for I am made in his likeness. You and I share these bonds with one another as well. When we love one another, we strengthen these bonds between us.

The same is true of our relationship with God. Earthly friendship, says Weil, reflects God himself. She reminds me that beauty "is a relationship of the world to *my* sensibility, the sensibility that deepens upon the structure of *my* body and *my* soul."[6] I am responsible for the well-being of my body and soul, and when I remove myself from the beauty of this world, I am essentially removing myself from one of God's gifts to humanity. Beauty is God's trap for the world, says Weil. He uses it to remind us, to win us, to open us up to the breath of heaven.

The Gathering of God's People

Now let's turn our focus to the church. One of the last things Jesus prayed for before he was crucified was that his disciples would be one, as he and God were one. He wanted his church to be a living testimony of oneness, of togetherness. We are his emissaries of hope for the world.

Hope does not grow in isolation. When we gather and lift each other up, our hope is stoked, our faith-coals are pushed together, igniting new flames.

When we neglect meeting together for the sake of stoking, we run the risk of falling into bad theology, weird teaching, or spiritual despair.

If you think "church" is about driving to a building or punching your spiritual time card or dressing up and looking the part of the put-together person, then you need some stoking, my friend.

Consider these three characteristics of gathering as we come together as the church:

1. **Worship**—We gather to worship the living God, first and foremost. Church is about him. Worship involves the common threads of surrender, confession, forgiveness, and communion. Worship requires a spiritual posture of humility and a bodily posture of praise. We lift our hands, we kneel, we bow our heads, we lay prostrate. The posture of worship invites communion with others. It says to them, "I am with you. I am not better than you. I need you."

2. **Sharing**—Sharing requires time. And time on Sunday mornings is scarce. We have over-produced our services to the point where sharing can only happen outside of church. Why sacrifice one for the other? Church leaders should consider this aspect of the gathering time. Deep sharing thrives in an environment of trust. We gather to hear stories of overcoming so that our overcoming-hope grows. We gather to share our own stories of pain and hurt and despair and how God met us in those dark places and delivered us. We share so that we can persevere through the muck life throws at us.

3. **Stoking**—We meet to spur one another toward love and good deeds. We are to encourage one another, building each other up in the faith (1 Thessalonians 5:11). Our talk as we gather should be beautiful, not corrupt (Ephesians 4:29). Hospitality should be our love language to one another (1 Peter 4:8–10). We stoke each other by the goodness and praise of our words. We encourage one another to never give up, to persevere, to fight.

If what I'm saying is true, then let's stop walking past one another in the halls of that monstrous church building and instead, stop to hug each other. Bear hug me because I need it. Bear hug me to stoke my fires. Because you'd better believe I'm going to hug you. I may even greet you with a holy kiss—watch out!

What if you and I woke up each morning and, as we scroll through our mental notes of what we need to accomplish, we add in ideas about how we can stoke someone's spiritual fire. It's time to reignite the flames of our faith, my friends. It's time to get the stoke back.

Be an Outsider

Earlier, I listed chasing the "inner ring" as a pursuit that moves against building togetherness. We live in a culture that says, "Pursue the in crowd if you want to be accepted." Since so many of us desire to be in the in crowd, we listen.

There is another way: the way of the outsider.

"But Tim," you say. "It's okay to desire acceptance. Surely you're not suggesting we drift out of the cultural discussion, live as hermits, and shun acceptance by others?

"Ah, yes," I reply. "Indeed, our desire for acceptance is good. But if we change our true selves to be accepted, then I'm afraid we've drifted from our intended purpose as created beings. We should always remain ourselves, even in the face of pressure to be accepted. Being accepted by the inner ring comes with a heavy cost."

The cost is a pleasure that will not last. Disappointment and emptiness. What you thought you saw from the outside vanishes once you get there. Why? Because it was never truly what you wanted. It wasn't just acceptance and friendship. It was status and popularity rather than, as C. S. Lewis writes, "loyalty or humour or learning or wit or any of the things that can be really enjoyed."[7]

Lewis says, "Until you conquer the fear of being an outsider, an outsider you will remain."[8] Speaking to undergraduates at King's College London in 1944, he warned the students about the temptation to get on the "inside," to be well-liked by the people who seem to matter most in society. Lewis himself was considered an outsider in the Oxford world, so he knew a thing or two about it.

Lewis's exhortation came with marching orders, as it were: stay busy honing your craft, become great in your own field, care less for what the so-called "inner ring" is up to, and care more about your own work and your own friends. I reread Lewis's address often as a reminder to keep my head down, do the work before me, and surround myself with the people I *really* like, instead of the people I'm *supposed* to like. We all want to be included. Everyone wants to feel appreciated. But we can end up trading off precious things if we blindly pursue the inner ring. Things like:

1. Sound thinking for pop-theology
2. True spiritual affection for cause crusading
3. Our integrity for influence
4. Loving relationships for transactional ones
5. Diverse relationships for relationships with people who only think like us

Being an outsider, says Lewis, is a matter of perspective. Lewis's perspective is, "Hang it all, I'll do my own thing, rather than give up whatever it takes to get in with the inner ring." Here's a quick hack for living life as an outsider: *realize that God appreciates you.* When you realize you possess a certain glory before God, then the desire to be included in the so-called "popular crowd" fades.[9]

So let's get to work, find good friends, and have at it. When we live like this, we become like another who lived his life as an outsider; a man who, though on the outside of society, created his own inner ring. Jesus was the original outsider.

PART 3

FOOTPATHS OF THE HILLS

Understanding the Mysterious Side of Beauty

CHAPTER 11

A Haunting Clack-Clack

The Footpath of Natural Mystery

I told you we'd need a sword.

"Why?" you ask.

To cut through the heart of the Dragon of Distraction of course. Imagine that? Dragons in the park, of all things!

We head out to the hills George described to Sam. I can almost see Sam, healed of his malady, heading out of the Park of Participation, and into a place more rugged and untethered: the hills. This is where you and I go now. I'm in Cumnor, just west of the city center of Oxford, heading out for a walk up Cumnor Hill—*Homo viator*!

LISTENING TO THE LANGUAGE OF MYSTERY

I walk across the moor, which is ancient and squishy. The long green grass pushes down into the saturated dark soil.

Squish, squish, squish. I'm grateful for my Gore-Tex boots. After cutting through the grass, I find my way back onto the footpath. "These footpaths are nearly a thousand years old, Tim. And the bridle paths, just as old. Horse and carriage pulled up and down the hills and villages, and we still use them today," said a new friend who took me on a drive into the Windermere countryside recently.

But now, I'm back from my late November trip to the Lake District and trudging through the hills that roll up behind our house in Cumnor village.

As I slog through the soaked countryside, I think about C. S. Lewis's love for walks and the outdoors in general. He was a rambler. He loved scrambling around the English countryside. He possessed a deep affection for the simple, rustic pleasures of the empty sky, the unspoilt hills, and the silent white roads on which you could hear the rattle of a farm cart half a mile away.[1]

He once told his older brother, Warren, how he wished he'd have had "gumboots and oilskins and a sou'wester" for outdoor play during periods of rain when he was younger. If Lewis were alive today, I'm convinced we'd most likely find him tramping some remote countryside in Gore-Tex boots and a Patagonia Nano Puff jacket in search of a quiet, beautiful place.

Footpaths trace patterns like scribbles all over England, across farmland and private estates. They connect the villages. Their entrances sometimes pop out at you, hidden between trees or along the wall beside a private residence or tucked behind a hedgerow. I didn't have to look far to find the footpaths near our house.

I turn right out of our driveway, walk down Cumnor Hill, and take Hurst Lane east to the old dirt road.

I walk the lane, and immediately, the hill of the Seven Sisters rises to my right. The locals named the hill after the seven large pine trees on top. The top of the Seven Sisters offers a sprawling view of the Vale of the White Horse. If you can catch the sunset up on the hill, you're in for a treat.

But today I'm walking further along the old dirt road to Boars Hill.

I walk another quarter mile, and a footpath cuts away to the southeast.

I take it.

The path rises into the woods. A shower passes.

Perhaps I should've stayed in, had some soup, and read with the girls. But the storm-laden sky drew me out, and it didn't disappoint. The woods on the hill are noisy with wind. It bangs branches back and forth and sprays rain, but not enough to soak anything except the grass.

The low clouds move like upside-down waves, white-capped and crashing further up into one another, filling the sky with billowing columns. The wind-rushed sky hurries along, brushed with blue-gray washes and sagging rain-droppers.

Dusk approaches, but I'm too far to turn back.

An iron gate obscures the trail's entrance into the woods. I unlock it and walk under a canopy of hardwoods. I pass Youlbury Scout Adventure Camp on my right. It's quiet there. No one is out.

Who would be? I say to myself. It's like a Washington Irving novel out here. The headless Hessian rides tonight, I'm sure of it.

The exasperated light dims above the barren winter limbs.

It's getting darker, I whisper, continuing my quiet conversation with myself.

The wind snaps, and the air dries out for a spell. Beneath a veil of straggly elms and ash trees, I walk, whistling like I do when there's no one around—loudly, with an overexaggerated vibrato.

Up, I continue, up to the gravel path, up to an unmarked road, over and up and along White Barn Road, then right, on a new footpath near the top of the hill toward the southwest.

The path hugs a wooden fence that outlines a large pasture.

A great white horse dines on the wet grass, unfazed by the turbulent weather. His mane hangs low around his neck and over his lazy eyes. The stout, white beast doesn't flinch as I pass. He chews as my eyes move from his mane to the undulating backdrop, a green field, and a line of woods.

THE MYSTERIOUS SIDE OF BEAUTY

I've taken you with me out here on this wet, wooded walk and detailed the experience so that I might tempt you with the haunting beauty of a simple walk in the woods at twilight. Beauty leaps out when we simply take the time to *see*, to participate. The lesson learned, however, reaches past the simple notion of getting outside and taking a walk. It even goes deeper than taking the time to see so that we might notice the intricacies of our kaleidoscope world. The lesson of this walk is to show you another side to beauty that we seldom think about but many of us love and are drawn to—*the haunting, mysterious wonder of our natural world*—and to encourage you. You don't need to be in a far-off land to experience the beauty and haunting wonder of the outdoors. You simply need to grab a jacket, step outside your door, breathe deeply, and start walking—preferably with a family member or friend, but God-walks, like my Boars Hill jaunt, always do wonders for the soul.

When I head out on walks like this one, or step outside to sit with my daughters and watch the storms roll in, I ask myself, *What might this mysterious side of beauty say about God?* I make sure I discuss it with someone close to me.

What might this mysterious side of beauty say about God?

Sometimes, beauty dresses up in haunting colors, misty lakes, or stormy woods. I find this beauty in the hills as I walk. The awe-inspiring landscape reminds me how I need mystery and wonder in my life. I feel a sense of terror and reverence as I walk the stormy hill, as though the presence of something full and beautiful yet dangerous looms close by. It's beyond me yet near me; big enough to feel in the wind, subtle enough to sense in my spirit. The feeling summons the words of John the Baptizer: *I must become less.* A characteristic of beauty I did not expect.

I'm alone in the hills, yet I'm still participating. I'm outside. No church building, yet I worship.

LEARNING FROM THE TREES

The outside world matters.

If you don't prioritize connecting with nature in your life, ask yourself, "If God made the mountains and the rivers and the ocean and the forests, might I find a piece of him there? Might I learn something of him that will draw me closer to him?"

You and I must be careful not to fall into the wrong thinking of our modern age, which views the outside world as a resource to be leveraged, a wilderness to be tamed, a possession to be utilized. Even Christians can fall into this thinking with skewed views of creation stewardship. The created world is not something we can fully understand, nor is it something we can begin to control. We must learn to live *with* the created order rather than viewing ourselves as controlling or subjugating stewards.[2]

Viewing the natural world as a resource further removes us from the creative hand of God. In the woods, we find breath, not just in a "Wow, I needed some time to clear my head" way but in a "Wow, look what I learned about God today by reflecting on the roots of a tree in winter" way.

The book of nature[3] longs for us to read it, not because it is itself a thing to worship, but because it was made and still holds the words of God.

The land speaks to me in a language I know but cannot speak. One I can read but cannot translate. If I listen close enough, it will tutor me on beauty's mystery and the haunting enigma of God's holiness.

THE UNKNOWN IN THE TWILIGHT

An age ago, the British poet Matthew Arnold walked these same footpaths. The westward view of the Vale of the White Horse, which is now obscured by ash trees, used to extend—on a clear day—to Berkshire Downs. The view inspired Arnold, so much so that the field was named the Matthew Arnold Field and Reserve. It explodes with yellow buttercups in late spring and summer—this I'd see firsthand on my spring return to the field. But today, gray has its way.

This is Boars Hill. An ancient rise a few miles southwest of Oxford as the crow flies, but one much changed over time. Another poet, Arthur Hugh Clough, lived here in the 1840s when the hill was still unwooded and offered spectacular views on all sides. It was Clough who introduced Arnold to the spot. Later, Arnold would describe the view of Oxford from the northeast side of the hill:

> And that sweet city with her dreaming spires,
> She needs not June for beauty's heightening . . . [4]

The dreaming spires, the assemblage of high steeples—exclamation points of the Oxford University gothic architecture and associate churches—vault toward heaven, and though I must walk a bit, I find Arnold's view of the spires. It does not disappoint.

Now the ash, elm, and oak trick you into thinking they've always been here. They creak and swoosh about in the west wind that sometimes deposits ocean salt on residents' windowsills. I'm not sure I believe this local legend, however. The ocean is some seventy miles away. The salty west wind, however, is at it this evening, and two loud, black birds now follow me along the road back to the footpath. They hop more than fly from treetop to treetop. Spies, no doubt, of the headless Hessian.

The walk and dimming light satisfy the yearning in me to get out, beyond the neighborhood and pubs, into a space alive with wonder. The trees, wind, and twilight create in me a healthy dread, like someone or something lurks in the woods or is watching—waiting for me. Probably just a mood brought on by the atmospheric landscape and weather, but it is palpable, nonetheless. Or is there something to my haunted feelings that begins to stir in me a spirit of longing for another time in the same place, perhaps a walking companion on this eerie, beautiful night, like Arnold or Clough.

Have you ever experienced feelings like this? Where the scene, the moment, all of it mixes into an elixir that makes you want to travel back in time? I like to tell my wife I was born in the wrong time. I long for an older age of castles and swords. Or have you ever arrived in a new town, or traveled to another country, and whispered to yourself, "This feels like home"?

Boars Hill, the twilight, the movement of the stormy sky, all coalescing—whisper to me hints of home. But of *another* home—out there. Heaven, perhaps?

HOW THE LIGHT WORKS ON US

I think of Peter Davidson's reminder of how twilight wields a kind of magical power that woos our hearts and arouses a "vague yearning for the place we haven't come to yet, or the place that we have left without hope of return."[5] England lies just above the 50th parallel, so it is not one of the "territories of true darkness," like our former southern home back in the States.[6] The sky looks different here. It's an island sky and yet also northern. The clouds, even billowing ones at dusk, possess a life unlike any I've seen. A pleasing melancholy resides in the European twilight, says Davidson; it's the way the light works on the people and the land, I suppose. So, this isn't just a chance evening spook I'm sensing on my walk. I am, indeed, experiencing a characteristic of the geography.

We become like the land in which we live.[7] Time and geography work on us, changing our moods, perceptions, and dispositions. The land touches our imaginations; it thrills, allures, and captivates. Even in our world, where virtually every land has been explored and mapped, you and I can still find ourselves in a place unknown, simply because it is unknown to us.

I love how geographer John K. Wright observed the importance of a term popular in his field: *terra incognita*, or "unknown lands."[8] He said that early explorers and geographers had the benefit of new lands. Why? Because unknown lands spark the imagination; they invite exploration, both physically and imaginatively. Unexplored lands, in older times, became thresholds for grand imaginative stories and legends. Think about how we see this same imaginative storytelling about space travel. Space is an unknown land to us, so we create landscapes within it—whole worlds, wrought by our creativity.

By nature, you and I fill in the cracks of the unknown. We imagine what a place might be like based on what we know of the place we're in.

Why?

Because the unknown enlivens our imagination and heightens our participation in the world. It breaks through to us. It stirs us and creates within us a desire to know more. It invites us to become seekers and questioners, so off we go![9]

Mystery and the unknown create a robust armor for beauty. Though we encounter the beautiful on our walk among the hills through our senses, we know *something else* hovers among the trees or lingers in the twilight or rings out in the *clack-clack* of the winter trees.

Beautiful moments like this remind us that beauty signals something far grander than even the most intense experiences of natural wonder.

Simone Weil considered beauty impossible to define because, in order to do so, one must try to wrap one's mind around God himself.[10] She considered beauty directly linked to God.

For Weil, our sense of the wonderful, the awful, the tremendous, the mysterious in our world is our sense of God. Something holy glimmers in beauty. Not the holiness we're used to talking about in American Protestant evangelical churches—something powerful, even dreadful, while also abounding in eternal wonder and beauty. This beauty calls us past the temporal things of the world, asks us to sit and be still, and to ponder God.[11]

My Boars Hill walk reminds me that the language of beauty consists of layers, one being the *numinous*—that strange feeling of awe and dread, mixed with wonder and fascination. I experienced what David Bentley Hart describes as the experience of beauty: "something mysterious, prodigal, often unanticipated, even capricious."[12]

In 1917, the German theologian Rudolf Otto combined the words *numen*, the Latin term meaning "divine power," and *ominous*, and formed the word *numinous* to describe a deep religious experience or mood brought on by inexpressible and terrifying feelings of mystery related to the divine. The kind one might experience during times of personal worship or when one participates in the event of beauty.

The *numinous* experience comes to us from outside ourselves. It creates the feeling that something "wholly other" is present.[13] In this way, the experience of the *numinous* is associated with religious experience. The Christian tradition names this "wholly other" *God*.

Consider how we find beauty in the mysterious when we read about the life of Jesus in the New Testament. Writers like Mark used "*numinous* elements of awe and fascination."[14] Mark "vividly portrays the impact made by the Son of God upon the apostles as he walked among men. They are dazzled and stupefied, as if by a brilliance too great for them to take in."[15] The *numinous* connects to beauty and frightens the Plastic People because it's not something that can always be controlled or quantified or defined. And yet the *numinous* draws us, fascinates us, fills us with dread, and we love it.

WAYPOINT

I took a walk to get out and clear my head, but as it turned out, a moment found me—one haunting, alive, and sacred.

Night, falling like a paperweight through spiderwebs, reminds me "that the best Nature does for us is to work in us such moods in which thoughts of high import arise."[16] I pray as I walk, caught in the mood of the raven-accompanied twilight and the banging branches; caught in the atmosphere of beauty.

What thoughts of mine might rise? How important will they be?

Smack!

Clack!

Bang!

I won't make it back before dark. And I don't have my headlamp. But do I even want to make it back before dark? Can I, for this last mile, let the landscape speak in the cloudy and raucous twilight?

How arrogant a thought.

Let it speak? No—I will listen to what it is already saying. I want to listen more, and now I have a chance to do so.

What do I hear?

I hear the beating of my heart at the falling dread of night.

I hear the storm wind and think of Ezekiel's vision of God shrouded by cloud, enveloped by lightning, burning like hot steel.

I hear my thoughts, whispered in prayers.

I hear fear, and I let it come.

I hear whole stands of trees bending in the wind. They sound like a treetop ocean, an unrelenting tide that gives the moment an unexplainable vitality. There is life in the storm. There is life in this "wolf light."[17] Even as night prowls, moments away.

It is a *numinous* moment.

Is this what I hear in the smacking branches and ripping wind? Is this the mood nature produces, or is it something else? Doubt always lurks behind moments of spiritual epiphany.

I hear the words of the landscape whipping in my ears as if God himself were speaking. I believe he *is* speaking.

What is he saying?

How can I discern his words?

In moments like this, I find myself praying for the strength of God to get past myself. To strip away the me that blocks the him around me. I try to empty myself into God's love for me.

I am so greedy. So full of worry. So full of anger. So distracted. How can I re-center myself? Do I even trust God?

I throw all of this at him, and he willingly takes it.

Something in the twilight sets me free, and I unload.

"God, I don't trust you to provide for me. I don't trust you to carry me when I can't walk. I don't trust you because I don't believe you invest yourself in my literal everyday life. So I worry. I fret over my bills and how to keep providing for my kids, how to set my wife at ease in this world.

"I am no farmer. I live in a post-industrial age. I don't depend upon the rains and the good earth to produce my sustenance. I must labor to earn money. You don't bring rains for me. Will you bring work? Will you help me in this toil? I don't see it.

"But I admit, I don't always look. I pray to you for guidance and help, but like the children of Israel who planted their crops, prayed to you, and then prayed to the pagan gods of rain and agriculture just to cover their bases, I pray to the pagan god of myself and work, and work, and work, numbing my hearing beneath the rattle of my metaphorical plow.

"The inner life? The spiritual life? What is it to me; a man in the world of incessant pressure to produce, to provide?"

I open up. My twilight jaunt becomes an evening prayer walk.

This happens to me often, and not always on walks. Sometimes, it happens during a quiet drive to the mountains. Or even waiting for my family to wake in the wee morning hours. I've discovered that the witness of the *numinous* beauty in my life manifests itself in a quieter husband, a steadier father, a friend who listens, and a community member who loves telling others why it is that I retreat so often to the mountains.

I've also learned of another *numinous* beauty that connects me to heaven: Jesus Christ. He is the bridge between the human and divine. It is because of him that I am able to approach the Father.

Reflect on these images of Jesus given to us in Scripture to draw you toward worshipping God in your daily life:

1. **Jesus as the pre-incarnate Son who created the world.** Earlier, we discussed the story "before the beginning" of time and how the Logos spoke the world into existence. Before the manger in Bethlehem, Jesus was. See him as Creator.

2. **Jesus as greater than Moses.** In Deuteronomy, God said to Moses, "I will raise up a prophet like you from among their fellow Israelites" (18:18 NLT) Moses met with God and led his people from the Egyptians. Jesus is seated next to God, walked on water, and covers over his people as the paschal lamb, rescuing the world from sin. See him as the Hope of the prophets. (Hebrews 3)

3. **Jesus as I Am.** Earlier, we looked at the wonderful mysterious name of God (the Divine Name): I Am. God identified himself to Moses as I Am. Throughout the gospel of John, Jesus famously refers to himself using seven I Am statements: I Am the bread of life (6:35), light of the world (8:12), the gate (10:7), the good shepherd (10:11), the resurrection and the life (11:25), the way and the truth and the life (14:6), the true vine (15:1). Twice, Jesus identifies himself simply as I Am. In John 8:58, the Pharisees pick up stones to kill him after he says, "Before Abraham was born, I am." And finally, in Gethsemane, when Judas and the soldiers come to arrest him, Jesus asks them whom they seek. "Jesus of Nazareth," they reply. "I am," says Jesus (John 18:5, 8). The "he" we find

in our English translations is implied. The Greek here is the same as the Septuagint (Greek translation of the Old Testament) when God identified himself to Moses at the burning bush: *egō eimi*. Jesus uttered the Divine Name, something the Jews would never do. Not only did he say the Divine Name, he also identified himself with it. And when he said it, the soldiers backed away and fell to the ground—a *numinous* moment. This is the One who walks with you daily. The One who tells you, "If you seek me, you will find me."

CHAPTER 12

THE RICHES OF SEEING

The Footpath of Regaining True Vision

How does one remember a time of hush? It's a sound, but not really. More like what a sound *feels* like when you live it. More like what a sound *looks* like when you remember it.

That's what I remember from the morning when Jessie, Sammy, my brother, Jon, and I camped in the pine grove off old Seglock Road. Eight inches of snow were on the ground, six more on the way. We hiked back in after dark because you're not supposed to camp in the Pennsylvania State Game Lands. We reached the pine grove Jon and I had found the day before. We dug out the snow and collected wood, built a fire, and ate Chunky Soup.

I woke early, just before dawn. The night's raging fire still smoked. We'd all slid into a bunch; crammed together, asleep, and warm.

I poked the fire and got it going. Each sound was something I could *feel*. The sun rose, but I couldn't see it. It just lit up the low-hanging clouds with a soft glow. The guys didn't move. I sat in the silence, watching the coals kindle and grow into flame.

Then, a flake.

And another.

More.

An even fall tumbled through the pines. The smoke rose, the snow fell, and my breathing slowed as the woods turned into an anechoic chamber of timber and white.

Then, quiet footsteps? Hooves? What was coming?

Through the pines, a lone deer walked toward the campsite. It stopped and looked at me. Was it inspecting the fire? Me? Then it continued, on and out of sight. The careful crunch of the deer's gait, the nothing sound of falling snow, the inaudible dance of the morning fire, and my own breathing.

A hush.

That's what I remember. A moment bottled up in my memory, silent, wonderful, beautiful.

The Fullness of Silence

That moment in the snow, with the deer, still stirs emotions within me. But when I reflect on that snapshot of beauty, I am struck by the audible silence of the experience. We tend to think of silence as the absence of sound, a kind of vacuity, and that is certainly an angle to consider. But this moment of beauty resounded with the hush of silence. Instead of thinking of silence as the absence of something, what if we thought of it as a framing for something *other*?

Silence cripples us. In South Minneapolis Orfield Laboratories built the quietest room on the planet, an anechoic chamber capable of absorbing 99.99% of sound. It is said a human being can last only forty-five minutes in the room before hallucinating or breaking down.

Founder Steven Orfield says that in a room such as the anechoic chamber, a person's ears will adapt to the silence and pick up sounds within the body, like a heartbeat or stomach churn. In a room of utter quiet, the human becomes the sound, and this reality can disorient a person, making it nearly impossible to even stand.

Silence also lures and woos us. On August 29, 1952, pianist David Tudor took the stage at the famous Maverick concert hall, which is located just south of Woodstock, New York. Over the next four minutes the musician made no audible sounds, played no notes on the piano, but simply turned the pages of the piece he was performing. The pages contained no notes.

When four minutes and thirty-three seconds passed, Tudor stood to a resounding ovation. The performance marked the debut of what would become John Cage's most influential and controversial work: 4'33" or "four thirty-three."

Cage described the sounds he heard during the three movements of "four thirty-three" on that summer day at the Maverick: "What they thought was silence, because they didn't know how to listen, was full of accidental sounds. You could hear the wind stirring outside during the first movement. During the second, raindrops began pattering on the roof, and during the third the people themselves made all kinds of interesting sounds as they talked or walked out."[1]

Composer and scholar Kyle Gann says that Cage himself considered "four thirty-three" not a piece of provocation, but "an act of framing."[2] The piece gathered the sounds from the immediate environment in a moment of attention. That moment of attention worked to open the mind to new possibilities in music; "it begged for a new approach to listening."[3]

Silences beg us to listen. Henry David Thoreau said the "orator . . . is most eloquent when most silent." It is silence, "the universal refuge," that gives those who speak well the wisdom to do so. The great orator becomes part of the audience and listens while she speaks. I wonder how many of us know what it is to listen more than we speak, listen when we speak, and listen to speak?

Silence, then, is more than absence. It possesses power, acts as a device for framing life, and instructs us on how to be attentive to others.

You and I grope for this feeling of fullness in our lives. That is what I'm describing to you now as I've felt it in my own life; from boyhood to manhood, I remember that feeling of fullness. I can feel that spiritual quality I might have labeled back then as wonder or beauty.

How can we discern this kind of fullness? Is it merely a feeling?

Charles Taylor helps us by explaining the experience of fullness as one that "breaks through our ordinary sense of being in the world, with its familiar objects, activities and points of reference."[4]

What does the act of seeing beauty require of us? A new framing of life and a willingness. We must recognize our need to adjust our pace of life and be willing to do so. Developing deeper sight into the soul also requires a willingness to live settled rather than chaotic. We can obtain the riches of seeing surface when we learn to be at home in silence. Silence breeds patience and humility.

Beauty is about seeing. And not just looking *at something* with the eyes in our heads. Seeing requires language. When the nature writer Robert Macfarlane discovered the Sussex word *smeuse*, which is the "gap in the base of a hedge made by the regular passage of a small animal hole left in a hedge,"[5] he made a mental note to notice these signs of animal movement in the hedges more often. The word *smeuse* informed his ability to see the landscape better. That bit of language enhanced his ability to see landmarks previously invisible to him.

Seeing is not about looking. I can look at the woods behind my house, caught in a blank stare, and see nothing. Or I can follow the flight of one of the pileated woodpeckers who like to dart and bob and burrow in the dying ends of pine trees around our property.

DIP, BOB, AND DIVE

I knew I was cutting it close. The woods grew dim, and the trees swayed in a strong spring wind.

But I wanted to see it—the trail I'd cut in.

A two-and-a-half-mile single-track greenway stretches across the contours of our neighborhood and into the woods, then dumps hikers, bikers, and equestrians out in a gravel parking lot.

We like to keep the section of greenway behind our house maintained, so I cut in a new section along the creek that led around a great muddy washout. I rode my mountain bike to the new section of the trail and stopped to take in the dusky woods. That's when I heard him.

Rat-a-tat-tat. Rat-a-tat-tat. Rat-a-tat-tat.

The unmistakable sound echoed in the empty woods. Just beyond the next turn stood a giant sycamore. It was three trees in one: a cluster lining the creek. I could see their tops, ninety feet or more above the forest floor. A pileated woodpecker perched above me, pecking the deadened sycamore tops as I watched from below. Back and forth, he skirted the tops of the far-right trunk and then rested, still and grand.

After he rested, he leaned back, turned his head, and let go.

But he did not spread his wings. He performed a free-fall dive through the quiet air. He fell fifteen feet with his broad chest facing me. Just before impact with the adjacent sycamore, he fanned his wings and magically turned upright, claws in trunk.

I shouted at the sight, a hallelujah to the God who saw his bird dip and bob in flight, feathering the treetops with silent grace. Every moment of every day fills up with bounty of this kind, beauty we do not see because we do not take the time.

In that moment of the woodpecker's dive, I thought of Job and how he questioned God; how God responded with stories of unseen wonders, untouched mysteries, and uncharted wisdom. Stories not meant to shame, but to remind Job that God's wisdom and glory remained unrivaled. In his wisdom, God cares for the silly ostrich and delights in the chaos of the leviathan. He sees the pileated woodpecker, alone in the dimming woods, and shouts his own hallelujah.

I was thankful to have taken the time that day, time to *see*. It reminded me that the days possess calamity and wonder, and both come under God's purview. But what he is most concerned about in both is whether I *see* him.

The Fingerprints of God

To *see* God does not require our physical eyes. Of course, no one can see God and live. But nature, with its glory, does help us see God in a way. The invisible qualities of God are visible in the beauty of natural wonders, but these qualities come more profoundly to us when we contemplate their meaning (Rom. 1:20). A lone woodpecker is beautiful. It performs woodpecker-type acts, its plumage unmistakable in the treetops, its flying pattern unique. But what is the significance of the lone woodpecker performing hidden acts of glory?

When we contemplate the beauty before us each day, we practice the spiritual discipline of seeing. Seeing is more than looking. It is *contemplating* the object, *reflecting* on the event, *considering* the person. Seeing is an act of *knowing*.

If God created the world, then his qualities rest like fingerprints all over it. His fingerprints tell us who he is just like ours tell who we are. They tell us that he is there, just like ours would reveal our presence if found by an inspector at a crime scene. But the fingerprint is only a door to the meaning of the presence.

Why did God create a bird so wonderfully adorned for no one to see?

Why do sycamores grow next to water?

Why does the wind blow through an empty wood? Why take the time to create this mysterious effect in a dusky forest?

The answer?

To remind us that he is near, even when it seems like he is not.

To remind us that his wisdom places him above all. He is not the god *of* thunder but the God who *created* the thunder.

To declare himself and his glory. For "the heavens declare the glory of God" (Ps. 19:1). We cannot understand God's closeness (immanence) without realizing the meaning of his distance (transcendence). He is with us in Christ through the Holy Spirit, yes. But he is also the great Maker who preserves creation. We've lost sight of the Maker

God. We pass by the sycamores without considering their glory or the glory of their Maker. What do the angels do when they recognize God as the one who *alone* creates and sustains?

They worship (Neh. 9:6).

The fear of God is the beginning of wisdom. And I am beginning to understand this.

Beauty Is a Gift for Every Person

Have you ever thought, *What would the world be like absent of beauty and wonder?*

Does the pileated woodpecker impact my day? Perhaps not directly, but what if woodpeckers didn't exist? What if God placed us in this world without the glorious bounty that surrounds us each day of our lives? What kind of sad life would that be? Nothing to see. Nothing to contemplate. Nothing to incite our curiosity.

But that's not reality.

Beauty explodes in and throughout our lives with profound effect. Beauty draws every person into a quest to discover what lies behind the wonder that dazzles our senses.[6] We just don't always realize it. I blame our modern reticence to use terms like *beauty* and *wonder*, which skew feminine, in a more generalized sense. Beauty is genderless. Beauty is deeper than our modern world presents. Beauty and wonder relate to so much more than mere gender affinities. Beauty is rooted in our very existence. It emerges in our desire for wholeness. It ignites our curiosity to understand our world more intimately.

How do I know this? Allow me to give you an example.

My friend Chad likes to say that when you sit any person around a fire ring with others, the fire acts as a truth serum. You hear the child come out in every person. You hear about their loves, fears, and dreams. Beauty, wonder, and curiosity drip from their lips like confessions to the priest of the bonfire. I could recount many stories testifying to Chad's observation. Bonfires act like beauty chambers. We fall under the spell of the crackling and popping and reveal our hearts. The beauty discovered around a campfire is far from one-dimensional. It touches male and female, old and young. It sets our hearts on fire. It touches eternity itself.

The bonfire shows us that every person wants to report on the beauty and wonder in their own lives just as much as the pain and disappointment.

The bonfire teaches us the convening power of the flames and the night sounds.

The bonfire reminds us of our thirst for glory.

Beauty touches our eyes and ears and even our noses.

Beauty is an invitation to go deeper with God. When I follow the woodpecker's movements, I learn about his routine, flight patterns, and work ethic. In the process of following him, I take in the glory of his red-cand black-speckled head and feathers. When I *see* the woodpecker, I can relay a story about his wonder, the way he free-falls from ninety-foot sycamores, carefree and effortless. The meaning is in the telling. And we are born storytellers.

But have we silenced our muse?

Rescuing Our Inner Richness

Beauty is about participation and attentiveness.

Earlier, we observed how society grooms us to be spectators rather than participants, and how the consequences of such a cultural education carries serious ramifications for the individual and the greater culture.

In 1952, Josef Pieper warned that so much visual noise in our world impedes our ability to "see."[7] He believed man's inner richness was at stake. But how did he connect the problem of noise to the inner parts of man?

The portal of the eyes.

We don't always consider the consequences of our actions, and our daily decisions to invite noise into our lives instead of the beautiful will do—indeed, has done—something to our insides. Humans, Pieper suggested, have lost the ability to see. The visual noise works on us. Over time, and without us realizing it, we begin to live and operate at an unsustainable pace, an inhuman pace, until we no longer take the time to see.

I can remember, as a young boy, sitting in the back seat of our old Chevy Malibu, watching those rows of corn we used to play in blur by. The speed of the car reduced the great field into a blurry green haze.

I can also remember walking down the old country lane that wound past our house. When I walked the lane with my dad, the corn looked different. The stalks rose to the sky, gigantic and emerald. The wind moved through their leafy stalks and made a flapping sound. The rain splatted on the stalks; a sound—much like the *shh, shh, shh* of running through them—I still find hard to explain. The rows stretched on forever.

When I walked, my senses came alive. When we drove, my senses dulled.

When we slow down, the world meets us with epiphany. When we attend, our eyes quicken our hearts. When we *see*, we notice God.

"But Tim, slow down. Aren't you sounding the alarm a bit prematurely? Aren't you overreacting? We'll correct our course, I'm sure of it."

I'm not sure about the course correction, but I *am* sure that the ability to see is essential to a human's ability to accurately make sense of this world. If we can't make sense of the world, how will you and I be able to know or define reality?

"But Tim, can it really be true that a little visual noise in my life can alter how I interpret truth?"

"I believe so, yes."

Truth is defined as that which affirms and corresponds to reality.[8] When we become unable to relinquish the pace that keeps us from seeing the particulars of reality, we risk losing our grasp of truth.

MARVELING

How do we regain our ability to *see*?

Bombarded with distraction and numbed by convenience, our eyes become lazy amidst the myriad photographic images that saturate our days through phone apps, internet browsers, and television. Distraction and convenience work in tandem. Everything lives within our phones. I can order dinner or groceries and download a movie while sitting on a lawn chair. People would rather pay for convenience than do something themselves. Writer, attorney, and Columbia law professor Tim Wu wrote on the dark side of convenience in the *New York Times*:

> Though understood and promoted as an instrument of liberation, convenience has a dark side. With its promise of smooth, effortless efficiency, it threatens to erase the sort of struggles and challenges that help give meaning to life.[9]

Created to free us, convenience constrains our willingness to do things on our own, and thus, in a subtle way, it can enslave us. We need to *get outside* and live with the earth beneath our feet and the sky above our heads. We were created to pursue beauty, not spectate from a lawn chair, drunk on the convenience of push-button life. But we pay no attention to the sloth encroaching on our ability to be human. Quite the contrary. We invite it into our lives by handing our children a device to keep them quiet, keep them busy, keep them out of our hair. Because *me time* is important. We indoctrinate our children with the orthodoxy of convenience and distraction and tell them, by the act of handing them a device, that the way the device tells you to interpret the world is okay. All of reality exists in that tiny rectangle.

The twentieth century novelist, philosopher, and essayist Susan Sontag wrote about how our photographic culture teaches us a "new visual code."[10] We think little of time spent scrolling through images. We don't realize we're training our minds to interpret the world a certain way and to make ethical conclusions about what is worth seeing.[11] Can photographs really alter our sense of reality in such a dramatic way? Sontag thinks so. She believes the "most grandiose result of the photographic enterprise is to give us the sense that we can hold the whole world in our heads."[12]

What is *worth* seeing. Think about that.

The moments we spend on our phones indoctrinate us to make value judgments on the worth of certain images over others. What does this "ethics of seeing" do to our ability to appreciate art or even pursue learning non-photographic arts, like watercolor painting? What does it do to our desire and ability to look upon the world with the eyes of a curious child?

Not everyone longs to be a painter. I get that. But the point of this notion of a new "ethic of seeing" rests in the pursuit of beauty. The painter, sketcher, or pianist pursues their craft, and, in that pursuit, they learn to *see* or *hear* in a way that fosters curiosity, spurs learning, and creates a longing for beauty. As children, we learn to see the world like the artist; we just don't realize it. Curiosity, learning, and longing work on us and help us derive meaning from our world. The pursuit of beauty reminds us that we cannot keep the whole world logged in our heads, as Sontag suggests. Likewise, the effects of beauty encountered in the natural world, like wonder and awe and terror, remind us of the inestimable nature of the universe.

GO MARVELING

You and I begin life as Beauty Chasers because it's hardwired into our human nature. But if we're not careful, we can lose that God-given sensibility as we grow up. So how can we remain Beauty Chasers? For starters, we need to go marveling.

A Methodist preacher by the name of Fred Craddock tells the story of how his ancestors used to take walks after church on Sundays. On the walks, they'd "admire nature and collect unusual things"[13] such as rocks or wildflowers. They called it "going marveling." The intentional observance and gathering of natural things we pass over every day or take for granted strengthens our ability to see the world.

The English poet Gerard Manley Hopkins believed, "What you look hard at seems to look hard at you."[14] It's the idea that the more time we spend observing something, the more knowledge we gain. Hopkins' observation suggests our need to see well and to understand our world specifically.

Specifics give us fits. We live in a culture in which leaders, politicians, and news anchors deal in sweeping generalities. We use generalizations to describe people. I've used generalizations in this book! At times, generalizing is appropriate; other times, the situation calls for a discussion of nuance. Hopkins was getting at our need to pause and see the specifics of a thing. When we do, the "instress" of the thing, or the "within-ness" or force of the thing speaks to us. This is no mystical mumbo jumbo. Hopkins, a Jesuit priest, believed the world was charged with God's grandeur. The instress of a thing is what Jonathan Edwards observed when he sketched the movements of a spider and noticed how even spiders engage in play and joy. This is what looking at something hard gets us: the joy of a thing.

Have you ever noticed that when you know little of something, you have a hard time describing it?

"That seems obvious," you say, "but so what?"

Well, have you ever considered how well we know how to describe a tree or the sky or the ocean? One of my favorite examples of this is Victorian British art critic John Ruskin's explanation of our common misconception about the nature of ocean waves:

Most people think of waves as rising and falling. But if they look at the sea carefully, they will perceive that the waves do not rise and fall.

They change.

Change both place and form, but they do not fall; one wave goes on, and on, and still on; now lower, now higher, now tossing its mane like a horse, now building itself together like a wall, now shaking, now steady, but still the same wave, till at last it seems struck by something, and changes, one knows not how,—becomes another wave."[15]

When I first read Ruskin's observation of the nature of an ocean wave, I sat stunned. *Of course*, I thought. I was amazed at my own inability to describe something so common as a wave.

Then I began looking at other natural things we (read: I) take for granted, like the sky and trees and pileated woodpeckers. When I considered their makeup, their nature, even their colors, I discovered I'd raced right past these objects, or even worse, I'd ignored them.

If I valued beauty, if I pursued beauty, would it not show in my understanding and appreciation of the world? Had I fallen prey to our photographic and convenience-drunk society, failing to look at things that I can't scroll through? Perhaps we don't see all that well because we lack the patience.

Our culture will continue to progress in the realm of digital technology. But we cannot abandon *real* life. Real life is served up away from the noise and distractions and involves things we can touch, see, and smell. It involves things that contribute to our inner richness.

I worry about the price we will pay in years to come from generations of individuals weaned on distraction. What will result from our culture of noise and from our own willful impoverishment of the mind and body?

What kind of people will we become? I hope we will be a people who chase after beauty.

The footpath that leads to regaining our true sight begins with *rest*. Perhaps this seems antithetical to you. After all, we just finished carving a trail that emphasized our ability to truly see the world. But visual sight accompanies spiritual sight. And Sabbath lies at the heart of both. I don't mean rest like lying on your back in a hammock, though I do not fault you for doing that right at this moment.

I used to think rest and weekends and holidays existed for doing nothing. But then I met my soon-to-be-brother-in-law, who raced mountain bikes. He introduced me to the idea of a recovery ride. Ride to rest. My journey of rest and leisure took a turn that year. And the learning and application continues.

One of my professors in seminary told me this about Sabbath: "No, we technically are not bound by the Sabbath day. But perhaps a better way to look at Sabbath is to view it as a chance to be heaven to someone." God himself describes rest as a place—his place, which you enter. Perhaps a wardrobe or secret passageway behind a bookshelf will lead you to his rest.

Interestingly, ancient pagan cultures understood leisure in the context of worship. A culture without worship (religious festival or holiday) was a culture that would become lazy. Without celebration and worship, our work becomes inhuman.[16] The do-nothing or numb-your-mind mentality associated with rest is the lie of the modern world. Rest restores. But not because it includes idleness. Instead, rest restores because it includes so much motion!

The motion of a mind awake.

The movement of joy in the glories of the domestic life.

The conveyance of activity with loved ones.

The conviviality of gathering with friends.

The stirring of the imagination through artful expression, reading, studying.

Days of rest are days filled with beauty-drops from God as we explore and contemplate his world—and with getting rest for our souls. Here's a short checklist for the footpath to regaining your sight.

1. **Celebrate**—*Celebration lies at the core of leisure.* And true leisure sets you on the footpath that leads to a marveling mind. Are you joyful in your opportunities to get outside and just be?

2. **Escape**—*Rest replenishes body and soul.* Don't get trapped in the binge-culture lie. Rest is not idleness, nor is it amusement.

3. **Activate**—*True rest includes the life-giving activity of body and mind.* You can activate your mind through hobbies. What have you always wanted to learn or do? Take a chance on something challenging. Since I was a young boy, I have always wanted to study martial arts. When my daughters were old enough, I took it up with all three of them. It's been the best decision I've made as a father. Challenging, fun, and focused.

4. **Wake Up**—*Rest is the plentitude of a mind awake, free-flowing with its surroundings.* Shake yourself from your stupor. The beautiful comes alive when we ourselves wake up to the world around us.

5. **Form**—*Rest forms heaven in your soul.* When we engage in healthy rest, something spiritual happens. If you want to train your spirit to see the world, rest activates heaven within you. By this, I mean that drop of eternity placed

in you by your heavenly Father. The deeper our rest, the more beautifully heaven shines through us.

6. **Imagine**—*Deep leisure sends your imagination soaring.* Don't neglect your precious imagination. Feed it with soulish things.

7. **Marvel**—*Gaze upon the beauty of God.* Put the marveling idea into practice. Use your Sunday afternoon (or any time that suits you) and set out to find a local trail or greenway. Don't rush. Make it your goal to find as many unusually marvelous objects as possible. These can be anything that sparks your curiosity. Take your journal with you, and write down your findings. Have children? Outfit your crew with journals, binoculars, and broad smiles, and see who can find the most marvelous things. Compare notes over a raucous dinner. Repeat.

CHAPTER 13

MAKE BEAUTIFUL SPACES

The Footpath of Place

Whered I was boy, I remember lying on my back beneath the "acorn tree," trying to count all the green and yellow acorns. I felt them, hard under my back, as I looked up through the limbs to the tiny patches of blue sky above. I was only about seven, but I remember feeling like something or someone was watching through those gangly limbs. As if the blue patches were peeking eyes, looking down on me from another place.

God, to me, was somehow the acorn tree.[1] And I found him in other places that also felt like that tree:

> The sinkhole across the street from our church, with its shadows and scary corners, and sheer depth.
>
> The field of high grass, where the spindly stalks rose up and made a "V" at the end, dotted by little black seeds.
>
> The old oak tree out behind my dad's church, the one my grand-pap helped build. It was the same tree where my dad would carry out all the metal chairs and set them up for potluck, or sunrise services. The same tree we tried our strength against, climbing it and skinning our knees on the rough bark.

The lake at 4 A.M., floating quietly with Dad, catching no fish, but
    catching the muted colors of the early Florida summer sun.
The dirty sand of the Gulf coast, muddy shells, and playing in
    the warm water.

The older I grew, the more the acorn tree looked like the glowing
snow across the midnight fields of Lancaster County, Pennsylvania,
the indigo sky dense with stars.

Do you have memories like these?

Memories of place and season and hot and cold and wonder and
play and delight; memories that make you cry, that make you shudder,
that still drum up a sense of awe in your bones. Beautiful memories
you'll never forget. The beauty we encounter throughout our lives
carves itself into our memories. Feeling beauty is not just a passing
experience. It is an encounter we take in with our senses. That vision
moves us through life and connects our exploration of the very real
world around us with the very real world inside us. Feeling beauty
expands who we are as people and paints seasons of our lives with
meaning.[2]

The places we inhabit matter. They not only serve as the backdrop
of our memories, but they also help form our memories and contribute
to the joy we experience daily. Land and place possess the power
to nourish us; as caretakers and creators, we serve ourselves and one
another by preserving their beauty.[3]

The land also teaches us. Some say this landscape of ours speaks.
It has its own language. But what is it saying?

THE LANGUAGE OF LANDSCAPE

Anne Whiston Spirn, a renowned landscape architect, says the language of landscape is our "native language," and that the language
of landscape can be spoken and read. "Landscapes are a vast library
of literature," she says. "And the library contains many genres like

worship, memory, play, movement, meeting, exchange, power, production, home, and community."[4]

Parks, hills, and mountains speak to us. They act as contexts for different times of our lives, and those contexts communicate meaning,[5] like the memories I've just recounted—each a place, a context sacred to my experience.

In the previous chapter, I told you of my experience with a beautiful silence in the snowy woods. The deer and the fire were woven with the pine grove and the snow on that wintry Pennsylvania morning, creating a context for my experience. I remember the acorn tree, not only because of the vividness of the tree and sky, but because of the meaning associated with my experience of wonder.

In all these places, I experienced the wonder and varied mystery of beauty. These were meeting places, sacred places—"Triggers for memory, the occasion of hope."[6]

How do we find these sacred places?

I did not *find* the sacredness of the acorn tree; it found me. And it did so only years later as I reflected upon its impact in my memory. A "sacred place is not chosen, it chooses."[7] I find this to be the way of it.

How many times have I walked a path, or lingered in a park, or ridden on the same mountain trail over and over until, all at once, I'm overcome with a holy experience? Was I not paying attention the first time? Was my imagination dull upon the landscape, seeing only the material elements in front of me? Dirt, sand, rocks, trees, shrubs, grass?[8]

If I've learned anything through my love for the outside world, it is that I must actually *go outside*. I must push away from the routine that usually consists of going back and forth between man-made buildings in man-made automobiles. I must step out in the rain every now and again. I must walk in the hills during a storm. I must take a trail alone in the mountains.

If I don't, I will not hear the language of the landscape, the language of beauty. And if I isolate myself from other people, and from trees, and hills, and mountains long enough, my ears will close, and I will become deaf to the language. I will live in a muted world of my own.

We get our word "idiot" from the Latin *idios*; it means one's own, personal or distinct. It can also mean an ignorant person, someone who cuts themselves off from the learning all around them. I suppose if I cut myself off from the outside world with its language of wonder, I will have become an idiot: alone, separate, ignorant. I do not want that for myself or my family.

PLACE MATTERS

Just as we become like the land we inhabit, so, too, do we reflect the structures that surround us. There is a rugged beauty to the old architecture in the world. My Boars Hill walk took me past several old structures—200 years old, maybe older. The main structure of the town pub was nearly 500 years old. Something wonderfully mysterious inhabits these structures.

Have you ever thought about what it is you sense when confronted with a beautiful object like an old building or an event like a sunrise? The splendor or grandeur or enormity—the *numinosity*—of the form draws us toward knowing whatever lies behind the grandeur. We explored this in connection to the natural world, but does the same principle hold true for something like an old pub?

Edwyn Bevan, the British philosopher and historian, says that when a person notices a sunset, the feeling evoked within him seems like a kind of knowledge of another world "spreading out like a halo from the object."[9] Something more exists beyond mere pleasant sensation or even intellectual knowledge. There is a "world of reality there behind the object."[10]

Bevan gives the beautiful a peculiar and unexplainable value. He attributes this same weightiness of meaning to an old brick house. The wood beams, large fireplaces, and low ceilings suggest the house was built in a bygone era. The patina, or the weathering of the house over time, is observed conceptually, so to speak. If you and I walked into this brick house when it was first built, we would not notice this particular beauty. We admire the house now because its beauty acts as a bridge into the past.[11]

"Eh, but Tim," you say, "is a house like a sunset? Does the beauty of one relate to the other? And if so, what does it matter for us in our daily lives?"

"Ah, yes," I reply. "It's an excellent point you raise. I, too, wonder often about the variety of beauty in the world and how it all weaves together to form our tapestry of reality. Here's a thought: if the beauty of the house and sunset are subjective (based on personal feelings), then I would say that that sort of beauty they possess doesn't really matter."

"But if both beauties are objective (not based on personal feelings), then we have something else entirely, don't we?"

The Plastic People want us to believe that when we say the house possesses a special beauty that takes us to a bygone era, we are, in essence, saying nothing about the object itself (the house). We are merely staining it with our own projected sentiment.[12]

If we return to that time before the beginning and remember how God covered over the chaos and breathed his words of beauty into time and space and pressed his fingerprints upon our reality, then everything we interact with in this world points to those first strokes of wonder. The world contains aspects of God's excellencies, his beautiful holiness. The various parts of the natural world work together in the dying of the day to display a cacophony of splendor in the form of a sunset. We cannot see the atmospheric water or minute particles in the air with the naked eye. We cannot sense the tilt of the earth toward or away from the sun at that exact moment, but all those elements work symphonically to give us the wonder of the dying of day. When we say the sunset is beautiful, we are not expressing something about ourselves and our feelings. We are making a statement about the properties of the sunset. So the beauty of the sunset is objective.[13]

And just as the symmetry and form of the earth coalesce in harmony to give us a cathedral of light and air, so, too, does the designer or architect of a home or government building or museum give us patterns unique to the human experience.

But something has shifted in the modern world. Just as we've alienated ourselves from the *numinous* wonders of God's creation, we've also neglected the structures we rush to build in the name of progress.

THE OLD WAY OF SEEING

In 1994 architect and critic Jonathan Hale wrote a brilliant little book titled *The Old Way of Seeing*. In it, he laments the loss of life and play in modern American architecture. Hale points to 1830 as the turning point. He claims that prior to the 1830s, architecture was focused on something altogether different. There was a magic to it—an intuitive beauty that made a person feel at home in their town.

"Architecture," he writes, "is the play of patterns derived from nature and us."[14] He says that design is play, and "the disharmony we see around us is the exception."[15] Architects now build lifeless structures that lack an identity and convey a kind of chaos rather than harmony. We feel this intrinsically, he says, though we may be unable to explain it fully. We sense it when we walk our neighborhoods, which tend to look monolithic, struggling under the burden of sameness. Instead of the patterns of architectural integrity speaking to us, we're confronted with drab buildings clad with veneers to make them look as if they're Gothic or Georgian when, in reality, they're fakes.

Hale attributes this loss of play and life in architecture to a lack of sight, a loss of the old way of seeing. Hale tracks this loss of sight to the 1820s, when architecture lost its charm and delight. Buildings began to strike poses using symbols, like pillars, to communicate architectural messages like heroic democracy or greatness of vision. Architecture turned from the play of design and pattern to symbolism.[16] A loss of magic and life.

Pattern ruled architecture before the 1820s. Patterns are ends in themselves and communicate directly to the viewer. After the 1830s, everyday architecture attempted to either communicate through symbols instead of patterns or not to communicate at all. The pressure for the modern designer of the nineteenth century was to be always doing something new. And by "new," Hale means strange. Not only is this a burden for the designer, but it also moves beauty further out of the reach of the everyday person. Beauty becomes the province of specialists.

The buildings that surround us contribute to our immediate environment and thus, to how that habitat affects us mentally, physically, and spiritually. If the buildings possess only brutishness in their design, we will respond with brutishness in the way we treat the town and our care for it. Consciously or not, the vision of our "main street" affects my mood, my visual delight or visual disgust. And that which comes into my line of sight does, indeed, affect me on a deeper level.

There is a sacredness to the places we build. You and I were created to create. We are, by design, builders and makers, and even if building and making are not our profession, we are wired to interpret the places we inhabit. A place of chaos breeds tension. A place of pattern and play breeds—well, magic. Whether it is a flower bed design, a perfectly patterned deck, or a playful chapel inviting us to worship, the places we inhabit connect us to something beyond the brick and mortar. Their pattern and play give us the joy of something familiar, the delight of home, and remind us that flourishing—that life itself—can and should be found in the places we gather.

Just Because It's Old Doesn't Mean It's Not Valuable

Think about how this same principle relates to the place where saints gather to worship God. When we reduce our gatherings and our modes of worship to what we think is relevant, we rob both ourselves and the spiritual seeker from experiencing the original and unique nature of God. Instead, we give them what is common in our culture, what they can buy in any store or experience at a rock concert or carnival or shopping mall (if those still exist). We offer spectacle when intimacy is what people desire. We produce transactional moments of emotionalism when we should be creating spaces reflective of the nature of the divine: symmetry of place, space for light, an invitation to the created order.

We think that methods must change but not the message. That might be true for evangelization, but worship is the primary purpose of the gathering of the saints. I suggest this "method/message" axiom to be another thoughtless evangelical trope used to justify entrepreneurial efforts to evangelize *en masse* rather than build God's kingdom through "making disciples." The *method* is the *medium* is the *message*.

Just like the pop culture icons of our time, the church perpetuates the astonishing movement of eliminating true culture altogether. We democratize the arts to bring high culture low, wanting common culture to be the seedbed of the gospel. But this reveals our own anti-intellectual desire for control and our contentment with artistic complacency. Cultivating high culture in our lives and in the church (*ecclesia*) means teaching ourselves and the young to discern that which is beautiful, good, and true.

Once, a good friend who'd pastored for decades asked me how to create a culture of prayer within his church. I attended his church, so I knew what he desired. I also knew what the culture of the church felt like. It felt like every other suburban church seeking to draw congregants—hip, contemporary, transactional. I told him if he wanted to change the current culture and invite a culture of prayer, he should get rid of the donut-and-coffee bar in the foyer.

I suggested worshipful music already playing upon entry, with elders and deacons already gathered for prayer. I recommended a quiet foyer rather than the pre-church donut party many refer to as "fellowship." I also suggested lingering in the musical time of worship and inviting prayer at the front. I said inviting people forward for prayer and leaving space for quiet reflection would encourage prayer. My friend instituted several of these ideas on creating a culture of prayer, The old way of seeing architecture carried with it a deep sense of space and the value of structures and how those structures affect us. The Protestant evangelical church prioritizes keeping up with cultural trends as they relate to structures and worship spaces, music, and interior environments. But it shouldn't. We love old structures and interior spaces and music *because* of the patina (the sheen on an object as it ages). Sometimes, the old way is the best way.

I spoke on this topic at a conference, and a man questioned me: "But I found Jesus in a place just like the one you are criticizing," he said. "Isn't it also true that these big, old medieval buildings are just empty shells? What counts the most is the people within the space. A building can look beautiful and still be dead spiritually."

I took his point. It is true that many people have come into the Christian faith in various gathering spaces. This seems to indicate that the building doesn't matter, that what matters most is Christian salvation. I'm in no way attempting to downplay the importance of salvation. But the argument falls in the either/or fallacy. Spiritual success does not negate God's call on our lives to be caretakers and preservers of beauty. Spiritual success can and does happen anywhere. We, however, are responsible for reflecting the excellent virtues of the Father in all we do and with the spaces in which we engage. This is as true of the buildings we construct as it is of nature and the land. Our aim in these engagements is to reflect the beauty and glory of God by either conserving and preserving and caring for the land, or by building structures that reflect the excellencies of the beautiful, the good, and the true.

While it is true that a beautiful structure can seem spiritually dead due to apostasy or heresy being preached within, it is also true that the structure itself embodies beautiful ideas. Notre Dame is beautiful, whether the gospel is preached there or not. The architects and artisans who built the structure aimed at the highest goal they knew—beauty. Why? To reflect the glory of God. For centuries, the cathedral has stood as testimony to this truth.

WAYPOINT

For this Waypoint, I suggest you find a good discussion partner, read the section together, and challenge each other to think imaginatively about how we, as Christians, can rekindle the beauty of *place* in our worship spaces and in our homes. Let's join together and think about what happens when we choose beauty over utility in our spaces. Could we create wonder-filled atmospheres for discipling world-changers and Beauty Chasers?

Reimagine Our Worship Spaces

Let's bring back the old way of seeing to our church buildings.

In the early 1960s, Bill Strickland was mentored by his high school art teacher, Frank Ross. Ross showed Bill the powers of art, community, and education. It was through these "tools" that Ross earned his way into the University of Pittsburgh. During his teen years, Strickland described himself as a "disengaged African-American man"[17] until Frank Ross showed him the power of beauty.

Their relationship was the seed that sprouted into the Manchester Bidwell Organization, an "adult career training school which offers vocational training at no cost to the student in medical services, horticulture, chemical laboratory technology, and culinary arts,"[18] which also offers programs in jazz performance and Grammy Award–winning recording production, an afterschool ceramics program for disadvantaged youth, and a center for horticulture. The organization maintains the philosophy that *environment shapes behavior*. The organization thoughtfully determines every detail of the centers, right down to how the light enters the rooms through the windows, the art they hang throughout the centers, and the friendliness of their staff. They believe every person "no matter their background deserves beauty, respect and the opportunity to learn in a safe space. When provided with these, the underserved will become world class, productive citizens."[19]

Their philosophy works. The affiliated jazz program features one of the longest running concert series in the country, a world-class recording studio, and educational programs for children and adults.

Imagine if the church adopted this philosophy. Imagine if the church shifted from being an organization that elevates utility over beauty to a body of believers joining together in reverent worship spaces that champion beauty in their cultural expressions?

We know environment shapes behavior, so what behavior are we shaping by creating worship spaces that bring to mind concert venues rather than beautiful, light-filled gathering spaces where congregants reverently worship the living God?

Cultivate Beauty in Our Homes

Place matters.

Did you know the structure of a house expresses our nature? A house is a composition of shapes and forms based upon the occupants: me and you. How we build homes, churches, and community structures matters. Why? Because the grammar of shape is intended to reflect life. An old cathedral? Life and harmony. A black box church with no windows? Well, you get the picture. God wired us to bring symmetry and beauty into our homes. We love patterns because they symbolize growth. And growth brings joy to life.

We naturally seek order and symmetry in our homes because the places we inhabit should reflect our very nature as human beings. Everything within a home is designed around the universal shape of the human body, no matter what size, from furniture to doorways. The golden ratio in architecture reflects the natural world and the objects within it that naturally possess that magic proportion. Think of a starfish, a conch shell, or even an egg. We physically and spiritually respond to the charm and glory of a well-appointed home design. Why? Because excellent design reflects human nature.

On the other hand, we bristle when chaos enters our spaces. We loathe buildings where disorder or lack of symmetry persists. Joanna Gaines isn't just a cool Texan with neat ideas that took the world by storm. No, she's touching on universal truths of proportion, harmony, and form. Every human being was designed by God to hunger for these magical characteristics of design.

We call the harmony of space "home," and for good reason. We sense something "other," something familiar but just beyond reach, yet, at the same time, something close, something we want to create in our gathering spaces and homes. That something is heaven.

I've mentioned Joanna Gaines as a leader in the space of bringing heaven into our homes, but I want to offer a few additional resources I recommend for kindling beauty in the home. Each of these resources touches an aspect of the home, whether it's actual design ideas or what it means to cultivate physical and spiritual beauty in your home or family. I have personally benefitted from these resources and count their authors as friends and leaders in this space.

1. **Christie Purifoy**, author of *Placemaker: Cultivating Places of Comfort, Beaut,y and Peace* and *Garden Maker: Growing a Life of Beauty and Wonder with Flowers*
2. **Myquillyn Smith**, author of *Welcome Home: A Cozy Minimalist Guide to Decorating and Hosting All Year Round* and *The Nesting Place: It Doesn't Have to Be Perfect to Be Beautiful*
3. **Ruth Chou Simons**, author of *Beholding and Becoming: The Art of Everyday Worship*
4. **Sara Hagerty**, author of *Adore: A Simple Practice for Experiencing God in the Middle Minutes of Your Day*
5. **Ann Voskamp**, author of *One Thousand Gifts: A Dare to Live Fully Right Where You Are*

PART 4

FOOTPATHS OF MOUNTAINS

Joy, the Life-Giving Mark of Beauty

CHAPTER 14

SHOUT WITH ME THE SOUND OF LIGHTNESS

The Footpath of Everlasting Joy

O ur walk now takes us to the mountains. Though they looked ominous from a distance, once we're among the peaks, they feel familiar and bursting with aliveness. The Plastic People are nowhere in sight. It's sad, really. The heights have so much to give. If you're willing to venture up the steep path, discovery awaits. But no one can ever fully explain the view from the top. You must experience it for yourself.

Thus far, Sam's renewed life and perspective have grown in the very real world of people, places, and things. He's adopted the cadence of beauty in his use of time, in how he interacts with people, in how he educates himself and others, and in how he observes the natural world. But the mountains move him beyond daily comfort and into the wilderness.

"The mountain wilderness" is an exciting phrase. As we learned earlier, God wired us for adventure. He built our hearts with sticks and stones and burly pines. He ingrained the wilds into our DNA. And not only the wilds we look upon with muted awe, but the wilds of worship, the wilds of pain and struggle, the wilds of war and peace. He set all of these in the mountains of life.

He also set himself on the heights. He lives there and invites us into his holy presence. Will we go?

The heights can scare us. Storms move in fast. The weather is unpredictable. The path narrows, grows steep and hard. But if we can put our fear behind us, we can discover untold joy. The heights can represent hard times in life, barren seasons of wandering. But remember Habakkuk's prayer: "He makes my feet like the feet of a deer; he enables me to tread oin the heights" (Hab. 3:19). God gives us the ability and strength to navigate rugged times. Joy follows travail.

The Silly Joy of Waterfall Way

The air cools, and glacial clouds descend. Two hours have passed; there are only two more to the summit. I can still see the Þórsmörk (pronounced "Thors-mork") hut in the valley behind me, but barely.

My legs burn.

My thirty-pound pack clings to my waist and shoulders like a gnome trying to pull me down.

Sweat soaks my base layer and steams around my neck.

My body feels hammered, and we've only just begun the final leg of our eight-day hike through the southern highlands of Iceland.

Jesse and I traversed the scraggly forest of Þórsmörk last evening. Now we ascend the most difficult section of the trail. Before we left, we asked the hut warden if he thought we could finish all 15.5 miles in one day.

His look said, "You Americans won't make it." Then he nodded and said diplomatically, "Probably."

It was during our hike, after talking with a couple French fellows, that we discovered Icelanders do it easily, but from the other direction.

Two ravens swoop overhead as we climb over a craggy switchback to a small lookout. One black bird alights on the volcanic rock outcropping just ahead. The other circles. I stop to rest and survey the view. I wonder if Óðinn, the Norse god also known as All Father, is nearby. In the Norse sagas, his two ravens, Munin and Hugin, fly throughout the land, gathering information to report back. Perhaps the raven was eavesdropping on our hike. My imagination sometimes gets the best of me.

Normally, hikers descend this section, and I can see why; it goes straight up. It's not the elevation gain you'd find in the Rockies or even Pisgah National Forest in North Carolina. The wet terrain gives no mercy to two Americans carrying too much gear. It does, however, provide a stunning view of Goðaland or "Land of Gods."

Above me looms Eyjafjallajökull (pronounced "no idea") and Mýrdalsjökull (pronounced "who knows"), two glaciers atop a volcano. Behind me, the Þórsmörk valley cuts through the highland range like a Viking longship through ice-cold river waters. The few remaining September wildflowers pop in purples and whites along the path that ascends 3,000 feet above sea level.

The clouds fall quickly. We reach the high plateau, then traverse to the narrow pass that connects to the peak. We race the clouds, trying to reach the summit before they veil our view. The clouds hover at the plateau. We turn again to look.

We stand above the clouds. Further up and to the south, blue sky cracks through the scattering clouds. Behind me, the valley falls asleep under a billowing blanket of white.

I listen.

Nothing but moving air.

I walk above clouds and feel as though I'm inhaling heaven with each labored breath.

My muscles ache as I stand there in the silence of moving air and clouds, hidden from the world for a moment.

We don't rest long.

We march over the Fimmvörðuháls (your pronunciation guess is as good as mine) mountain ridge, through the wind and swirling mist, then descend into Skógar.

We follow the glacial river toward the coast. The river cuts and dives and crashes its way through the Icelandic peat and rock.

Twenty-six multitiered waterfalls greet us at every turn. We view the waterfalls from above because the water cuts a canyon into the volcanic landscape, giving us a bird's-eye view of the majesty and immensity of the water crashing toward the coast.

The low mists lift, exposing the naked landscape and the tumbling white water navigated by an undulating path. Moss electrifies the volcanic earth as far as I could see.

If you research this trail, you'll find images and short articles describing the eight-mile descent known as "Waterfall Way." I feel like a child running down the stairs at Christmas. The anticipation of the next stunning view makes Jesse and me laugh as we trek faster in unbelief at the overwhelming beauty.

"No way!" Jesse shouts.

"I can't believe this!" I shout back.

You can imagine the exclamations and ear-to-ear smiles as our exhaustion dissolves. The uncommon scene fills us with new life. I walk as though drunk, tripping down the path in disbelief. The glacial water pounds down its ancient path toward the sea. At the moment, my anxious thoughts about my graduate school course of study, making enough money to stay abroad to finish my research, and my lingering doubts about if this was the right path for my family dissolve in the sound of water crashing down the back of a volcano. Nature's tumult brings immediate perspective to my anxious thoughts and notions.

We end our jaunt at the iconic Skógafoss waterfall, one of the most recognizable and most photographed waterfalls in the world. We snap multiple photographs of each other in front of the mammoth falls, attempting to show its magnitude. A few shots succeed, but how do you communicate the sound and fury of such a natural wonder? The mist alone soaks us, and we're still over a hundred yards from the base.

The crashing water sounds like a sustained roar. I think of John's and Ezekiel's descriptions of God's voice as rushing waters, and I picture myself beneath the vast expanse with the cherubim who shout and sing praise to God in Ezekiel's vision. I think of Psalm 29:

> The voice of the LORD is over the waters;
>> the God of glory thunders,
> the LORD thunders over the mighty waters.
>> The voice of the LORD is powerful;
>> the voice of the LORD is majestic.

David knows what he's talking about. Because if God's voice sounds even one iota like Skógafoss, I'd be shouting and laughing in praise every chance I got, just like the cherubim and seraphim.

Describing Iceland is like chasing the Northern Lights. You can run further into them, but you'll never exhaust their glory. You want to relay its form but fail to describe its quality. On the bus ride back to Reykjavik, I couldn't wipe the smile from my face or the yearning from my heart. I wanted to keep the sound of Skógafoss in my ears. I wanted to capture the Goðaland view forever in my mind's eye.

AN UNTAMED GLORY

"But Tim," you say, "I've never been to, nor do I ever plan to visit Iceland. How does your story tell me any more about beauty?"

"Ah, yes," I reply. "Of course, you're right to ask. And you don't have to travel all the way to the southern highlands of Iceland to experience such a joyous moment. But when I close my eyes and think about the indelible moments in my life, in which beauty jumped out and grabbed me by the throat, Iceland springs into my imagination."

When I think about Sam, healed and walking into the park, I wonder if, when he saw the mountains in the distance, his heart jumped at the possibility of reaching them, or if doubt crept in.

"I'll never be able to visit those peaks," he might have said.

Or, "I can't wait to reach those peaks."

I like to think it was the latter. I like to think the looming peaks created a longing to experience the mountains in all their wild glory. My own experience of mountains reminds me of the inexpressible joy that accompanies a mountain trek. The mountains, as I've come to know them, represent not craggy uncertainty, but untamed joy. Joy moments jump out of my memory as mountain-top experiences. Jubilation is a response to the beauty I beheld.

Can you think of such moments in your own life?

Consider this mountain moment of joy that occurred in my backyard.

I was hammering the throttle of my John Deere across our "second acre"[1] field when I spotted my then-six-year-old, Brielle, waving her hands wildly at me. I stopped, idled down, and waved her over to the mower.

"Can I ride with you?"

I hoisted her up, and we took off. I let her drive down the hill. And then, there it was.

A huge doe leapt across our neighbor's garden and right into our path. Like a slow-motion scene in a movie, I released the throttle and stopped. We gaped at the bounding deer as it took off through our backyard and over to the hedgerow.

Brielle immediately turned to me, her eyes the size of UFOs, her smile latched to each ear, as she shouted over the mower's growl, "Did you see that! That was AMAZING!"

We laughed and shouted our jubilation to each other, then finished mowing the second acre.

It was a mountaintop moment.

Now think of your own. We'll let others distinguish between joy and happiness and how joy transcends circumstances. Right now, think of a moment of joy, and reflect on the life-giving nature of it. There's more to joy than meets the theological eye.

Joy Is Our Gasp at the Beautiful

Joy.

It's an emotional and spiritual reaction to beauty.

We experience beauty with our whole being. The joy experience pulls on our hearts and minds. It irrupts into our lives, opening our eyes, changing our perspectives, and molding our desires.

I liken it to yet another personal experience. This one was with the ocean. The joy moment is that moment when the anticipation of running into the Pacific Ocean meets with the cold crash of the wave hitting you for the first time. It's an explosion of feeling. An event of mad pleasure. It's the gasp of delight that blurts out in wild euphoria as you rise from the foamy water: "AH!"

Imagine if you could bottle up that moment. What would it sound like? Look like? Taste like? What if you lined up hundreds of those moments, transitioning from one to the other in a never-ending succession? It would be heaven itself, would it not?

And so it is.

I call those successive moments all lined up *beautiful.*

The event of it.

The ocean-ness of it.

Me in the ocean.

The cold water waking me, bringing me to life. An occasion shocking me with its beauty, filling me with nostalgia even as I tell my friends about my ocean experience.

The theological definition of joy is "a state of delight and well-being that results from knowing God." I can see the truth of the definition through my own experience of joy. There exists a relationship between the subject and the object of the joyful experience. That's plain enough as I shout with my daughter or scream as I surface in the Pacific. I respond to the moment with visceral praise. The moment catches me.

Joy gives movement to beauty. Let's break down the progression of seeing, then experiencing the ocean with our bodies, shall we? Like a movement in music, the joy movement begins with our eyes seeing the ocean. Then, our body touching the ocean. Then, our body engulfed in the ocean.

We see.

We touch.

We praise.

We remember.

The Irish writer John O'Donohue says, "Movement is a sign of life."[2]

Joy breathes out of us, our gasp at the beautiful. It is a moment, an experience, a remembrance. If we were to cut open a moment of joy, we'd see a portal gushing with the blood of life itself. Leonardo da Vinci called joy an "eternal object" within our universe.[3] Like a vagabond shard of heaven let loose on the prairies and mountains and shores. That shard of heaven cuts us with its poignancy because it makes us long for heaven.

Why else do we recall the beautiful with delight, accompanied by a sense of the thing slipping away?

How is it that we can feel melancholy as we remember the beautiful?

When I play in the Pacific's waves, I feel delight and also a keen sense of horror. Once, during my romp, a wave pummeled me to the ocean floor. The weight of the water pushed my breath from my lungs, and my eyes opened to the stinging salt. The swirling water pushed me down onto the sand, and for a moment I thought about death.

Then, tucking my feet up beneath my body, I pushed upward with all my strength. The kick up was barely strong enough to push me to the surface. When I did emerge, I ducked back into the water, just missing another wave. Finally, I rose between the waves, and with adrenaline pulsing through my body like a drug, I pushed my way through the chest-deep water back to the shore, coughing and spitting, salty mucus hanging from my nose, and a smile tethered to my now-pale face.

I sat on the hot sand while a cool breeze swept over me. I shook with heat and cold. I smiled at the ocean, laughing more, marveling at its strength, which I'd felt all over my body. From a distance, I delighted in its beauty, caught in the joy that only crashing waves can produce.

That was God's hand, that heavenly shard, dazzling through water and sand and the weight of the wave. The infinite, caught in a moment by the finite. Each time I visit the coast, I remember the weight of the Pacific, the taste of sand, and the overwhelming joy of that moment. And I want it again. Only I'm scared. And then not. And then I'm running headlong into the waves once more.

Have you ever loved a moment so much that you longed for it, over and over and over? Have you felt a keen sense of pain in your longing—your desire pushing you to somehow find the experience again?

I am not always pining for the Pacific. Instead, I long for that *moment* where my reaction to the beautiful caused me so much joy. I wasn't expecting joy that day. Just to play. And I found the truth that it is in our moments of play, where expectations scatter and can be found no more, joy finds us, unguarded.

JOY AS THE EVERLASTING NATURE OF BEAUTY

Joy reflects the everlasting nature of beauty.

Joy lasts. No, perhaps not on and on as a feeling that never subsides. More like waves. They begin far off, in the middle of the sea, and travel far, gathering immensity before crashing upon the shore and foaming up onto our toes. Crashing waves and foaming sea water—we crave that feeling. We crave the waves of joy in our lives, too.

Joy looks like God's hand reaching for us in and through the world. It wants to lure us to the Father. The reaching hand seeks to move us in our deepest parts. Karl Barth, the twentieth century German theologian, says this about joy: "If we can and must say that God is beautiful, to say this is to say how He enlightens and convinces and persuades us . . . He acts as One who gives pleasure, creates desire and rewards with enjoyment . . . And this persuasive and convincing form must necessarily be called the beauty of God." Barth says God's glory is his "overflowing self-communicating joy."[4] Joy is God reaching through the beautiful moment, the beautiful vision, the beautiful event, and pulling us toward him. He pulls us to life with beauty.

JOY AS A SIGN OF LIFE

If we look at Scripture, joy carries with it all the signs of life itself. We see joy in our gestures. A smiling face, a change in posture—we sit more upright or lean into a moment of beauty. Our eyes brighten, our cheeks squish up under our eyes in a broad smile. The ready smile gives up joy. Think about the imagery of light in Scripture and how it communicates a life-sustaining sunshine. We see this in the priestly blessing found in Numbers 6:22–27 (emphasis mine):

> "The LORD bless you
>   and keep you;
> *the* LORD *make his face shine on you*
>   and be gracious to you;
> *The* LORD *turn his face toward you*
>   and give you peace."[5]

Have you ever wondered why the blessing includes God's face turning toward you and shining on you? The blessing imparts *life* to those upon which it falls. Like Moses, who remained in the glory cloud for forty days, sustained only by the food of God's presence, the prayer asks God to do the same to us. To cover us in his presence. In his presence, he literally sustains us with life. When God turned his face away in the Scriptures, it was not good.[6] When you and I pray this blessing for our families and friends and ourselves, we are seeking the life brought by God's gaze upon us. In his gaze, we find everlasting joy.

But this light and life gained from his presence is not an item for personal consumption. Remember, Moses' face radiated the brilliance of God's countenance and nature. When he left the glory cloud of Sinai, the people saw him and were awed by the radiating light beaming from his face. He had to cover his face for the brilliance. The light of God's countenance also resides in us through the Holy Spirit. So, we too should radiate God's light and life as a testimony of his saving power and glory to the world.[7]

Think about how the Old Testament describes joy in worship, even with animals, as the ox flings his head (gesture), or leaves clap their hands (gesture). Have you ever flung your head back and forth in wild jubilation in worship? Have I? Maybe we should. Consider the wild vitality present in Psalms 29. In this raucous poem, "lightning and thunder make the wilderness dance or 'writhe.'"[8] The lines direct us to worship in which the glory and majesty of God sizzles with vitality.

Have you ever turned to a friend in a moment of rapture and exclaimed your jubilation with words like "Wow!" or "Did you see that?" or "Oh my word!" or "YAWP!" (my personal favorite)?

Joy takes us over. It is our response to the moment—and our response usually takes the form of praise or some other verbal form of jubilation.

Remember when Jonathan ate wild honey when he was hungry, and his eyes brightened?[9] Life! Joy!

The Hebrew Bible and the New Testament both communicate joy as *vitality* and as emotional response to an experience or an object. In the Hebrew word *simcha*, we find this meaning: "the state of joyful well-being, but also its expression, rejoicing." In the New Testament, the words *chara* and *agalliasis* also communicate a personal reaction from the individual to the object of jubilation.

Joy reminds us that we are alive. And not just us. The world teems with vitality, a cacophony of endless jubilation.

JOY CONNECTS TO HOPE

In Scripture and in storytelling, hope looks toward a future state of joy. This joy might be deliverance, like Israel's hope in future joy to be found in the promised Messiah, here sketched through the poetry of Isaiah the prophet:

The wilderness and the dry land shall be glad;
>   the desert shall rejoice and blossom like the crocus;
> it shall blossom abundantly
>   and rejoice with joy and singing . . .
> And the ransomed of the LORD shall return
>   and come to Zion with singing;
> everlasting joy shall be upon their heads;
>   they shall obtain gladness and joy,
>   and sorrow and sighing shall flee away.
>   (Isaiah 35:1–2, 10 ESV)

J.R.R. Tolkien coined a new word related to his storytelling and all storytelling in the fairy tale genre: *eucatastrophe*. Quite simply, it means the opposite of catastrophe. Instead of a downward turn in the story, it is an upward turn—the happy ending.

Tolkien modeled this idea after the Good News message found in the New Testament; the joyous upturn in human history when Jesus is sent by the Father to bring restoration to the relationship between God and man. Tolkien writes, "The Birth of Christ is the eucatastrophe of man's history. The Resurrection is the eucatastrophe of the story of the Incarnation. The story begins and ends with joy."[10]

Joy possesses a strong forgetfulness. It flourishes more greatly without the weight of expectation. This is why, when you and I walk the park, or the wood, or the seashore with eyes wide open, we often find ourselves mesmerized by what we find. We stand spellbound, caught in a moment of eucatastrophe.

These spellbinding moments water our hearts with delight. We mustn't think *delight* is merely a word for children. That would be a mistake. Delight works in our hearts and minds as a prompt. We encounter beauty; it triggers, even awakens joy; and we feel ourselves grow in the desire to know more, to go further, to understand better. Joy leads curiosity in and past the boundary lands of beauty.

Think about how curiosity spurred on our friend Sam. He wanted to see outside, to see the beautiful park so badly that he endured great personal pain. It was joy, however, that whetted his appetite for the daily vision of the park vividly described by his good friend, George.

What is going on here in Sam's mind? What is it that drives this curiosity incited by joy?

Earlier, I described joy in the world as God's reaching hand, luring us to himself through the beautiful. Sam found himself pulled by God's creative energy in the world. It actively pulls on our hearts and minds. It revitalized our imaginations. Joy, like the waves, crashes into us, then subsides. But we know it's still out there, gathering velocity, foaming toward us again like a freight train of wonder.

WAYPOINT

When we sense that mysterious vitality in the world we inhabit, we become hunters for its source. Joy reaches beyond mere feeling and reminds us that something deep within us resonates with our experiences of beauty in this world. Joy speaks of the life within life. It awakens our desire to discover the place from which all the beauty comes. Joy is the "exhilarating moment when one is drawn out of oneself by the lure of something grander, higher, and elusive."[11]

When we reach beyond pleasure, we discover the prismed world of joy. It's a forgetful world, one where the worry of "self" falls away, replaced by the beauty of presence.

It is the resounding moment of life being lived.

Joy shakes our hearts and our hands as we steady the camera or phone in order to capture the first steps of our child, the first kiss of wedded lovers, the final moment of a graduation. Joy looks like an elegant collection of fine friends gathered in one place.

Joy calls through the resounding landscape.

You and I dip into joy's world, and we feel strangely at home.

"Do we have to leave the Blue Ridge Parkway just yet? Can't we drive a few more miles? Can't we stop for one more hike? Can't we explore that orchard? Can't we grab a few moments at that pub? Can't we . . . ?"

The Chorus of Joy's Manifesto

Blare for me the sound of lightness that echoes in the gestures of life; the cataract and the stallion stomp; the echo from the blast. Shout with me, O Pioneers, into the holy tempest called life. Dance in song with me as we seize glory's power and compress it into a dainty yet holy thunder of everydayness.

I am joy's talon, shredding, digging, being; into, in which, before, below, through, and seeing.

Rage, sun. Roll, clouds, and proclaim your surly wild. I ramble with you; me, the broken and strong heaven child.

Sing with me, O Hunters, let our chorus lift, an everlasting raucous of rambling toward home.

If the song of joy proclaims life and draws my attention beyond myself, then is it any wonder the things that promise to satisfy us in this world ring with vacancy?

I will not allow the pace of this world to steal joy from me. I will pause.

I will not allow the digital world to taint my moments of wonder.

I will not allow your pace to dictate mine. I live and breathe and have my being from the One beyond.

What is this ambition that whispers lies in my ear?

What is this ugly call to provoke, divide, and be heard?

I refuse to listen to the gongs of a joyless world. I sing to the uncommon commonality of our holy moments. They remind me that joy's prismed world is not my destination. It is my now and evermore. How will I let joy—my joy—influence the world for good. How will you?

CHAPTER 15

RECLAIMING OUR WONDER

The Footpath of Spiritual Intimacy

I found God on a snowy January night as I was sitting alone at a bonfire. It was the loneliest I'd ever been in my life. Recently expelled from a prominent Christian university for various offenses, all of which related to some seething anger at the church, I found myself adrift. I questioned the faith of my parents and the *realness* of God.

Until that night, he represented distant ritual to me. The fire, however, was my homecoming. In those quiet moments, beneath the starry hosts, with my life laid bare, I finally saw myself how I'm sure others saw me: monstrous.

That night, I came face-to-face with something beyond religion, beyond ritual, beyond the stale mantras of western evangelicalism. C. S. Lewis says, "Men are reluctant to pass over from the notion of an abstract and negative deity to the living God."[1] We're reluctant, I think, because we fear the encounter with a real, living God.

But I wanted something *real*. I thirsted for something beyond my own rage to consume me.

I had bottled up hurts and disappointments by an abstract deity with no name. But by the fire that night, I found something tugging on the end of my line; I felt someone breathing in the darkness just beyond the pines.

I found, as Lewis says, "God himself, alive, pulling at the other end of the cord, perhaps approaching at an infinite speed, the hunter, king, husband."[2] When I realized that God was not a far-off negative deity, I cowered like a wolf before the flame—transfixed by the wonder and beauty of that which can truly consume.

It is when we come face-to-face with the beautiful that our brutishness shows itself in all its appalling glory.

It was then that my focus shifted. It was then that my desire turned inside out. It was then that I began the never-ending homecoming of going "further up and further in,"[3] as Aslan says, into God himself. I started reading the New Testament, especially the words of John the Beloved. I dove into the narrative of Jesus's life, death, and subsequent resurrection.

Jesus was radical, and he demanded those who follow him to do so with like radicalism. I heard him whisper, "With abandon" in my prayers and felt my bones burn with life. I wasn't moving into some tepid, politicized movement. I was moving into *the Way* itself. Love, resurrection, life—Jesus didn't possess these things; he *was* these things.

Years ago, I was looking for the passionate, the otherworldly, that which would make me want to soar. I didn't find a sensual satisfaction. Rather, I found a dying, a melding, a vanishing into the *Other*, which came in the quiet moments beside a fire beneath the stars. I found the beautiful. I found Jesus.

THE COMING OF THE BRIGHT SHADOW

Our quest for intimacy with God began at the moment Adam and Eve wandered from the holy presence. Intimacy with the Almighty is the jewel of our adventure with God.

From the last of the Hebrew prophets to the emergence of John the Baptizer, Israel longed for a Messiah—a political deliverer. What they received was something far more profound: the jewel of a spiritual kingdom.

Here now, in the throes of another industrial revolution and the shifting of political ideologies in the west, we find ourselves bereft of a center that holds us together as Christians. Indeed, we live in a splintered *ecclesia*, where some follow "Paul" and others "Silas." The Hebrews fell into the great silence of God because they lost their way and invited pagan idolatry into their hearts. In so doing, they removed YHWH from the centerpiece of their spirits and exchanged the Creator for dumb gods made of stone and bronze. It was the rugged words of Isaiah, a fringe speaker of truth who encountered the awful beauty of God himself, that rang through the silence with the hope of one who might bring back the glory of God (723 years earlier).

The arrival of Jesus of Nazareth was 2,100 years after Abraham set out to establish the family of God. And here we stand, another 2,000 years after the incarnation of the Son of God, bereft of hope and praying for the return of the King. Throughout God's sojourn with the stiff-necked Hebrews, he appeared to them in glory. He spoke with Moses on the mountain and sent his radiance among his people by way of the glowing face of that greatest of all prophets. He swept over the mountain cave at Horeb with the voice of roaring thunder, making the prophet Elijah shudder, causing him to hide beneath his cloak. He blew before Ezekiel in a raging storm cloud, took him before the throne of heaven itself, and revealed the glory of angels and things indescribable. The encounter left Ezekiel staring mutely by the river Kadesh for seven days.

God's next revelation to his people, however, would not come through the storm cloud of theophany. Instead, it came through a wandering commoner whose words spoke life into his hearers. The commoner became a prophet, the greatest since Moses (Deut. 18:15; Acts 3:18, 22–24). He was despised by his own people and executed on trumped-up charges. But the religious leaders misjudged him. He did not come to mount a political coup or begin social justice reform. He came to conquer death—the consequence of the people's revolt against their Creator.

The resurrection of the Christ ignited a movement of spiritual renewal unlike any the world has ever seen. But before Jesus of Nazareth departed from his disciples, returning to celestial glory with God the Father, he promised *another*, One who would abide within the very tabernacle of the human soul. The spirit descended upon the followers of Jesus in fire just as God had done before the children of Israel as they wandered the wilderness for forty years. The Spirit of God, the same avian figure who *covered over* the deep and went forth with the Logos to create the cosmos, now fell upon every son of Adam and daughter of Eve, igniting the fingerprint of heaven that lay dormant on so many.

The blaze of the Holy Spirit enflamed the human spirit with a beauty uncommon in a world that had grown fat with its own achievements. And as it has been since the advent of the Spirit, spiritual revival enflames whoever awakens to the glory of the Spirit, reestablishing their reverent fear of God and calling them to worship him in spirit and in truth.

It is to this conflagration of spiritual upheaval we now turn to regain our perspective of divine glory. Without realigning to God's holiness, no amount of social good will bring us one iota closer to the God of creation who seeks not only our devotion, but also our reverence.

How do we recapture the wonder of the divine? It's simple. We must hike up the mountain, as Moses did before us, stand within the glory cloud, and see what happens.

What We Missed at Sinai

"Come up to the mountain," God says to Moses, "and I will show you my glory."[4] And God both does and doesn't. In the most iconic of theophanies, God covers the mountain with storm and fire before he passes by Moses, but he also does something extraordinary. He says who he is.

What is Moses asking of God? The Hebrew term *kabod* here

translates to "glory" and means "weight" or "splendor."[5] The glory of God (luminosity) is his essence, and that essence is weighty; it is "good"—as "good" relates to virtuous—and thus refers to God's nature, the truth of his being.[6] Jonathan Edwards puts it like this:

> The word *glory* denotes sometimes what is *internal*. When the word is used to signify what is within, or in the possession of the subject, it very commonly signifies *excellency*, dignity, or worthiness of regard. This, according to the Hebrew *idiom*, is, as it were, the *weight* of a thing, as that by which it is heavy; as to be *light*, is to be worthless, without value, contemptible.[7]

God is altogether glorious, which is to say he is altogether weighty in his goodness; a goodness so transcendent a person cannot look upon it in full, or it will physically overwhelm him or her. When God refers to "my glory" he is literally saying "myself."[8]

Moses does not *see* God, but he does *hear* him. He hears God's name as "YHWH" or "Lord." And in God's name, we find so much goodness for our souls.

In the glory cloud, Moses encounters the radiance of God's character and the wholeness of who he is.[9] In God, we lack nothing. He alone sustains us with who he is.[10]

God communicates his utter goodness to man through the symbolic notions of radiance and light. God draws us to himself through the very real created order and the beauty within it. In God's self-sufficiency, humanity finds another aspect of God's essence—*joy*. It is the idea that in drawing man to himself, God fulfills man's desires through *spiritual relationship*.[11]

When I think of Moses on the mountain, I always ask myself, "What was in Moses' heart and mind that prompted him to ask to see God's glory?"

He wanted to know God's ways. Is this curiosity? Arrogance? Innocence?

When he asked to see God's glory, Moses said, *Your presence sets us apart.* We might say, "Your presence makes us holy." God's presence with his people has been the point since the beginning. Moses desperately wanted God's presence with Israel, and with him.

The act of sanctifying is the act of setting something apart for sacred use. The life of the Christian is one of sanctity, a setting-apartness. *God desires to set apart your life and my life for sacred use.* It's easy to make holiness formulaic, something achieved. But the distinct life God desires of us is not something based in humanity's achievement or moralism. Instead, it emerges in the relationship between God and us. And such a relationship requires presence: God's presence in our lives.

The temptation is to skip to the part when God passes by and hides Moses in the cleft of the rock. But don't miss the heart behind such an ask. Moses' request possesses an innocent audacity.

My friend Lacey told me she likes to think about the humility of Moses' inquiry.

"Can you explain that?" I asked.

"It would take someone of humility to ask something a child would ask," she said. "There's an innocent audacity to such a question. Think of a child and their ability to ask parents the most innocent and intimate questions."

Remember, before Moses asked to see God's glory, he met with God regularly in the Tent of Meeting. Such a question reveals beautiful intimacy. Moses was asking from a humble heart. Think about when the Israelites encountered God's glory. They feared it would consume them. They didn't want to die, so they sent Moses. He had no trouble going because he longed to see God's glory.

Moses wasn't acting out of spiritual hubris. His desire was for greater intimacy.

I also believe his question came from an innate desire to be at rest with God. Augustine said we struggle with restlessness until we find our rest in God. Why? Because being *with* God is our proper place, our intended home. Remember our little sketch of Adam and

Eve enjoying Eden with unfettered access to God? They communed with him in the Park of Delight before sin entered the picture. Eden provides us a picture of human beings in their proper home, in their intended relationship with God.

Sin broke this relationship.

After Adam and Eve ate the fruit, God came to them, speaking out of the storm, which became the new normal for man's interaction with God. Unfettered glory and wholeness and a sense of home fell behind the buffer of human sin. The rest of the theophanies in the Hebrew Bible occur with God speaking from the storm.

After Moses asks to "see" God's glory, YHWH (which is the Hebrew substitute for God's personal Divine Name) consents and explains how their meeting will happen.

"But no one can see me and live," says God. "So I will hide you in the rock."[12]

Throughout the Old Testament, whenever God reveals himself, he does so concealed by natural phenomena. Now, the moment arrives for God to show Moses his glory. And just before God moves past him, he proclaims *who he is* to Moses. This is the big reveal, but it wasn't something seen by Moses, it was something *heard*.

The passage reads: "The LORD passed before him and proclaimed, 'The LORD, the LORD, a God merciful and gracious, slow to anger, and abounding in steadfast love and faithfulness!'" (Ex. 34:5–7 ESV).

In this wonderful, terrible, intense, moment—a moment in which Moses hoped to see God, God lets him *hear* him. Moses hears God describe what kind of God he is. At this moment, as the mountain stands drenched in holiness, God identifies himself to man.

Who is this God?

He is merciful, gracious, slow to anger, abounding in steadfast love, and faithful.

For so long, whenever I read this passage, I passed over God's proclamation so I could get to the fire and glory of the scene. But God's proclamation is the main point of the scene.

He reveals his identity, his character—the kind of God that he is.

Before Moses sees the back of God, he *hears* who he is. YHWH sets up the story of his love through the beauty of his glory and holiness. The awe-filled encounter steals our breath as Moses falls to the ground in *worship* (v. 8).

And yet my mind returns to Eden before the fruit and expulsion. Will God and humans ever regain their edenic communion?

FROM PROCLAMATION TO ENFLESHMENT

Moses *hears*, then *sees* God—at least a portion of his presence as he passes by him—while God shields him, hiding him from the fullness of his splendor. Richard Bauckham shows us an interesting tidbit in John's prologue.[13] In John's theological memoir, he revisits the world pre-creation and describes the mysterious Logos that was with God and was God. The Logos became flesh. After John tells the reader the Logos became flesh, he stops referring to him as the Logos and calls him the Son of God.

In Moses, we have a human asking for deeper intimacy with God. He wants to *see* God's glory. But God's holiness does not allow this. Only while hidden by God can a person even catch a glimpse of his presence. On Sinai, God showed Moses his back, or the trail of his glory, but only after he proclaimed himself.

In John's prologue, however, God does not speak to human beings from the storm or consume a mountain with fire. Instead, he comes in flesh and bone—a vagabond man without home or food—and consumes their hearts. He lives among the people, cloaking his glory in the flesh of humanity.

He touches the blind eyes of man.

He reaches out and heals the sick.

He shouts with a grief-stricken voice and snatches his friend from the grip of death.

He prays with his friends.

He eats with his enemies.

He tells stories to anyone who will listen to him.

He protects the weak from the unjust.

He speaks truth to power.

And shows everyone the Way.

Down from heaven, the incarnate Son of God shows the world the splendor of his holiness, but not through the wind, fire, an earthquake, or the crushing voice of thunder that Elijah heard. Instead, he shows the world his beauty and splendor through the rustic wonder of a life given up for the ones he loves. The Logos comes, and what was before only heard and seen as the cloud-and-fire God now walks among his people. He takes on the lowliest form to bring them back to life and to show them the beauty of himself.

THE LOVELINESS AND BEAUTY OF CHRIST

In the spring of 1721, a seventeen-year-old named Jonathan Edwards found Jesus, too. He struggled with his view of God as a sovereign tyrant. He could not stomach the thought of God choosing to save some from damnation while sending others to hell. This philosophical and theological struggle caused him to rebel as a young boy. But he did not resign himself to bitterness. It was as if he wanted to believe in God's grace, but something was keeping it from him.

After graduating as valedictorian from the newly established Yale College in New Haven, Connecticut, Edwards stayed on to study for a Master of Arts degree. It was while returning home for a break that he experienced a profound spiritual breakthrough. In his writings, Edwards explains how, as a boy and as a teenager, he loved religion not for God himself but because it was what he was *supposed* to do.

This is the religious way, isn't it? It can be nothing but empty ritual. If it's not ritual, it can become something we wield rather than a path we walk toward God. Without God's *presence* in it, it gets twisted to something very much human and ugly.

Something, however, changed in Edwards's spiritual life when he was struck by the simple delight of the Scriptures. He experienced in his contemplations of God that same bright shadow of beauty C. S. Lewis experienced when he read *Phantastes* by the Scottish poet and minister George MacDonald for the first time. It was a bright shadow—an oxymoron—because that was the best description for the *numinous* delight Lewis experienced. Only later in life did Lewis understand that what he was explaining was holiness. Something similar gripped Edwards. It was a divine holiness that wakened Edwards's spirit to the wonder of God and his eyes to beauty he encountered in creation. Edwards called what he saw in nature the language of God.

Throughout the ages, other spiritual thinkers—such as Augustine, Coleridge, and Simone Weil—also looked to the book of nature to unravel the deep mysteries of God. They believed that creation, in a sense, held the fingerprint of God, and that if one spent time in meditation and prayer, pursuing quiet and solitude, one could understand more keenly the excellencies—the beauty and holiness—of God.

The lightning of epiphany also hit Edwards when he read 1 Timothy 1:17 in the King James Wersion: "Now unto the King eternal, immortal, invisible, the only wise God, be honour and glory for ever and ever. Amen." When he read this verse as a young man, Edwards's soul was touched with "a sense of the glory of the Divine Being; a new sense, quite different from any thing I ever experienced before."[14]

He had a similar spiritual sense as he meditated on the writings of the Canticles, or Song of Songs, what he took as a description of Christ as "the rose of Sharon, and the lily of the valleys."[15] He believed these words described the loveliness and beauty of Christ. It was Edwards's contemplation of divine things that took on deeper significance in his spiritual life.

Prior to this moment of revelation, he'd experienced three years of depression. It was the character of God, however, that broke through the dark clouds hanging over his spirit, as well as the wonders of nature that captured his imagination and led him to explore the deep and mysterious wonders of God's character more deeply.

Edwards practiced *being* with God. He contemplated the wonder of God in a spiderweb. He saw God's glory in the thunderstorm, in the trees of the forest, and in clouds and sky. Edwards saw God's holiness as altogether lovely, delightful, and nourishing to the soul. It was where Edwards wanted to be. The holiness of God "ravished his soul"[16] so that he longed for it, like a small white flower bowing low to the ground, drinking in the life-giving glory of the sun's rays.

The Tender Disciple

This symbol of the white flower bowing reminds me of the tender relationship between our holy God and his children. The beautiful is not only something we see, though that's part of it. It is something we *become*.

How? Through the crucible of humility, of self-abasement, of lowliness—the bending low of the white flower.

In struggling to break free of a view of God he didn't understand, Edwards discovered God's tender holiness.

These words might not excite us. But remember who came to us as one "humble, riding on a donkey."[17] The beautiful contains the lowly of heart and position. For only in the act of giving up the self do we discover the truth of God's love, his *hesed*, or steadfastness.

If Edwards's view of holiness seems strange to us in the twenty-first century, perhaps it's because we too often relate moralism with holiness. We think of holiness as only referring to one's behavior and moral decisions. But that is not the entire picture of holiness, and it is nothing close to what Edwards describes in his journals. And remember, it was this lightning-bolt discovery that fueled Edwards's affections for God, and his devotion to prayer that enflamed the Great Awakening.

God speaks to us through beauty, mystery, wonder, awe, and the unknown. But if we want to hear him speak to us through the created world, we must get out in it, as Edwards did, *see* God's grandeur, and learn from the book of nature. This requires us to *slow down*.

Eugene Peterson writes, "A disciple is a learner, but not in the academic setting of a schoolroom, rather at the work site of a craftsman."[18] In our information-driven society, we're accustomed to cramming our heads full of insipid facts, useless information about trending, then fading topics.

Keep pace.

Speed up.

But the life of a disciple of Jesus is not about keeping pace. It's about the splintered hours spent in intimacy learning the trade from the craftsman. It takes time, an eye for beauty, and the patience to let something form out of the formless.

WAYPOINT

I could share several spiritual disciplines with you that might invigorate your spiritual intimacy with God. Practices like silence and solitude, study and prayer are time-tested. They work. But I want to focus on one specific discipline we, as Christians, tend to marginalize. After I share this discipline, I want to conclude the chapter with a fictional sketch meant to inspire spiritual renewal in the church.

Do You Love the Word?

Once, I led a discussion at a men's retreat about the power of God's Word. I don't apologize for the simplicity of this phrase, "the power of God's Word." In fact, it reminds me how people regard the power of beauty in their lives: they don't. If we believe God is who he claims to be through Jesus, then why do we fill our days with everything but the quiet beauty of listening to him speak through his Word?

I used this phrase in discussion with the men when our conversation opened the topic of past wounds and experiencing spiritual distance from God. They told stories about their experiences with counselors and spiritual directors. I listened as many of the men present shared similar stories and encouraged each other with practices derived from psychology on how to deal with their hurt, relational estrangement from God, and alienation as a man in the church. Not one of the men present mentioned their experience with God's Word playing any role in their healing.

Now, before you write me off as anti-counseling, hear me loud and clear. I believe in counseling. I believe we can learn much from the social sciences about the life of the mind and spirit. But I found it extraordinary that when it came to spiritual estrangement or distance, no one spoke of their love for the Scriptures.

Why is this?

Let me offer a suggestion by way of a personal story.

Simple Hacks for Cultivating Spiritual Intimacy

I arrived at my tutor's home for my lesson. Dr. Randolph was the kindest and meekest of spiritual leaders. His vision had failed him, but that did not hinder his study of the biblical languages.

He opened our session with a question: "Tim, why do we study the Scriptures in the original language?"

I stammered, thinking to myself, *To get a good grade*, but said nothing.

After an awkward pause, Dr. Randolph answered his own question: "Because we love God's Word."

I was struck to the core. I trembled in my heart. I did not

love God's Word. I studied it for the grade, the prestige, to be in "the know." *Look at me, I know Greek.* My exchange with Dr. Randolph was the preface to all my further study. As I slowly fell in love with God's Word, I found that my study was no study at all. It was a journey into intimacy with the Almighty.

This journey teaches me still. It shows me portraits of my Eternal Lover. How silly I feel even now when I think of how I expected God to be just as I thought he'd be—a humanlike equalizer for the unjust, or a moral watchdog. How embarrassing to think he is anything like me or thinks like me?

On the journey toward intimacy, I've encountered many fellow pilgrims. Augustine, Tozer, Lewis, Chesterton, Dr. Randolph, my own father. All leaders in the church. And all somewhere out there, off the beaten path.

It's easy to think of religion or faith as an artifact that molds culture. And it does. But the golden turning points of Christian history did not come from an organized strategy, a program, or from leaders seeking influence. Instead, seminal shifts in church history resulted from individuals on their knees, pursuing intimacy with the Almighty. Dr. Randolph's question still rings in my ears. It reminds me that to lead, I must become small. I must disappear. I must follow the Shepherd of my heart.

For so long, I approached the Bible with hubris. It's embarrassing. I treated it like a *gotcha!* book or a moral checklist or a weapon to wield. It wasn't until Dr. Randolph's simple question that my spiritual pride was exposed, laid bare before me.

That's the point, isn't it? To realize that the footpath of spiritual renewal begins in the dirt of confession, confessing pride, selfish ambition, and greed. On my adventure into loving God's Word—and I have not yet arrived and remain on this adventure—I've discovered other pilgrims who have walked similar footpaths.

What I experienced at the men's retreat applies to women and young people as well. The Christian life can become rote, stale, and formulaic. But as I shared the story about Dr. Randolph, I asked the one simple question that continues to shape me as a disciple of Christ: *Do you love the Word?*

Consider this simple hack for cultivating a life of spiritual intimacy:

1. Find a chronological Bible to work through. A chronological Bible will present the story of the Bible in a more cohesive form and allow you to immerse yourself in the narrative. It will also shake up what might be a dull routine of Bible reading.
2. If podcasts and audiobooks are pushing Scripture reading to the margins in your daily life, stop listening to them for a time. Get intense and intentional about your time in the Word. Digital content that is not the Bible can feel like it's giving you something, but beware of the trick. The Word of God is living, but it's not an instant fix-it-button remedy.
3. Start a Bible study at your home or join one at your church. Make sure it's not a study in which the attendees share their feelings about the passages every week. Find a good teacher or an older mature Christian to guide the study. You and I must commit to reading Scripture, pray through it, and be willing to change when confronted with its truth.
4. In your study, work through an entire book of the Bible. Study the cultural context, the perspective of the author, and the purpose of the message or story.
5. Familiarize yourself with reference sources like commentaries, word study books, and deep dives into theological ideas. But be careful not to let your time be consumed with the extra-biblical study. The point is to

dive into the Word and use the additional resources to help bring it to life in your imagination.

The Renewal of the Church

The church's cultural influence will not improve from pursuing societal acceptance. It will come from the wonder of rugged intimacy with God.

How do we find intimacy with God?

Intimacy with God comes at a price. Are we willing to pay it?

The price of intimacy looks like a constant emptying; like pouring water from a bucket that never runs out. Intimacy's invitation asks for confession but in turn gives grace; it desires repentance while granting mercy.

We find intimacy in the quiet places, in the away places, in the high places—it is the fruit of solitude. The wilderness forges the beauty of intimacy. In barren times, lonely times, times of going without, intimacy looks like the footpath of healing. Of surrendering a painful burden over and over again to a God who holds the universe even as he cares for you.

The spiritual adventure of Edwards took him along the path of revival. The spiritual fire ignited in him and spread to the church. What I see in Edwards, I also see in myself. And I see it in you. And I see it in the church. It's the potential for revival!

For Augustine, knowing God more intimately is accomplished through human contemplation in the soul—the outside world of beauty can only bring a sketch of God. Without the Word, without the Holy Spirit, the ordered cosmos, spiritual practices, whatever, all ring hollow. God is spirit, and you and I must engage him in spirit and in truth.[19]

When I look out across the landscape of the church, I

find that in the land of plenty, spiritual fervor wanes; in the land of want, spiritual fervor blossoms. I wonder if this is the way it needs to be in this country for God's beauty to ignite our hearts for revival.

But then I look at Edwards and say to myself, *No, Tim, nothing can obscure the power and glory of God. We need only the willingness of a few incongruent people to advance the kingdom of God here on earth.*

Once, after reflecting on the deep divisions and consumptive mentality of the modern American church, I sketched a short story of fiction. In the past, church leaders or academics have warned me about offering critiques of the church without also offering a remedy or answer to the problems facing us. I offer this fictional sketch to you now not as a tiny work of skepticism, but as a herald of hope. For I believe beauty will save the world. And beauty is spelled J-E-S-U-S.

A Visit from the Angel of the Lord

You'll never believe who stopped in yesterday.

"Tim, my friend, how are you?" said the visitor, as he walked right past me and into my living room. He's *that* kind of friend.

"I'm good! To what do I owe the pleasure?" I asked, not surprised by his rather dramatic entrance.

"Well, I wanted to show you something. Do you have a few minutes?" he asked, looking around the room at nothing in particular.

"I'm a little busy," I said, "but I think I can spare a moment or two."

"Great! Let's go. Hold on, now."

Before I had a chance to ask why I needed to hold on, he lifted me on his back, the ceiling of my foyer opened, and we rocketed up into the stormy sky.

"Where . . . are we going?" I shouted into the wind as I held on for dear life.

"To the battlefield!" he shouted back.

As you may have guessed by now, my visitor was the Angel of the Lord. He drops in every now and again, usually with some kind of major interruption that "just can't wait."

We landed hard in a desolate place. No trees, just an open plain. But I could see mountains in the distance on either side.

"Where are we?" I asked, trying to get my bearings.

"We're at the battlefield," he said again, now very calm.

I took a look around and noticed that we stood among the dead. Thousands, maybe hundreds of thousands, of dead soldiers.

"What happened here?"

"A great battle was fought here," he said, now sounding like a storyteller. "As you can see, it was a massacre."

As the Angel of the Lord spoke, the stench of the place hit me. Vultures descended. The wind kicked up, and my eyes watered from the smell.

Then the wind blew harder. And with the wind, night fell; the stars, then the moon, then morning came, all in a flash. I felt like I was standing in a time-lapse photography video.

When it stopped, I looked again. No more rotting corpses. Just a battlefield of bones and armor and swords. The wind stopped.

"Who were these people? What did they do to deserve such an end—to be annihilated like this?" I asked.

"This, dear friend, is the Church. Do you know them?"

I looked at him, as if struck dumb.

"I can see you've heard of them," he said. "They were once a great nation. A vibrant people who lived like the wind. Death hates people like that— so unpredictable, yet so powerful in their devotion."

"But if this is the Church, who was their enemy? You said they, whoever it was, had just departed."

"Yes, the enemy," he repeated. He began pacing. "I will just say this: they are much closer than you think. Perhaps they've fled to the nearby mountains."

Walking slowly around a small part of the battlefield, I looked more closely at the carnage. I stopped at a pair of skeletons that wore the same shields, their swords lodged in one another's chests.

And then it dawned on me.

"There is no enemy fleeing to the mountains, is there?" I asked, a pit growing in my stomach.

"No, friend. There is not."

"They killed each other," I said flatly.

The Angel did not respond. He continued pacing.

"Why did you bring me here?" I asked.

"You knew this was happening, old friend. But you've been ignoring it. Look over there." He pointed to the horizon, to a ridge of mountains.

"That city on the hill? That's their home. A beautiful place. I prepared it especially for them. They lived there for so long. But their arguments and bickering led them to this desolate valley. No water—*my* kind of water. No springs. Just hard, dry ground. A perfect place for a battle. Like dogs, they snapped and snarled their way out here, not realizing how far from home they'd wandered."

He stopped pacing and stared out at the mountains.

"Is there no one left, over there, in the mountains?"

"There are some left. But they are very young. And scared. There's no one to lead them," he said. He turned his gaze on me, but I looked away, down at the bones.

"What are we to do with these bones? Just leave them?" I asked.

"Oh no. I have a plan for the bones."

He stepped close to me and whispered in my ear.

I listened, pulled back, looked at him in disbelief, then leaned in again.

Again, he whispered. I nodded.

I stepped away from his side and walked onto the battlefield, among the bones. I breathed deeply and began to sing.

I had learned the hymn as a child. The words back then loomed large in my mind. By the time I became an adult, they'd become somewhat forgettable.

"Amazing grace, how sweet the sound, that saved a wretch like me . . ."

I choked on the word "me," and the weight of the song rushed in on me like a raging, white-capped river. I heaved. I felt the bones. The waste. The despair.

"I once was lost, but now I'm found, was blind, but now I see . . ."

I barely got the words out. I buried my head in my hands, shaking. Though the wind was still, I heard a cagey rattling.

I looked up, astonished.

The bones shook on the ground. They rose up and began to shake and dance in the air, rattling through the valley like a war song.

"What's going on?" I shouted to the Angel.

"Keep singing!"

"When we've been there, ten thousand years . . . bright . . . shining as the . . ."

I couldn't finish.

The words echoed in the empty valley as a fierce wind brewed. Dust, stirred up by the wind, whipped around the bones, covering them. Sinewy figures rose to stand around me, erect but lifeless.

"What's happening?" I yelled, trying to shout over the echoing, rattling, and blowing. My hands shook, and my face felt hot, windblown and sand blasted.

"Hope!" the Angel shouted. "Hope is happening!"

"How? *How* is it happening? Will they live again?"

He came toward me, drawing me close to whisper in my ear once more. More instructions.

I nodded and dropped to me knees with a sob. And the words rose out of me like birdsong in a springtime wood.

"Our Father, who art in heaven . . . hallowed . . . be . . . thy . . . name . . ."

As the words fell off my lips, a great and terrible wind blew through the valley—mightier than the one before. It sounded like a shrieking banshee, but I knew it was no mythological force. I crouched low, burrowing into the hard ground, afraid.

"Thy kingdom come . . ."

I looked up just in time to see the heads of

the standing dead snap back. The air filled with screams, the unholy kind. So many screams. I covered my ears and bent low once again.

Then, I felt warm hands around my hands. It was the Angel. He pulled my hands away. The screams had stopped. I heard singing. He bent low over me, bringing my hands close to his heart.

"Do you hear what they are singing?"

I listened for a moment and nodded.

"Yes, yes. I hear it. It's wonderful. What song is it?"

"Hope, Tim. It's the song of the wind—the song of hope!"

"I want to learn it!" I shouted, half laughing, half crying.

"You already know it. It's the song you sing to me in the morning—remember that prayer you sang the other day?"

I stared at him.

"Remember when you took the children so your wife could get some rest and go shopping? Well, she spent time with me, too. And the song struck deep in her heart."

"What?"

"Remember when you prayed with your neighbors before they moved? You felt so insecure, so afraid. But you listened to the song in your heart, and you prayed. They're attending a church in Jersey now. Remember that annoying man at the retreat? How unfairly you treated him in front of all those other men? When you sought him out and asked forgiveness, he returned home and asked his wife for forgiveness—they were very close to ending their marriage."

"How . . . how is this possible?"

As we crouched on the valley floor, the dead sang and danced around us. The Angel held me, still whispering in my ear.

"You put that song into their souls, Tim. Just from listening to my daily whispers. You already know the wind song because you sing it. Almost daily. You have sung it enough for it to take root in your life. The tune comes to you, and sometimes it scares you. But when you really listen, and heed its melody, beauty awakens."

He helped me up, wiped my face with his hands, and kissed my forehead.

"What am I supposed to do now?" I asked.

"Sing," he replied.

Suddenly, I was standing back in my house, hearing the kettle boil on the stove.

"Tim . . . Tim?" It was my wife. She looked concerned.

"Huh?"

"Is the coffee ready? Are you okay?"

"Yeah . . . oh, yeah. Just thinking about hope."

CHAPTER 16

A REBELLION THEY WON'T FORGET

The Footpath of Beauty Chasing

The world barges in on us.

    We let the world barge in on us.[1]

Which is it?

Both, probably.

We don't chase beauty anymore because we live lives that are too *affected* by the world. I'm not suggesting some new-fangled theological separatism here, in which we live in communes on the edges of town—though that does sound good to me some days.

I'm saying I believe God created us to partake in this world, to cultivate it, to preserve its beauty, but chiefly to commune with him. We achieve the latter by engaging in the former. But working the garden, so to speak, gets tough when we allow the world to saddle us with its own agenda: get more, be something great, find fame, look out for yourself first, scream your pain, embrace victimhood, voice your outrage, champion the profane.

We can't chase beauty if we're chasing our own tails and growling our discontent like everyone else. That's what the world's agenda for life amounts to, doesn't it? I believe chasing beauty looks a lot like finding your voice. Here's what I mean.

THE IMPORTANCE OF DISCOVERING YOUR TRUE VOICE

The analogy of "finding your voice" might, at first, sound like a journey for the artist. But finding your voice does not only apply to artists or musicians or writers.

Do you *have* a voice?

See?

Here we go.

Once, I sat in on a recording session with a friend of mine who produces records in Nashville. He was producing a new album for one of those classic rock bands that has endured, a band everyone continues to love.

"Their voices were so *affected*," said the lead singer, recounting a scenario in which he met with a famous rock producer for lunch. The producer lamented his failed efforts to get the lead singer of a new rock band to record an authentic vocal track.

"He couldn't sing a straight note. Their producer pleaded with him to sing the notes with his own voice. But his own voice was so layered with the inflections of his influences, he didn't know how to sing a straight note in his own voice."

I sat in my friend's studio, listening to this story, when it hit me.

"Affected," I whispered to myself.

It's almost impossible to live unaffected by the world. So many influences roll into our lives. Like the ocean's tide, they crash in and move out, each time washing away more and more of our shoreline.

Think about the lament of that famous rock producer. When we hear a unique singing voice, we know right away. We love it because it possesses something so real, we almost can't explain it. In today's world, we call this realness "authenticity." I don't want to use that word because it comes with philosophical baggage. The realness I'm referencing is the kind we intuitively understand. It draws us to it. We feel as though we're hearing from the person's soul.

Does someone's voice come to mind for you?

For me, it's Eddie Vedder, the lead singer of the band Pearl Jam. I remember where I was when I first heard "Even Flow," one of their most popular songs and a modern classic. I was driving my 1984 Chevy Luv pickup, headed back to what became my last partial semester at Liberty University, when I had to pull over.

"Who *is* this?" I muttered to myself, looking around the cab of my truck for the CD case. That voice. Raw, gritty, passionate, baritone. It wasn't long until every other singer in the modern rock genre began mimicking Vedder's earthy baritone. When smart industry people find a successful formula, they mimic it. This is natural. The music industry is a copycat industry. At least, that's what my producer friend told me.

The Affected Voice Syndrome or AVS (note: I made this up) also exists in the writing world.

HOW TO LIVE UNAFFECTED

When I began my full-time writing career in 2005, I wanted to write like my favorite authors: George MacDonald, C. S. Lewis, Frederick Buechner, Annie Dillard, James Joyce, T. S. Eliot, Ernest Hemingway. Remember, "Imitation is the sincerest [form] of flattery."[2] Like the rock singer who couldn't shed his AVS to sing a pure note, I drizzled their voices all over my prose. I had to get it out of my system. I'm still getting it out of my system.

Mimicking the popular is a natural cultural phenomenon. William Zinsser, author of the bestselling classic *On Writing Well*, recounts how he imitated his favorite writers for much of his early career. It wasn't until he was in his mid-fifties, and his wife encouraged him to turn his Yale course on writing into a book, that he discovered his own style—another term for voice. Until then, his writing took on the voice of the person he wanted to be perceived as: a youthful, witty critic. Once he shed his AVS, he found his voice.

Zinsser realized that, for years, he had tried to write like the famous essayist E. B. White. He also tried to *be* E. B. White. But when he stepped away from his infatuation with White, he saw himself, *unaffected*. He saw a unique person who loved to participate in the world, a teacher who valued interaction with his students. When he taught his classes, he was warm and encouraging. And that's who he wanted narrating his book on writing.

Himself. His *unaffected* self.

The unaffected self. That is the goal, right?

I need to issue a word of caution here, because in our modern world, embracing your unaffected self means something different than the idea I'm getting at. The world's version of the unaffected self can easily be turned into a monster bent on satisfying the self. I again turn to the wisdom of Zinsser. He addresses this "me-monster"[3] with a short essay in which he gives every reader permission to write their own story.

His permission, however, comes with a caveat: *the writer must abide by the unwritten code of modesty.* Why? Because Zinsser says that in our age, humility has left the building. Every inch of a person's life is fair game. In fact, you're encouraged to share your most squalid acts—the more detail, the better. Reality TV, news, social media—they eat it up. This shamelessness now passes for *authenticity.*

"Memoir," Zinsser writes, "became the new therapy. Everybody and their brother wallowed in their struggle with alcohol, addiction, recovery, abuse, illness, aging parents, siblings, teachers, coaches, and everyone else who dared misunderstand them. It was a new literature of victimhood."[4] He reminds us that timeless memoirs, like *Angela's Ashes*, work through the muck but only in order to get to the beautiful themes of love and forgiveness. When I mention the unaffected self, I'm *not* talking about the kind of unfiltered, unchecked whining Zinsser describes so well. Instead, I'm envisioning you and me, finally standing before God, at ease with our muck because we're standing in the brilliance of glory. In the shadow of his glory, we don't see the muck. We see ourselves as God sees us: drenched in his presence.

I'm reminded of the apostle Paul's words about casting off anything that hinders his pursuit of Christ. It's a Greek image of a naked runner sprinting unencumbered to the finish line. The runner runs *unaffected*. No AVS. This is the picture I'm trying to paint when I say we need to chase beauty as unaffected participants in God's universe.

THE REBIRTH OF THE ORTHODOX MYSTIC

Zinsser's story arms me with three important reflections that can encourage us along the pilgrim way of chasing beauty.

First, his story inspires me to stop comparing myself to others and to listen to God's voice—the only one that matters. The path God sets before me will not look like your path. How boring if it did! No. It looks a lot like the green dotted roads we find on the old Rand McNally road maps. It's unique to me; but not in a self-serving or egocentric way. In a life-giving way. When Zinsser discovered his own unique, unaffected voice, it changed his life. The discovery breathed new life into his writing, gave him a newfound confidence in his abilities, and gave him the strength to cast off the influence of those writers he admired. It's time to pull ourselves away from the dark voices in our lives and live the adventure of chasing beauty, of chasing God.

Second, I must cultivate a cultural and spiritual awareness. If I'm racing through life without taking the time for reflection and self-evaluation, how will I ever realize the extent to which the world affects me?

The spiritual life requires us to maintain intimacy with God. The apostle Paul desired the same for himself. "What is more," he writes, "I consider everything a loss because of the surpassing worth of knowing Christ Jesus my Lord, for whose sake I have lost all things. I consider them garbage, that I may gain Christ" (Phil. 3:8).

What does intimacy with God look like? It looks like a Christian who lives as if God's existence and companionship is reality.

"But Tim, isn't all this intimacy talk a bit too mystical?"

Perhaps. But I believe we must revive the orthodox mysticism A. W. Tozer defined and practiced. In his final work, *The Christian Book of Mystical Verse*, published posthumously, Tozer defines what it means to be an orthodox mystic:

> [The orthodox mystic] differs from the ordinary orthodox Christian only because he experiences his faith down in the depths of this sentient being while others do not. He exists in a world of spiritual reality.
>
> He is quietly, deeply, and sometimes almost ecstatically aware of the presence of God in his own nature and in the world around him. His religious experience is something elemental, as old as time and creation.
>
> It is immediate acquaintance with God by union with the eternal Son. It is to know that which passes knowledge.[5]

Orthodox Christian mysticism doesn't need to entail strange, theological-sounding words from medieval times, or odd practices that require incense and candles, or living as a recluse. Christian mysticism, simply stated, looks like a Christian who has a close relationship with God through his Son, Jesus Christ.

The times when I am closest to God are also the times when I'm most culturally aware. Many Christian mystics returned from their places of solitude and intimacy and were better equipped to critique a culture in need of healing and restoration. In this way, our spiritual awareness empowers our cultural awareness. We cannot pretend to care about the so-called Christian cultural impact or "engaging culture" when our own spirits wheeze with the sickness Sam and George struggled with.

Third, his story challenges me to cast off my AVS. When we cast off the expectations and pressures of the world, we can walk our unique paths once again. In walking them, we find ourselves like Sam stepping through the doors of the hospital: healed, revived, ready to explore and to give chase to the beauty before us and around us, capturing us with every step, every conversation, every loss, every triumph.

When I experienced freedom from AVS, it was as if I woke to a new spiritual reality in my personal relationship with God. Walking my unique path unencumbered allowed me to pursue intimacy with Christ in a profound way. This new freedom, however, does not imbue me with unchecked hubris. It frees me to joy in who God created me to be, yes. But such freedom should create meekness.

When Jesus said the meek shall inherit the earth, he was not suggesting that you and I become weak and feeble-minded Christians. In the ancient world, meekness was often associated with horses. A meek horse was one who obeyed its rider. Imagine the racehorse or warhorse in all its strength, speed, and glory. Unbridled, the horse runs wild. But when it comes under the careful guidance of the rider, all that strength, speed, and glory are used for a specific purpose.

When I cast off my AVS, draw close to God, and submit myself to his careful guidance, he takes the reigns, and I run free. It's a beautiful paradox. Running free requires not a filling of confidence for the journey ahead, but an *emptying*. The Beauty Chaser invites emptying.

The modern creative spirit is misconceived as self-effusive; the more we express ourselves, the closer we come to imaginative nirvana. Not true. What you and I receive from our experiences, along with the insights we gain by participating with the natural world, comes to us from God. We do not work in the world as co-creators with God. That is theological hubris.

> "We are creatures who *derive* from God
> a wonderful ability to make something
> of what God has given us."[6]

We live as recipients of God's gifts to us.
We steward God's glory.

We shape our voices with God's wonder.

We churn the soil of God's beauty.

All under the careful tug of the reins by our Heavenly Rider.

Lewis Hyde, in his classic work, *The Gift*, reminds the artist that the imaginative bounty comes to her as a gift, and that gift must stay in motion. "The gift turned inward," he writes. "Unable to be given, [it] becomes a heavy burden, even sometimes a kind of poison. It is as though the flow of life were backed up."[7]

I believe this concept of keeping the gift in motion relates to every person, and it is primary to the Christian life. Teresa of Avila says, "The point is that we should make a gift of our hearts, emptying them of ourselves that they may be filled with God. What power lies in this gift! Our almighty Father becomes one with us and transforms us, uniting Creator and creature."[8]

Do you see the contours of our sketch yet—this Beauty Chaser sketch?

Beauty Chaser: *the heaven-focused orthodox Christian mystic riding under the eternal twilight of our Glorious Heavenly Rider.*

Or something like that.

CHASING DRAWS US INTO THE UNKNOWN

When it comes to metaphors for life, my friend Kevin prefers the idea of the chase rather than the idea of the journey. The word *journey*, he says, implies that we might govern our own pace. *Chase*, on the other hand, paints the picture of something out ahead of you, compelling you on, over the crest of the next hill. The chase draws us out into the unknown.

The fires of the unknown call to us. Are we brave enough to venture out and give chase?

Why don't we chase beauty?

Because the world barged in on us?

Because we got distracted?

Probably both.

Your voice is who you are. It's the same with chasing beauty.

You were created to chase, to hunt, to live on the edges. *Homo viator!*

But beware the Plastic People. They'll call you inside, where it's safe, then choke you with the status quo. You and I must resist. We must embrace our pilgrim status, open our eyes, and walk further into the unknown than we ever thought we could.

Life is not some relational or cultural monolith. It's a kaleidoscope of activity, desires, passions, failures, interests, and relationships. You and I do not live in a digital world. We live out there, on the edges, where the wildness of life meets the beauty of it. Out there, amid the parks and hills and mountains Sam longed for each day.

When I think about the grizzled prophet John the Baptizer, I think about how Jesus described him: as one crying out in the wilderness. For John, it was all about paving the way for his cousin, Jesus. And I wonder if, like John out there on the edges, we can become that same kind of voice.

I'm not suggesting we move out to the desert and eat locusts and honey and wear animal skins—well, *I* might—but what if we metaphorically moved to the wilderness and became voices of and for beauty and joy? Testimonies of "that something more" everyone senses but can't describe.

How would that collective voice rattle and paint our world?

CHASING PATCHES OF GODLIGHT

For C. S. Lewis, beauty possessed a mysterious relational quality that invites those who witness it to take up the life-giving quest of chasing beauty. I sensed this life-giving quality in some of his other work as well. Like this line from his novel, *Till We Have Faces*, for example: "The sweetest thing in all my life has been the longing—to reach the Mountain, to find the place where all the beauty came from—."[9]

This quote now hangs on my wall, etched in wood. I love it because it doesn't say that beauty itself is the sweetest thing. Rather, the sweetest thing is the longing to find that far-off place where beauty comes from. *Homo viator!*

Lewis described himself as a hunter of beauty. I cannot see ol' Jack (that's what his friends called him) strapping on an over-under Browning Citori (that's a shotgun) and heading out into the field—he'd spook everything with his pipe—but that's the image he uses to describe chasing beauty.

> Yes, you are always everywhere.
> But I, Hunting in such immeasurable forests,
> Could never bring the noble Hart at bay.[10]

The elusive stag (beauty!) leaves us chasing shadows. Lewis compares chasing patches of light in a wood to chasing beauty. For him, beautiful things we love to pursue are "patches of Godlight in the woods of our experience."[11] If we're attentive, we can learn from these patches of Godlight.

Chasing patches of Godlight will fill us with anticipation, which will then be our constant posture and perspective. When you and I view our journeys as adventures, chasing beauty on a daily basis, our perspectives will inevitably shift. Our eyes will look past the profane and the cynical. We'll live preoccupied with scanning relationships and daily experiences for Godlight.

Our hearts will stand at attention, waiting for arrows of joy, as Lewis liked to call them. My friend Jason tells me that a hunter notices the details of the wilderness and interprets them as clues to where the deer or elk or, in Lewis's case, the noble stag, might be. Likewise, a Beauty Chaser notices the details of this world and interprets them as clues to the unfolding love of God, wrapped up in Godlight.

It all sounds so grand, doesn't it?

Keep in mind, however, that chasing beauty is not safe. Quests never are. Why? Because beauty is not something we can define and slap into a book. Beauty is not pragmatic. It resists homogeneity. It throws things off-balance. It embraces pain. It drenches us in emotion. It rests at ease with loss. It comforts us in despair. It floods us in love. We must prepare for both pain and glory, epiphany and despair, longing and joy.

The more we chase beauty, the more it affects our voices and actions in this world. Beauty molds our voices with patience as we engage with the world of the park, with the people who mark our existence with theirs. It calls to us through the delight of deep friendships.

Beauty also acts upon us. It comes bounding to us in the turbulence of mystery and wonder. When we get out of our boxed-up existence, beauty claps in winter-tree-branch glory and gives us something to dread.

Beauty comes to us in the infusions of joy that abound in our daily existence. That joy-whisper in our work, for example, reminding us that our daily grind is anything but.

What are we to do when we find something so mysterious and wonderful in this world? Something so abundant? Something that seems to move throughout all of creation? Something that seems to speak through the space of artwork and the time of music?[12] Something we see in people and experience in special situations?

Doesn't this mysteriously wonderful thing we call beauty seem to be saying, "Hey, you! Do you see me? Over here! Yeah, this is only a sliver of what I am. Don't you want to know more? Well, then, come on!"

You don't have to be an outdoor enthusiast or adventurer to experience beauty. You don't have to be an artist to communicate through beauty. You don't have to possess an advanced degree to understand beauty.

But you do need to do one thing.

You need to answer beauty's call. Beauty does not exist for us to simply notice and move on with what supposedly matters most.

Beauty exists to remind us that there's something more, something beyond us. Those of us who take the time to notice it will find themselves changed.

The World Needs Incongruent People

Jesus invited those who follow him to live counter to the world's thirst for the profane and violent and its idolatrous focus on self.[13] His call is to the Beauty Chasers, whose duty is to possess the courage to rebuke our culture.[14]

And who is that brave?

Revolutionary voices rise not because people want them, but because the culture needs them. The revolutionary listens to her instinct to follow the path of Beauty Chaser. What is the person of faith if not a saint who is incongruous with the modern world? Like that weird uncle of yours who lives on a farm and seems a little off because he doesn't like the internet, but you know he knows something more, something deeper, about life and beauty and living well.

The world needs incongruent people who stand not against it but outside of it, calling it to something *other*. Who are those people—those saints—who walk the path of enchantment? Who speak in songs? Who live in wonder?

As people of faith, this is a calling given to all of us. If we don't see it as our calling, we must regain our grasp of God's beauty and rethink how we formulate our theology for practical, everyday living. Then, we might see God as "the foundation and fountain of all being and all beauty,"[15] beauty not as consolation, nor as a refuge, but as the platform of faith and thought. When we calibrate our sensibilities toward a way of living and being that champions beauty, we reposition beauty as the crown of our thoughts.

Beauty requires curiosity and sight. It requires us to think. It does not passively move upon us or this world. It makes demands upon us. It says, "Be attentive. Be still. Be reverent. Give life!"

When we see beauty, either with our physical eyes or the eyes of the heart, we somehow find focus and the ability to hope again. Beauty beckons us. It eases and calms. It causes joy. It gives life. It begets and creates in us the desire to beget works of art, acts of kindness, crafts, thoughtful business models, an engaging lecture, a dinner table, a stew—I could go on, right?

We began this little adventure of a book imagining what it might look like if Sam were healed and headed out on a walk through the park, the hills, and the mountains. Then you and I ventured out on our own walk, and I told you stories about some of my favorite walks. Being out here, taking these walks, beauty reconnects us. Not only with the outside world, but with one another. We see the people in the park feeding the ducks at the pond, holding hands along the path, and our hearts quicken. Seeing the path winding toward the hills, our minds come alive with curiosity. Don't you want to see what's just over the hill? It calls to us with the promise of joy. What are we waiting for?

It seems almost silly that to be an incongruous people, all one needs to do is take a walk. But perhaps it is just that simple.

A New Beginning:
Recapturing Our Wonder

Strength Found in Meekness

I want to close with a reflection on Paul's prayer at the end of his letter to the Christians in Ephesus:

> For this reason I bow my knees before the Father, from whom every family in heaven and on earth is named, that according to the riches of his glory he may grant you to be strengthened with power through his Spirit in your inner being, so that Christ may dwell in your hearts through faith—that you, being rooted and grounded in love, may have strength to comprehend with all the saints what is the breadth and length and height and depth, and to know the love of Christ that surpasses knowledge, that you may be filled with all the fullness of God.

God loves you with a cosmic love. Paul's prayer is a cosmic prayer for Christians. Paul's use of "Father" is the Greek word *patera*. Though we like to think of God as our Father in the parental sense, *Father* can also be used to mean "originator." Paul says all the families of heaven and earth originate with God, and he pleads for these Christians to comprehend the four-dimensional love of God. He prays the Holy Spirit will be able to give them the wisdom no human has on her own.

I'm reminded of God telling Job, "Brace yourself like a man, because I have some questions for you, and you must answer them." God intended to help Job comprehend his glory.

By the spirit of God dwelling in them, the Ephesians might be able to comprehend his love.

"But Tim," you say, "we all know what love is. And that Christ died for us and all that jazz. Aren't you telling us something we already know?"

"Yes," I reply. "But the idea is that we continue to pursue this love instead of taking it for granted. We need strength to go 'further up and further in,' as it were, to search out this four-dimensional love of God."[1]

"What is this four-dimensional love you speak of, Tim?"

It's like when I say to my daughter Brielle, "I love you, Bri." I mean something different than her reply, which is, "I love you, Daddy."

Time works on us. We age, and our souls grow—hopefully they grow closer to God. In that growth, our ability to love grows. Brielle can't know the true depth of my love yet, for she is only a child. Life has shaped me in ways that only come with time. I think about the moment when I saw her born, when the midwife raised her up, new-birthed. That experience shaped my love. It opened a reservoir in me I didn't know existed.

Brielle doesn't know what happened to my heart at that moment. And at that moment, neither did I. It was a moment held in eternity; a moment in which heaven itself seemed to fill my heart.

Here's what Brielle doesn't know.

When I say, "I love you, Brielle," what I'm really saying is, "I would die for you, Brielle."

And when she responds, "I love you, Daddy," she's saying something like, "I feel safe with you, Daddy." I know this is what she means, and it is beautiful. But one day, her heart will open even further, and it will grasp more clearly how wide and deep and high my love for her is.

This is what I think about when I contemplate God's four-dimensional love. I think about something I cannot know right now without the Spirit of God stretching my heart in ways I don't understand.

When God says to me, "Tim, I love you" what am I hearing?

When I say to God, "I love you, my Father," what am *I* saying?

Perhaps I am saying, "I feel safe with you, God." Yes, probably. And, "I am thankful for how you provide for me, God." This is right and good.

But what is God saying when he says he loves me? I believe it is something I don't quite know or understand. I may never know this side of heaven. He speaks of a love that spans eternity. A love that existed before time, before the foundations of the cosmos were set. When he says, "I love you, Tim," he is speaking as one from whom love itself comes. He is the Fountainhead of love, the Originator of love. Love, for God, is natural because it is one of the many excellencies of his character. It is a love that makes me lovely to him. It possesses the power to change me.

I thank God that I did not come up with this thing called love. Imagine humans thought it up—what might it look like now? Perhaps our culture reflects this very thing in that it places love and lust in the same position of self-gratification. Love in our fallen world looks selfish and grim and idolized and bent.

God does not speak from the experiences of life, like I do when I tell my daughter I love her. His experience is outside of time, and it reaches to infinity. How can I fathom a love that holds all the mysteries of the world within it *and* expresses itself to me? What does that mysterious love look like here on earth? What would it do to and for others if I could somehow grasp it and reflect it back to my Originator?

When God says, "I love you, Tim," he is saying, "I will die for you, Tim." This is the pinprick of eternity I felt at the birth of Brielle—at the births of all three of my daughters—when my entire life was compressed in one moment of wonder. And it reflects this four-dimensional love from the Fountainhead of love itself.

My daughters Lyric, Brielle, and Zion will push into my love their whole lives. My wife and I will hold them and say, "I love you," and they will say it back to us. It is not the same, and it *is* the same all at once. It is the same because it is the seed of eternity, the seed of a love that will grow into a dying love—an expanse they can't understand right now.

And that, my friend, is you and me with God our Father, our Originator. You, pushing into him. Getting enveloped in your love for him, pushing through to a love that can finally say to others, "I will die for you" as a reflection of the beautiful love you've discovered as you fall endlessly into him.

Perhaps this willingness to die is the beginning of all that is.

This love I find to be the heart of beauty, the cosmic Lover of the universe. It is the reason I long to push further up and further in, to let go of distractions, to throw myself off the cliff of his love, diving deep into the four dimensions of God.

A Note from Behind the Bookshelf

I know. I said I wasn't telling what I found behind the bookshelf, but I couldn't resist.

I found a note behind the bookshelf. It was tightly scrolled and placed within a sandy bottle, washed up from an ancient shore. It was written in the language of heaven and addressed to you and me. The note contained instructions and coordinates to a place called "The Far Beyond."

I followed the instructions and found a high country with sprawling terrain. I spied a woman sitting by a river that carved through the countryside.

"Did you send me the note?" I asked her.

"Oh, no," she said, "all the notes come from the coastal mountains." She pointed me to a well-worn path and said, "This footpath will lead you there."

I walked the trail until I encountered with an older gentleman. His smile invited conversation.

"Good afternoon," he said, raising the tattered hat from his head.

"And to you," I said. "Do you know if this is the way to the coastal mountains?"

"I'm returning from that very place," he said. "The name is George. I'm off to greet my friend Sam, who arrives today. He finally found his way beyond the bookshelf."

"George!" I exclaimed. "I was just telling my friends your story. But—you're no longer blind!"

"Indeed! This place restored my sight and so much more."

George told me how describing the beautiful world to his friend Sam in their hospital room helped him find his way to The Far Beyond.

"I realized," he said, "that for so much of my life, I'd looked ahead to the next thing instead of being in the moment. True life, I discovered, is *recognizing the moment of glory when you're standing smack-dab in it*. Don't look ahead. Be here, now. See this moment for what it is. Each step in this land behind the bookshelf is a step towards what our hearts yearned for in that hospital room."

With that, George raised his hat, waved goodbye, and marched on to meet Sam. I wondered if I'd find the place C. S. Lewis described—the place all the beauty comes from.

As I walked the path, I happened upon so many friends and family who helped me tell the story of beauty you now hold in your hands: my wife Christine, who never flinches in the face of new adventures and will love until the sun fails to shine; and my daughters Lyric, Brielle, and Zion, who inspire me beyond what I ever thought possible. Phyllis and Whitie Willard, who never told me not to chase my dreams; and my siblings and their spouses, Renee and Mike Husovich, Jon and Kathy Willard, Robin and Jeff Troyer, Michael and Katlin Willard, plus all sixteen cousins—all of whom are my haven and my strength. Ken and Marlene Mottin, and Kenny and Lisa Mottin, who give, love, and pray and pray some more. My visionary-surrogate-siblings Kevin and Danielle Sterner, who years ago challenged me to chase my calling as a writer.

Then, there are all the Beauty Chasers who helped send me to England, where beauty unfolded before my eyes: Ravi and Sajan George, Jay Williams, Jessie Mutchler, Holly Moore, Cindy and Chris Haughey, Chris and Monica Van Allsburg, Brian and Mandy Miller, Heather and Jason Locy, Gabe and Rebekah Lyons, Steve Graves, and Bill Voge. In Oxford, my soul expanded through deep conversations with Alister McGrath, Malcolm Guite, Michael Ward, and Sarah Clarkson—here's to a Blackwell's tea and a gushing discussion about writing. Esther Fleece Allen—here's to *orthodoxy!*—Matthew Anderson, and Matt Benton. Jason and Tamy Elam, who walked with me and Christine during the midnight snow when we met Mr. Tumnus. A serendipitous encounter and conversation with the late Walter Hooper at The Bear and the Ragged Staff pub, which turned into tea times and discussions about C. S. Lewis and Northernness. The discovery of a life-long friend in Bernard Cadogan at Blackwell's—he was the first who told me to trust my voice. If you've noticed, most good things begin at Blackwell's Bookshop—you should visit when you can.

The journey continued back in the States with Lil Copan; my narrative mentor John Sloan; my "bossy big sister" Myquillyn Smith and her husband-turned-forever-mountain-brother Chad, the forested cul-de-sac family of Huntcliff; Sara, Nate, and Lily Hagerty and our continual conversation about beauty, God, and *Till We Have Faces*; Brent Cole, who sat with me in the morning rain and helped me remember George and Sam. Alex and Christie Kennedy, John Snyder, Sam Casey, Chip Cash, Michael Hawn, Bethany Douglas, John Sowers, Adam Weber—a brother who drops exhortation on me at the perfect times—and both Mitchell families. My cosmic twin sister, Roberta Ahmanson, and our love for Augustine and beauty. Ruth Chou Simons, who taught me about generosity in writing. Ann Voskamp—"What is there to fear?" Lacey and Josh Sturm—we walk with angels. Christie Purifoy—my fellow Beauty Chaser and digger of dirt and words. Shawn Smucker—North Carolina midday coffees. Sean Dietrich—the bloodhound of writers. Edie Wadsworth—whose infectious joy ignites mine, daily. Leah Boden—across the pond, but kindred through and through.

And then the patient ones at Zondervan Reflective: Ryan Pazdur, Jenny-Lyn de Klerk, Harmony Harkema, and Alexis DeWeese, along with the design team at Fivestone. And finally, Chris Ferebee, my literary agent who never says never.

I could show you where to find my bookshelf, and you could crack it open to find my secret path, but the truth is, you have your own. It's waiting for you right where you are. It's the *presence of God*, disguised as popping daisies, quiet conversations over a tasty beverage, and the rattling leaves beneath thunderclouds.

Beauty is an event, and it is unfolding upon you right now. Look around you, seize the moment, and find your way back to the wonder.

Notes

Chapter 1: The Window

1. I'm thankful to my friend Brent Cole, who joined me one afternoon on a cabin porch to watch the rain. We sat by a fire, and he reminded me of this story. The author of the story is unknown, and Brent and I both have heard it told with different settings, like a prison cell instead of a hospital room, for example. In any event, I'm including a link to one version I found online. I've taken some liberties with the story and added some dialogue. See To Inspire: Quotes for the Mind & Soul, http://www.toinspire.com/Stories/Inspirational%20Stories.html, accessed March 6, 2018.

2. Frederick Buechner, *The Sacred Journey* (London: Chatto & Windus, 1982), 4–5.

3. Gerard Manley Hopkins and Walford Davies, "God's Grandeur" in *The Major Poems [of] Gerard Manley Hopkins* (London: Dent, 1979), "The Windhover," 67.

Chapter 2: Curiouser and Curiouser

1. Roger Scruton divides beauty into four categories: human, natural, "everyday," and artistic beauty. See Roger Scruton, *Beauty: A Very Short Introduction* (Oxford: Oxford University Press, 2011), 29, 49, 67, 82.

2. For more on this kind of dualist approach to beauty, see Patrick Sherry, *Spirit and Beauty: An Introduction to Theological Aesthetics* (London: SCM, 2002), 35. In my doctoral research I came across Sherry's wonderful introduction to theological aesthetics and return to this small volume often and recommend it for further reading.

3. Gerard Manley Hopkins, "The Windhover," in *The Major Poems [of] Gerard Manley Hopkins* (London: Dent, 1979), 64.

4. "YAWP" comes from Walt Whitman's poem, "Song of Myself: 52." The line reads: "I sound my barbaric yawp over the roofs of the world." Walt Whitman, *Leaves of Grass*, A Bantam classic (New York: Bantam Books, 2004), 73.

5. Sherry, *Spirit and Beauty*, 35. Sherry recommends we cast a broader net for our definition of beauty. And so here I borrow the reference and agree with the idea that beauty requires us to open our minds and allow more information and experiences to inform our working definition of it.

6. John O'Donohue, *Beauty: The Invisible Embrace* (New York: Perennial, 2005), 12–13.

7. C. S. Lewis, *Surprised by Joy* (New York: HarperOne, 2017), 186–87.

8. C. S. Lewis, *The Weight of Glory and Other Addresses* (San Francisco: HarperSanFrancisco, 2001), 14.

9. C. S. Lewis, *Perelandra: A Novel* (New York: Scribner Classics, 1996), 261.

10. In the western world, our concept of beauty originates with the Greek thinkers from antiquity, Plato, and Aristotle. Plato's more objective view of beauty described it in terms of copies and archetypes. Meaning, the beauty we see and experience in this world mimics (mimesis) the original form of beauty (archetype). The archetype of beauty lies somewhere out there in the beyond. It transcends this world. Aristotle viewed beauty more subjectively, rooting the concept in the real objects. Beauty was something that characterized things, people, places, and events. Variations of the Greek view of beauty trickled down through the ages. Plato and Aristotle influenced thinkers like the early church fathers like Cyril of Alexandria and St. Basil the Great as well as others like St. Augustine of Hippo, Thomas Aquinas, and Immanuel Kant from the modern era.

11. Sherry, *Spirit and Beauty*, 31–33.

12. Paul Guyer, *Values of Beauty: Historical Essays in Aesthetics* (Cambridge: Cambridge University Press, 2005), 3.

13. Beauty's fall from philosophical conversations and conversations related to the world of art culminated in the twentieth century. Though

beauty's banishment seemed final, some thinkers have called for its
return, like the provocative art critic Dave Hickey and philosopher
Mary Mothersill, who, in *A Companion to Aesthetics*, called for a
"return to the question of the nature of beauty." See Mary Mothersill,
"Beauty" in David E. Cooper, Joseph Margolis, and Crispin Sartwell,
A Companion to Aesthetics (Oxford: Blackwell Reference, 1995), 51.
See also Laurie Fendrich, "Dave Hickey's Politics of Beauty," *CHE*,
last modified January 2, 2013, accessed March 11, 2021, https://www
.chronicle.com/article/dave-hickeys-politics-of-beauty/. See also Dave
Hickey, *The Invisible Dragon: Essays on Beauty* (Chicago: University of
Chicago Press, 2012).

14. In his famed Symposium, Plato does everything but define beauty. It's
from Plato that we get the idea of beauty being a copy of something
else, of beauty's begetting power that roots itself in human desire.
Plato's more objective view of beauty described it in terms of copies and
archetypes, meaning the beauty we see and experience in this world
mimics the original form of beauty. This original form of beauty is
known as an archetype. The archetype of beauty lies somewhere out
there in the beyond. It transcends this world. See Plato and W. R. M.
Lamb, *Plato Volume III: Lysis, Symposium, Gorgias* (London: William
Heinemann, 1967), 203–12.

15. For Moses' perspective of beauty, I am using William Dyrness' study
on the seven Hebrew word groupings that convey the idea of *beauty*.
William Dyrness, "Aesthetics in the Old Testament: Beauty in
Context," *JETS* 28, no. 4 (December 1985), 421–32.

16. Christy Wampole, "Why Simone Weil Is the Patron Saint of
Anomalous Persons," *Aeon*, accessed December 2, 2021, https://aeon.co
/essays/why-simone-weil-is-the-patron-saint-of-anomalous-persons.

17. The Turf is a popular pub tucked between colleges at the University of
Oxford.

18. Psalm 104:1–2: "Praise the LORD, my soul. LORD my God, you are very
great; you are clothed with splendor and majesty. The LORD wraps himself
in light as with a garment; he stretches out the heavens like a tent." (NIV)

19. J. Lust, "A Gentle Breeze or a Roaring Thunderous Sound? Elijah at
Horeb: 1 Kings XIX 12," *Vetus Testamentum* 25, no. 1 (1975): 110–115,

accessed April 14, 2021, http://www.jstor.org/stable/1517376, 115. The article explores the Hebrew language used in this phrase and concludes that "a gentle whisper" does not articulate the Hebrew well at all. In fact, the more appropriate translation of this passage is, "a roaring and thunderous voice." See also Jeffrey Jay Niehaus, *God at Sinai: Covenant and Theophany in the Bible and Ancient Near East*, Studies in Old Testament Biblical Theology (Grand Rapids: Zondervan, 1995), 31–42, 248.

20. Simone Weil, *Gravity and Grace* (London: Routledge, 2002), 150–51.

21. The aesthetic intention of the adjective *tov* carries the idea of enjoyment and satisfaction in an object or person. The Septuagint, perhaps more accurately, uses the term *kalos*. *Kalos* is most often associated with beautiful, "pertaining to having acceptable characteristics or functioning in an agreeable manner, often with the focus on outward form or appearance." See Johannes Louw and Eugene A. Nida, *Greek-English Lexicon of the New Testament Based on Semantic Domains* (United Bible Societies, 1988). If you and I substitute the English "beautiful" for "good" throughout the Genesis 1 account of creation, we can see how beauty and vitality, or life, are so closely associated. "God called the dry land Earth, and the waters that were gathered together he called Seas. And God saw that it was beautiful" (Gen. 1:10 NIV). See also Paul Evdokimov, *The Art of the Icon: A Theology of Beauty* (Redondo Beach, CA: Oakwood Publications, 1990), 2–3.

22. I am referring to William Dyrness' work on beauty with the Old Testament context. Dyrness groups seven Hebrew roots that refer to beauty. See William Dyrness, "Aesthetics in the Old Testament." See also David Lyle Jeffrey, *In the Beauty of Holiness: Art and the Bible in Western Culture* (Grand Rapids: Eerdmans, 2017), 22–27.

23. Augustine, in his *City of God*, observed how humanity's chief sin was pride or the turning away from God and the turning to the self (the theological idea of *incurvatus in si*). See Augustine and Marcus Dods, *The City of God*, Modern Library ed. (New York: Modern Library, 1993), Book XII, Ch. Vi.

24. Psalm 50:2 (ESV).

25. Augustine, *Confessions* (Oxford: Oxford University Press, 1998), I. 1. Augustine wrote at great length about beauty. He used unity, equality, number, proportion, and order to describe beauty. See Burleigh and Augustine, "Of True Religion" in *Augustine: Earlier Writings*, ed. John S. Burleigh (Philadelphia: Westminster John Knox Press, 1953), 245, 252. See also 1.12, in which Augustine refers to God as "The supreme beauty, you give distinct form to all things and by your law impose order on everything."

26. G. Gabrielle Starr, *Feeling Beauty: The Neuroscience of Aesthetic Experience* (Cambridge, MA: The MIT Press, 2013), 66.

27. Martin Luther King Jr., *Strength to Love* (Minneapolis: Fortress Press, 1980), 91–92.

28. C. S. Lewis, *The Abolition of Man* (New York: Simon & Schuster, 1996), 27.

Chapter 3: Where Beauty Begins

1. See Acts 17:16–34. Keep in mind, Paul's engagement with the philosophers at Athens was provoked by their idolatry. Paul was greatly stirred in his spirit because of their devotion to idols rather than the Creator God.

2. In the Old Testament, one of the seven-word groupings for beauty relates to the beauty and glory of nations. Nations that rise up and in pride claim their glory for themselves, forgetting God as their source, will face destruction. A prime example of this in the Scriptures is Sodom and Gomorrah.

3. I use Christian love here in a deliberate way to distinguish Christian love from pagan or secular love. Kierkegaard makes this same distinction in his *Works of Love*, chapter 11, "You Shall Love Your Neighbour." See Søren Kierkegaard, *Works of Love* (New York: HarperPerennial, 2009).

4. William Wordsworth, "Intimations of Immortality from Recollections of Early Childhood" in *Poetical Works [of] Wordsworth; with Introductions and Notes* (London: Oxford University Press 1969), 462.

5. Richard Bauckham, *Who Is God? Key Moments of Biblical Revelation* (Grand Rapids: Baker Academic, 2020), 39–45. Here, Bauckham walks us through a wonderful discussion about God's Divine Name. Our modern translations of the Old Testament name God as "I Am" when

he talks to Moses through the burning bush. "I Am" conveys the idea that "God is self-subsistent and self-determining. He will be who he chooses to be." God allows himself to be addressed with a "name" because of his love for Israel. He *chooses* to reveal himself. And yet even when he reveals himself through the "I Am" phrase, his Divine Name remains a mystery to humanity. Richard Bauckham reminds that when God refers to himself as "I Am," he is giving Moses (and us) a clue to how he intends to act.

6. For more on how the Holy Spirit works as God's beautifying agent, see Patrick Sherry, *Spirit and Beauty: An Introduction to Theological Aesthetics* (London: SCM, 2002), 100–20.

7. See Bauckham, *Who Is God?*, 35–59. Here Bauckham helps us understand that when God reveals his name to Moses, the revelation itself is an act of love toward Moses. Even "YHWH" does not convey the full name of God, which remains a mystery to human beings. God does, however, reveal his character to us, which is bound up in the Hebrew word *chesed*, which means steadfast, love.

8. Richard Bauckham, *The Bible and Ecology: Rediscovering the Community of Creation* (Waco, TX: Baylor University Press, 2010), 20–25, 103–40.

9. For superb analysis of the anthropic cosmological principle, see Alister E. McGrath, *A Fine-Tuned Universe: The Quest for God in Science and Theology: The 2009 Gifford Lectures* (Louisville, KY: Westminster John Knox Press, 2009).

10. John D. Barrow and Frank J. Tipler, "Introduction" in *The Anthropic Cosmological Principle* (New York: Oxford University Press, 1986).

11. I'm not attempting to offer a God of gaps argument here. Though evidence of the validity of the "God hypothesis" for the creation of the universe has recently gained new traction with Stephen Meyer's bestseller, *Return of the God Hypothesis: Three Scientific Discoveries That Reveal the Mind Behind the Universe* (New York: HarperOne, 2021).

Chapter 4: The Life of Practical Romance

1. I am drawing here on Dallas Willard's definition of "life" he sets forth in his classic *The Spirit of the Disciplines*. See Dallas Willard,

The Spirit of the Disciplines: Understanding How God Changes Lives (San Francisco: HarperSanFrancisco, 1990), 56–57.

2. I'm indebted to my long-time friend Dr. Bernard Cadogan (DPhil, Oxford) for his insights into how the Hebrew languages fractures, showing in language what is happening in the relationship between God and human beings. Upon their expulsion from the garden, they set off as wanderers. Imagine the drift, from living in the wonder of God's presence within the Park of Delight to living apart from the glorious light of heaven.

3. H. W. F. Saggs, *Civilization before Greece and Rome* (New Haven, CT: Yale University Press, 1989), 267–73.

4. Ibid.

5. Martin E. Marty, "Introduction" in William James and Martin E. Marty, *The Varieties of Religious Experience: A Study in Human Nature* (New York: Penguin Books, 1982), xxi, 26–27.

6. Annie Dillard, *Teaching a Stone to Talk: Expeditions and Encounters* (New York: Harper Perennial), 88.

7. Religion will play a key role in defining any culture, as will the lack of religion or acknowledgment of the supernatural. See Roger Scruton, *Modern Culture* (London: Bloomsbury Continuum, 2019), 1–4. For a more psychological conception of culture see Peter Berger, *The Sacred Canopy* (New York: Anchor Books, 1990), 6–18.

8. Erich Auerbach, *Dante, Poet of the Secular World* (New York: New York Review Books, 2007), 11–19.

9. C. S. Lewis, *The Collected Letters of C. S. Lewis*, vol. 1 (San Francisco: HarperCollins, 2004), 176. A young man when he coined this word, Lewis was using it in his correspondence with Arthur Greeves to affirm his friend's hope "that something strange and wonderful ought to happen" in life. He was not necessarily using it as I am here, to describe God's awesome and terrible and beautiful holiness.

10. G. K. Chesterton, *Orthodoxy* (Garden City, NY: Image Books, 1959), 10–11.

Chapter 5: Beware of the Plastic People

1. Radu Bordeianu, "Maximus and Ecology: The Relevance of Maximus the Confessor's Theology of Creation for the Present Ecological Crisis,"

The Downside Review 127, no. 447 (April 2009): 103–126, accessed December 16, 2018, https://journals.sagepub.com/doi /10.1177/001258060912744702?icid=int.sj-abstract.similar-articles.2.

2. Hans Boersma, *Heavenly Participation: The Weaving of a Sacramental Tapestry* (Grand Rapids: Eerdmans, 2011), 118–19.

3. Richard Dawkins, *Unweaving the Rainbow: Science, Delusion and the Appetite for Wonder* (Boston: Mariner Books, 2000), 6–8.

4. Roger Scruton, *Modern Culture* (London: Bloomsbury Continuum, 2018), 2–12.

5. I'm indebted to my friend John Snyder for this notion. When I asked him what he thought the opposite of plastic was, he replied with one simple word: oak. He was right.

6. William Least Heat-Moon, *Blue Highways: A Journey into America* (Boston: Back Bay Books, 1999), 241.

7. "Suicide Rates Rising across the U.S.," CDC Online Newsroom, accessed September 15, 2019, https://www.cdc.gov/media/releases /2018/p0607-suicide-prevention.html#:~:text=Suicide%20rates%20 rose%20across%20the%20US%20from%201999%20to%202016 .&text=Suicide%20rates%20have%20been%20rising,or%20older%20 died%20by%20suicide. Perhaps this truth is most lucidly displayed in the number of people taking their own lives. Suicide rates, especially among young people, have increased across the United States—in some states, an increase as high as 58%—since 1999. Suicide is one of only three causes of death that are on the rise. See also "Depression, Anxiety Rising among U.S. College Students," *Reuters*, August 29, 2019, accessed September 2, 2021, https://www.reuters.com/article/us -health-mental-undergrads-idUSKCN1VJ25Z.

8. Wesley A. Kort, *C. S. Lewis Then and Now* (New York: Oxford University Press, 2001), 33–37.

9. Due to the progress in modern physics, philosophers prefer the term "physicalism." See Simon Blackburn, *The Oxford Dictionary of Philosophy*, (Oxford: Oxford University Press, 2016), 294. For a lively discussion that touches on many of the dominant voices in the New Atheism who espouse physicalism and reject the idea that science and theistic belief can coexist, see Stephen C. Meyer, *Return of the God*

Hypothesis: Three Scientific Discoveries That Reveal the Mind behind the Universe (New York: HarperOne, 2021), 17.

10. For more on the power of innovation over people, see C. S. Lewis, *The Abolition of Man* (New York: Simon & Schuster, 1996), 67–91.

11. Klaus Schwab, *The Fourth Industrial Revolution* (New York: Crown Business, 2017), 7–8. For a shorter synopsis of it, see "The Fourth Industrial Revolution: What It Means, How to Respond," World Economic Forum, accessed March 20, 2018, https://www.weforum .org/agenda/2016/01/the-fourth-industrial-revolution-what-it-means -and-how-to-respond/. For more on what this means for the world of religion, see "Globalization, Governance, and Norms," Berkley Center for Religion, Peace, & World Affairs, Georgetown University, accessed March 20, 2018, https://berkleycenter.georgetown.edu /forum/globalization-governance-and-norms. Schwab outlines humanity's progress since the first Industrial Revolution (1760–1840), which brought the advent of railroads and the steam engine and all they allowed humans to produce. The Second Industrial Revolution, from the late nineteenth century to the early twentieth century, brought the birth of electricity, assembly lines, and mass production. The Third Industrial Revolution, the digital revolution in the early 1960's, brought the boom in the computer world. Computers morphed from semiconductors and mainframes to personal computers.

12. World Economic Forum, "The Fourth Industrial Revolution," YouTube, https://www.youtube.com/watch?v=SCGV1tNBoeU.

13. For more, see Roger Scruton, *Beauty: A Very Short Introduction* (Oxford: Oxford University Press, 2011), 146.

14. Scruton, *Beauty*, 159, 147–61. See also Roger Scruton et al., "Beauty and Desecration," *City Journal*, accessed March 8, 2018, https://www .city-journal.org/html/beauty-and-desecration-13172.html. See also "Dr. Roger Scruton: Beauty and Desecration," Franciscan University of Steubenville, accessed February 24, 2021, https://www.youtube .com/watch?v=uIKoPCouhHc.

15. Laurie Fendrich, "Dave Hickey's Politics of Beauty," *CHE*, accessed March 11, 2021, https://www.chronicle.com/article/dave-hickeys

-politics-of-beauty/. See also *Dave Hickey, The Invisible Dragon: Essays on Beauty* (Chicago: University of Chicago Press, 2012).

16. Scruton, "Beauty and Desecration." See also Scruton, *Beauty*, 147–61. Art critic Roger Fry wrote a collection of essays between 1900–1920 titled *Vision and Design*. In it, he articulates the modern view of morality as it relates to art. He writes, "Art, then, is an expression and a stimulus of the imaginative life, which is separated from actual life by the absence of responsive action. Now this responsive action implies in actual life moral responsibility. In art we have no such moral responsibility—it presents a life freed from the binding necessities of our actual existence . . . Morality appreciates emotion by the standard of resultant action, art appreciates emotion in and for itself." The absence of moral responsibility rose to preeminence during the twentieth century, notably expressed in the aforementioned *Piss Christ* (1987), as well as works such as Ridgeway Bennett, *Reactive Armor* (semen, wax, vinyl, and resin on lutrador with aluminum studs, 1990) Sue Coe, *Rape, Bedford* (1983), and Barbara Kruger, *Untitled (It's our pleasure to disgust you)* (1991). See Jerry D. Meyer, "Profane and Sacred: Religious Imagery and Prophetic Expression in Postmodern Art," *Journal of the American Academy of Religion* 65, no. 1 (1997): 19–46, accessed May 13, 2021, https://www.jstor.org/stable/1465817. For more on Roger Fry's essays, see Roger Fry, *Vision and Design*, ed. J. B. Bullen (Mineola, NY: Dover Publications, 1998), 15, 19.

17. Robert Hughes, *The Shock of the New*, Rev. ed. (New York: Knopf, 1991), 149.

18. Ibid.

19. Ibid.

20. Scruton, *Beauty*, 157. Scruton summarizes the definition of *kitsch* made by Clement Greenberg's article, "Avant-Garde and Kitsch," which was published in the Partisan Review, 1939. See Clement Greenberg, *Art and Culture* (Boston: Beacon Press, 1981).

21. Ibid., 160.

22. Ibid., 161.

23. Ibid. Here Scruton quotes the poet Rilke from the "Archaic Torso of Apollo": "you must change your life." Such an admonition leads us to

realize that contemporary modern culture needs far more than surface aesthetics; we need beauty imbued with relational value and divine quality.

24. Scruton, "Beauty and Desecration."

25. Swift was announced by the cosmetic company Cover Girl as the face of a new generation on December 14, 2010. See "Taylor Swift Announced as the Face of New COVERGIRL Cosmetic Line, NatureLuxe," accessed September 13, 2021, https://www.prnewswire .com/news-releases/taylor-swift-announced-as-the-face-of-new -covergirl-cosmetic-line-natureluxe-111521939.html.

26. In our present age, many institutions, such as politics and even theology, are downstream of culture. If the culture deems that beauty begins with the unique self, then that is what many will believe.

27. "Quentin Tarantino: Violence Is the Best Way to Control an Audience" *Telegraph*, accessed March 8, 2018, https://www.telegraph .co.uk/culture/film/film-news/6975563/Quentin-Tarantino-violence -is-the-best-way-to-control-an-audience.html.

28. Iris Murdoch, *Existentialists and Mystics: Writings on Philosophy and Literature* (New York: Penguin Books, 1999), 290–91.

29. Erich Auerbach, *Dante, Poet of the Secular World* (New York: New York Review Books, 2007), 18–21. See also Erich Auerbach and Edward W. Said, *Mimesis: The Representation of Reality in Western Literature*, trans. Willard R. Trask, (Princeton: Princeton University Press, 2013), 170–202. It was at the height of this change that Dante burst onto the scene with a work of literature revolutionary in its day. Unlike ancient writers such as Homer, Dante wrote his timeless work from a mature medieval perspective, one that interpreted the world as a "unified culture which here rose above vulgar spiritualism" and "sprang from a sure, direct perception; it was perception that gave rise to the ideal . . . of the perfect, well-formed life devoted to the service of love." Dante's realism, as Erich Auerbach has so masterfully critiqued, was the early tremor of the modern consciousness.

30. Thomas F. Mathews, *The Clash of Gods: A Reinterpretation of Early Christian Art*, (Princeton: Princeton University Press, 2003), 6. Matthews puts this stunning religious displacement in perspective. He

observes that in one fell swoop, a nuanced visual language that had been used to express man's understanding of the cosmic order, help him grasp the cosmic forces beyond his control, and provide order for the seasons as well as his social life, abruptly ended.

31. Stephen Richard Turley, *Awakening Wonder: A Classical Guide to Truth, Goodness & Beauty* (Camp Hill, PA: Classical Academic Press, 2015), 9–13.

32. David Hume, *Selected Essays*, ed. Stephen Copley and Andrew Edgar (Oxford: Oxford University Press, 2008), 136–37.

33. Mark A. Noll, *Turning Points: Decisive Moments in the History of Christianity* (Grand Rapids: Baker Academic, 2012), 2. Here, Noll lists three core advantages to studying historical turning points in the history of Christianity. His third advantage is worth noting for our purposes: "Studying specific turning points also provides opportunity to interpret, to state more specifically why certain events, actions, or incidents may have marked an important fork in the road or signaled a new stage in the outworking of Christian history" (2).

34. Oliver O'Donovan, *Self, World, and Time*, vol. 1, Ethics as Theology: An Induction (Grand Rapids: Eerdmans, 2013), 116.

35. C. S. Lewis, "The Weight of Glory" in *The Weight of Glory* (New York: HarperOne, 2001), 31.

36. See "Introduction" in Charles Taylor, *A Secular Age* (Cambridge, MA: Belknap Press, 2007). Taylor also ends his tome with more discussion on the idea of what he calls fullness. I will be coming back to this idea several times. Taylor offers excellent insight here, though the concept is as old as Plato.

37. See Kevin J. Vanhoozer, *First Theology* (Downers Grove, IL: IVP Academic, 2002), 16–17, 23–25.

38. G. K. Chesterton, *St. Thomas Aquinas* (San Francisco: Ignatius Press, 2002).

39. Ibid.

40. Søren Kierkegaard, *The Sickness unto Death: A Christian Psychological Exposition for Edification and Awakening* (New York: Penguin Books, 1989), 47–49.

41. K.E. Kirk, *The Vision of God: The Christian Doctrine of the Summum Bonum* (New York: Harper & Row, 1966), 1.

Chapter 6: Walking the Path

1. C. S. Lewis, *Till We Have Faces: A Myth Retold* (San Francisco: HarperOne, 2017), 75.
2. C. S. Lewis, "Meditation in a Toolshed," *God in the Dock; Essays on Theology and Ethics* (Grand Rapids: Eerdmans, 1970), 212.

Chapter 7: The Adventure of Holy Wayfinding

1. G. K. Chesterton, *Orthodoxy* (Garden City, NY: Image Books, 1959), 67–80.
2. J.R.R. Tolkien, *The Hobbit: Or There and Back Again* (New York: Ballantine Books, 1984), 18. For some reason, I can half see C. S. Lewis joining old "Tollers" (that's what he called Tolkien) at The Eagle and Child pub and reading this chapter aloud and the two of them sharing a laugh at Bilbo's reticence for adventure. And that thought makes me happy. That is all.
3. "Ferdinand Magellan: How Did the Pacific Ocean Get Its Name and What Did This Portuguese Explorer Have to Do with It?" Royal Museums Greenwich, accessed April 5, 2021, https://www.rmg.co.uk /stories/topics/ferdinand-magellan.
4. J.R.R. Tolkien, *The Fellowship of the Ring* (New York, Ballantine Books, 1983), 171.
5. John Edward Huth, *The Lost Art of Finding Our Way* (Cambridge, MA: Belknap Press, 2015), 403.
6. Alexander Nehamas, *Nietzsche: Life as Literature* (Cambridge, MA: Harvard University Press, 1985), 66.
7. Augustine, *Confessions* (Oxford: Oxford University Press, 1998), I.
8. Ibid., V, xxvii.
9. Here, I am using a phrase I first read in a small and wonderful book titled *Intimacy with the Almighty*, by Charles Swindoll (Nashville: Thomas Nelson, 2000). I highly recommend this little work for those interested in deepening their Christian devotion.

10. Here I am borrowing from the now popular passage in Charles Taylor's *A Secular Age*. See Charles Taylor, "Introduction" in *A Secular Age* (Cambridge, MA: Belknap Press, 2007), 5.

11. 2 Corinthians 10:12: "We do not dare to classify or compare ourselves with some who commend themselves. When they measure themselves by themselves and compare themselves with themselves, they are not wise."

12. Galatians 1:10: "Am I now trying to win the approval of human beings, or of God? Or am I trying to please people? If I were still trying to please people, I would not be a servant of Christ."

13. Philippians 2:3: "Do nothing out of selfish ambition or vain conceit. Rather, in humility value others above yourselves."

Chapter 8: Stop Spectating, Start Participating

1. Andrea Cavagna et al., "Scale-Free Correlations in Starling Flocks," *Proceedings of the National Academy of Sciences* (June 12, 2010), http://www.pnas.org/content/early/2010/06/11/1005766107.abstract.

2. Ibid. No doubt you've seen a murmuration on a cold winter's day. You might look across a harvested cornfield and see a flock of starlings, hundreds of them, flying in one harmonious wave, back and forth and up into the sky. A murmuration is an unsolved phenomenon known as a scale-free correlation: "The change in the behavioral state of one animal affects and is affected by that of all other animals in the group, no matter how large the group is. Scale-free correlations provide each animal with an effective perception range much larger than the direct interindividual interaction range, thus enhancing global response to perturbations." For a view of a murmuration in Oxfordshire, see "Oxfordshire Starling Murmuration 'Fantastic Phenomenon'," *BBC News*, accessed January 18, 2022, https://www.bbc.com/news/av/uk-england-oxfordshire-35534081.

3. George Pattison describes the now-familiar results of the technological revolution as follows: "Destruction of tradition; the acceleration of change to a rate human beings cannot bear; rationalization; standardization; automatism; the subordination of the individual to the mass; the suppression of freedom and, indeed, of nature."

Though less publicized, it is a subtle shift in culture that impacts our interaction with beauty, muting it as we replace walks with virtual reality, video games, and social media. For more on this, see George Pattison, *Thinking about God in an Age of Technology* (New York: Oxford University Press, 2007), 52–53. For the creative or entrepreneur or artist, chapter nine of this volume will come in handy.

4. I am here referencing the act of the triune God creating not only the earth and the heavens and the animals, but also human beings represented by the first beings, Adam and Eve. The poetic rendering of the creation account in Genesis 1 (1:1–31), followed by the more detailed version in Genesis and augmented by a few of my favorite scenes in John Milton's *Paradise Lost*, show God the Father giving the Son freedom to create the world and mankind. The creation of Adam was an act consistent with Christ's own character, the love within the community of the Trinity. From love, he created mankind to love. In Genesis 2 (2:15–25), we find God and Adam discussing a helper suitable for Adam. God brings the animals before him and Adam names them all. But none is found suitable for Adam. Finally, after God causes Adam to sleep, he brings forth Eve from Adam's bosom. When Adam wakes up and sees the woman, he names her. She is "bone of my bone, flesh of my flesh." Immediately, we see that God intended human beings for fellowship with God, but also with his own kind, man for the woman, and the woman for man. Man was created to participate in the Park of Delight, enjoying the presence of God—communing with him. Again, participation. When pure spectating comes into the picture, it is with the serpent directing Eve to look upon the fruit that was pleasing to the eye.

5. George Sayer, *Jack: A Life of C. S. Lewis* (Wheaton, IL: Crossway Books, 1994), 416.

6. Ibid., 344.

Chapter 9: Soul Leadership

1. Charlotte M. Mason, *A Philosophy of Education* (Australia: Living Book Press, 2017), 56.

2. Georgia Wells, Jeff Horwitz, and Deepa Seetharaman, "Facebook

Knows Instagram Is Toxic for Teen Girls, Company Documents Show," *Wall Street Journal*, September 14, 2021, accessed September 15, 2021, https://www.wsj.com/articles/facebook-knows-instagram -is-toxic-for-teen-girls-company-documents-show-11631620739.

3. For more one what is referred to as "ordinate affections" see Plato and Robin Waterfield, *Republic*, Oxford World's Classics (Oxford: Oxford University Press, 2008), 402A. See also chapter 11, as Plato explains how warped minds form warped societies. Here, Plato describes the three areas of a person that drive their ambitions: intellectual, passionate, and desirous. A person's desire proves to be the strongest driver of the human being, as it is desire that drives us toward food, drink, and sex.

See also Jeffrey Henderson, "Aristotle, Nicomachean Ethics," *Loeb Classical Library*, accessed October 17, 2018, https://www.loebclassics .com/view/aristotle-nicomachean_ethics/1926/pb_LCL073.79.xml, 1104b., See also C. S. Lewis, *The Abolition of Man, or Reflections on Education with Special Reference to the Teaching of English in the Upper Forms of Schools*, (New York: Simon & Schuster, 1996), 29. See also Augustine and Marcus Dods, *The City of God*, Modern Library ed. (New York: Modern Library, 1993), 15.22.

4. For more on how we have done this as a culture, I recommend Lewis's *The Abolition of Man* (New York: Simon & Schuster, 1996). You may also want to use Michael Ward's excellent *After Humanity: A Guide to C. S. Lewis's The Abolition of Man* (Park Ridge, IL: Word on Fire Academic, 2021).

5. Plato's thoughts on the importance of cultural education are worth including here: "Isn't the prime importance of cultural education due to the fact that rhythm and harmony sink more deeply into the mind than anything else and affect it more powerfully than anything else and bring grace in their train? For someone who is given a correct education, their product is grace; but in the opposite situation it is inelegance. And isn't its importance due also to the fact that a proper cultural education would enable a person to be very quick at noticing defects and flaws in the construction or nature of things?" In other words, he'd find offensive things he ought to find

offensive. Fine things would be appreciated and enjoyed by him, and he'd accept them into his mind as nourishment and would therefore become truly good; even when young, however, and still incapable of rationally understanding why, he would rightly condemn and loathe contemptible things. And then the rational mind would be greeted like an old friend when it did arrive, because anyone with this upbringing would be more closely affiliated with rationality than anyone else. See Plato, *The Republic*, 4022.È.

6. Hannah Richardson, "Children Should Be Allowed to Get Bored, Expert Says," *BBC News*, accessed October 17, 2018, https://www.bbc.com/news/education-21895704.

7. "This Is Your Brain on Nature," *National Geographic Magazine*, last modified December 8, 2015, accessed October 17, 2018, https://www.nationalgeographic.com/magazine/2016/01/call-to-wild/.

8. Samuel Hall Young, *Alaska Days with John Muir* (New York: Fleming H. Revell Company, 1915), 204.

9. Mason, *A Philosophy of Education*, 1.

10. Charles Williams, "The Concept of Co-Inherence," St. Bonaventure University, accessed August 25, 2021, http://web.sbu.edu/friedsam/inklings/coinheretance.htm.

Chapter 10: Get Stoked

1. G. K. Chesterton, "A Ballade of an Anti-Puritan" in *The Collected Poems of G. K. Chesterton* (London: Methuen & Co. Ltd., 1933), 91–92.

2. Simone Weil, *Waiting for God*, (New York: Harper Perennial Modern Classics, 2009) 105.

3. Wendell Berry, *The Art of the Commonplace: The Agrarian Essays of Wendell Berry* (Washington, DC: Counterpoint, 2003), 61.

4. Sherry Turkle, *Alone Together: Why We Expect More from Technology and Less from Each Other* (New York: Basic Books, 2011), 1.

5. "VI. Quotation and Originality. Ralph Waldo Emerson. 1904. The Complete Works," accessed November 12, 2018, https://www.bartleby.com/90/0806.html.

6. Weil, *Waiting for God*, 103-104. In this extraordinary passage, Weil

recounts how the beauty of the world had a very important place in the lives of human beings. From Greece to China to India, the beauty of the world was primary to life. She also notes how much the Christian tradition emphasized love for the beauty of the world. This love indicated a relationship humans enjoyed with the physical world.

7. C. S. Lewis, *The Weight of Glory and Other Addresses* (San Francisco: HarperSanFrancisco, 2001), 155.

8. Ibid., 154.

9. Being famous with God is the crux behind Lewis's famous address "The Weight of Glory."

Chapter 11: A Haunting Clack-Clack

1. Warren Lewis, "Memoir of C. S. Lewis" in *Letters of C. S. Lewis* (London: Geoffrey Bles, LTD, 1966), 2.

2. Richard Bauckham, *Bible and Ecology: Rediscovering the Community of Creation* (Waco, TX: Baylor University Press, 2010), 12–18.

3. The Christian tradition has a long history of thinkers who view nature as a book from God—Thomas Aquinas, St. Augustine, Jonathan Edwards, John Ruskin, Simone Weil, and C. S. Lewis, among others.

4. "Thyrsis: A Monody, to Commemorate the Author's Friend, Arthur Hugh Clough by Matthew Arnold," text/html, Poetry Foundation, accessed October 8, 2018, https://www.poetryfoundation.org/poems/43608/thyrsis-a-monody-to-commemorate-the-authors-friend-arthur-hugh-clough.

5. Peter Davidson, *The Last of the Light: About Twilight* (London: Reaktion Books, 2015), 9.

6. Ibid.

7. Richard Muir, *Approaches to Landscape* (Basingstoke, England: Macmillan, 1999), 115–145. This statement might sound "poetic" but in fact it is true. Or at least it's suggested by Muir in his wonderful chapter titled "Landscapes of the Mind," in which he discusses, among other things, how two landscapes exist—the one we're standing on, beneath our feet, and the one we end up creating in our minds; it's our perception of the landscape that comes to us in our memories. That perception and memory give meaning to the landscape. It's a

remembered context; it possesses a familiarity that we sometimes feel in other places too. Why? Because perhaps we sense the same thing that is brought on by similar forms in the landscape—perhaps the hills or streets or mountains or the way the landscape interacts with the light of the land. Light is also a contributor to landscape, as it not only paints what we see, but also indicates weather and brings our senses into the context and memory.

8. Ibid., 118.

9. Jerome A. Miller, *In the Throe of Wonder: Intimations of the Sacred in a Post-Modern World* (Albany: SUNY Press, 1992), 4.

10. Patrick Sherry "Simone Weil on Beauty" in Richard H. Bell, *Simone Weil's Philosophy of Culture: Readings tToward a Divine Humanity* (Cambridge, MA: Cambridge University Press, 1993), 268. Sherry explains here how other great thinkers, such as Schiller, Baudelaire, and Kant, also found it difficult to define the concept of beauty.

11. Augustine "On True Religion" in Burleigh and Augustine, *Augustine: Earlier Writings*, ed. John S. Burleigh (Philadelphia: Westminster John Knox Press, 1953), 251–55.

12. David Bentley Hart, *The Experience of God: Being, Consciousness, Bliss* (New Haven: Yale University Press, 2013), 279–81.

13. The *numinous* is not just something for the religious. It surfaces in places such as the literary world as well." You might recall the famous scene in Lewis's *The Lion, the Witch and the Wardrobe* in which Mr. Beaver tells the Pevensie children that Aslan is on the move. Each child experiences a unique feeling at the mere sound of Aslan's name. Lewis, here, connects mystery and beauty in this scene to achieve terreauty—which, you might recall from an earlier chapter, is Lewis's coined term for combining terror and beauty. This is the numinous as work in his literature.

14. Hart, 24.

15. Ibid.

16. George MacDonald, "The Fantastic Imagination" in *The Complete Fairy Tales* (New York: Penguin Books, 1999), 9.

17. Davidson, *The Last of the Light,* 17.

Chapter 12: The Riches of Seeing

1. Kyle Gann, *No Such Thing as Silence: John Cage's 4'33"* (New Haven, CT: Yale University Press, 2011), 4.

2. Alex Ross, "Searching for Silence," *The New Yorker*, September 7, 2010, accessed September 15, 2021, https://www.newyorker.com/magazine/2010/10/04/searching-for-silence.

3. Gann, 11.

4. Charles Taylor, *A Secular Age* (Cambridge, MA: Belknap Press, 2007), 5.

5. Robert Macfarlane, *Landmarks* (London: Penguin Books, 2016), 5.

6. Writers and thinkers down through the ages have directed our attention to the phenomenon of questing for beauty. Plato observed beauty's begetting power; we encounter the beautiful, and rush to reproduce it. Beauty draws us by way of creating desire within us. See Plato, *The Symposium*. St. Augustine of Hippo observed how God stirs us with beauty, making us restless until we find our home in him. See Augustine, *Confessions*. C. S. Lewis in several of his writings noted how beauty prompted him with a desire to discover the place of its origin. See C. S. Lewis, *Till We Have Faces*, "The Weight of Glory," and *The Pilgrim's Regress*, for starters.

7. Josef Pieper, *Only the Lover Sings: Art and Contemplation* (San Francisco: Ignatius Press, 1990), 31–36.

8. Here is a handy little book I like to consult on matters of truth: Kevin J. Vanhoozer, J. P. Moreland, and R. Albert Mohler Jr, *Whatever Happened to Truth?* (Wheaton, IL: Crossway, 2005).

9. Tim Wu, "The Tyranny of Convenience," *The New York Times*, February 16, 2018, accessed September 15, 2021, https://www.nytimes.com/2018/02/16/opinion/sunday/tyranny-convenience.html.

10. Susan Sontag, *On Photography* (New York: Picador, 2001), 3.

11. Ibid.

12. Ibid.

13. Dr. Fred Craddock, *Craddock Stories*, (St. Louis: Chalice Press, 2001), 65. See also William P. Brown, *Sacred Sense: Discovering the Wonder of God's Word and World* (Grand Rapids: Eerdmans, 2015), 1.

14. Joseph J. Feeney, *The Playfulness of Gerard Manley Hopkins* (Burlington, VT: Routledge, 2008), 14.

15. John Ruskin, *The Works of John Ruskin*, vol. 5, E. T. Cook and Alexander Wedderburn, eds. (New York: Longmans, Green & Co., 1904), 211.

16. Josef Pieper, *Leisure: The Basis of Culture* (San Francisco: Ignatius Press, 2009), 68.

Chapter 13: Make Beautiful Spaces

1. No, I'm not promoting pantheism. I'm merely connecting my vivid boyhood memory of a tree I used to lie under as the acorns fell. I remember thinking thoughts about God beneath that tree at a very young age.

2. G. Gabrielle Starr, *Feeling Beauty: The Neuroscience of Aesthetic Experience* (Cambridge, MA: MIT Press, 2013), 80–81. Starr relates our experience of feeling beauty to the nurturing of meaning in our lives. I love this connection of beauty to meaning. There are others who also connect the making of meaning in our lives to how we engage with the natural world or landscape. See Belden C. Lane, *Landscapes of the Sacred: Geography and Narrative in American Spirituality* (Baltimore, MD: Johns Hopkins University Press, 2002), 131.

3. In Genesis 2:15–25, when God places Adam and Eve in the garden (literally called "garden of delight"), one of his directives is "keep." This word carries rich meaning, with one being "to preserve" in the same way a gardener preserves the garden, beautifying it. A beautiful garden is one in which the gardener works to preserve it both practically and aesthetically.

4. Anne Whiston Spirn, *The Language of Landscape* (New Haven: Yale University Press, 1998), 15, 21.

5. Ibid., 133. Spirn directs our attention to the meaning of the word "context." It comes from the Latin "*contexere*," meaning "to weave." Spirn writes, "Context weaves pattern of events, materials, forms and spaces." It is through the weaving together, through context that objects or materials acquire meaning. A rock by itself might be round, gray, wet, dry, large, or small. But a stack of rocks signifies a marker for hikers. The "sarsen" stones of Stonehenge signify meaning and create a context for religious rituals, perhaps.

6. Lane, *Landscapes of the Sacred*, 18.

7. Ibid., 18–19.

8. Ibid., 131.

9. Edwyn Bevan, *Symbolism and Belief* (Andesite Press, 2008), 276.

10. Ibid.

11. Ibid., 277.

12. It is one thing to say that beauty and the sublime are two separate qualities, thus bifurcating the related terms due to their lexical value. But it is difficult to make this contention in light of Hume and Kant's notion of beauty containing nothing, meaning that it does not possess any *ganz andere* element such as the *numinous*. This Kantian conception of subjective beauty mutes the notion of the *numinous* within an object of beauty and, therefore, negates any higher (i.e., divine) quality governing the form. See "*De Vera Religione*" in Augustine and John Henderson Seaforth. Burleigh, *Earlier Writings* (Philadelphia: Westminster, 1979), xxi, 57.

13. Anthony O'Hear, *Beyond Evolution: Human Nature and the Limits of Evolutionary Explanation* (Oxford: Oxford University Press, 1999), 187.

14. Jonathan Hale, *The Old Way of Seeing: How Architecture Lost Its Magic (and How to Get It Back)* (Boston: Houghton Mifflin, 1996), 2

15. Ibid., 2–5.

16. Ibid., 3–8, 26, 67–72.

17. "Our Story," *Manchester Bidwell Corporation*, accessed September 14, 2021, https://www.manchesterbidwell.org/our-story.

18. Ibid.

19. "Our Philosophy," *Manchester Bidwell Corporation*, accessed August 3, 2021, https://www.manchesterbidwell.org/our-philosophy.

Chapter 14: Shout with Me the Sound of Lightness

1. The girls named our first house in Charlotte, North Carolina, "The Second Acre." It was our first house upon returning from living in Oxford, England, for two years. The Second Acre yard was filled with tall Carolina pines, and an acre field stretched out behind them.

2. John O'Donohue, *Beauty: The Invisible Embrace* (New York: Harper Perennial, 2005), 117.

3. Giorgio de Santillana, *Age of Adventure: The Renaissance Philosophers* (New York: Mentor Press, 1956), 75.

4. Karl Barth, qtd. in Richard Viladesau, *Theological Aesthetics: God in Imagination, Beauty, and Art* (New York: Oxford University Press, 2012), 26.

5. In the Scriptures, we often see joy expressed through light imagery (Prov. 16:15; Ps. 89:15; Is. 60:1–15).

6. See Deuteronomy 31:17–18, 32:20; Ezekiel 39:23–24; Micah 3:4; Isaiah 59:2; Psalm 30:7; Jeremiah 33:5; et al. See also Jeffrey Jay Niehaus, *God at Sinai: Covenant and Theophany in the Bible and Ancient Near East* (Grand Rapids: Zondervan, 1995), 311–15.

7. Ibid., 312.

8. Robert Davidson, *The Vitality of Worship: A Commentary on the Book of Psalms* (Grand Rapids: Eerdmans, 1998), 103.

9. 1 Samuel 14:27.

10. J.R.R. Tolkien, Verlyn Flieger, and Douglas A. Anderson, *Tolkien on Fairy-Stories*, (London: HarperCollins, 2014), 78.

11. Wesley A. Kort, *C. S. Lewis Then and Now* (New York: Oxford University Press, 2001), 124.

Chapter 15: Reclaiming Our Wonder

1. C. S. Lewis, *Miracles: A Preliminary Study* (San Francisco: HarperSanFrancisco, 2001), 150.

2. Ibid.

3. C. S. Lewis, *The Last Battle* (New York: Macmillan, 1970), 155–171. The "further up and further in" theme runs through the ending of Lewis's final installment of the Chronicles of Narnia. The idea expressed is one of a person moving further into God's unending joy.

4. My paraphrase.

5. *Kohlenberger/Mounce Concise Hebrew-Aramaic Dictionary of the Old Testament*, Accordance Bible Software, electronic ed., n.p.

6. *New Bible Commentary*, ed. D. A. Carson et al., Accordance Bible Software, electronic ed., 117.

7. Jonathan Edwards, *Works of Jonathan Edwards: Volume One* (Carlisle: The Banner of Truth Trust, 1995), 116 (emphasis mine).

8. *Kohlenberger/Mounce Concise Hebrew-Aramaic Dictionary of the Old Testament*, Accordance Bible Software, electronic ed., n.p.

9. Richard Bauckham, *Gospel of Glory: Major Themes in Johannine Theology* (Grand Rapids: Baker Academic, 2015), 50.

10. Richard Viladesau, *Theological Aesthetics* (Oxford: Oxford University Press, 2012), 26. Viladesau attributes this notion (that sufficiency manifests itself in man not lacking anything) to Karl Barth.

11. Ibid.

12. My paraphrase.

13. Bauckham explains this idea in two sources. For a more in-depth explanation, see Bauckham, *Gospel of Glory*, 46–55. See also Richard Bauckham, *Who Is God? Key Moments of Biblical Revelation* (Grand Rapids: Baker Academic, 2020), 61–71.

14. Edwards, *Works of Jonathan Edwards: Volume One*, xiii.

15. Ibid. (emphasis mine).

16. Ibid.

17. Zechariah 9:9 NLT.

18. Eugene H. Peterson, *A Long Obedience in the Same Direction: Discipleship in an Instant Society* (Downers Grove, IL: IVP Books, 2000), 17.

19. Henry Chadwick, *Augustine of Hippo: A Life* (Oxford: Oxford Univ. Press, 2010), 27–29.

Chapter 16: A Rebellion They Won't Forget

1. The Johannine description of worldliness seems *apropos* here. First John 2:15–17 instructs readers not to love the "world" (*kosmos*). See Mounce, *Mounce Concise Greek-English Dictionary of the New Testament*, n.p., "*kosmos.*" *Kosmos*, in this particular passage, is best defined as "the present order of things." The passage then lists the ways the world stands at enmity with God: the desires of the flesh or the cravings associated with the fallen human state, the desires of the eyes or those aesthetically pleasing objects which tempt and arouse a desire through their external show (this would also include "the love of beauty divorced from the love of goodness") and, finally, the pride of life or those external material objects or circumstances that may incite

human arrogance, such as wealth, status, etc. See John R. W. Stott, *The Letters of John: An Introduction and Commentary* (Downers Grove: InterVarsity Press, 1988), 104.

2. Charles Caleb Colton, *Lacon, or, Many Things in a Few Words: Addressed to Those Who Think* (New York: S. Marks, 1824), 114.

3. I am referencing a phrase used by the comedian Brian Regan. See "Brian Regan: I Walked on the Moon Video Download," accessed August 18, 2021, https://brianregan.shop.musictoday.com/product /3BDD02.

4. William Zinsser, *The Writer Who Stayed* (Philadelphia: Paul Dry Books, 2012), 75.

5. A. W. Tozer, "Introduction" in *The Christian Book of Mystical Verse: A Collection of Poems, Hymns, and Prayers for Devotional Reading* (Chicago: Moody Publishers, 2016), 16.

6. Richard Bauckham, "The New Age Theology of Matthew Fox: A Christian Theological Response," 125. *BiblicalStudies.Org.Uk*, accessed January 11, 2019, https://biblicalstudies.org.uk/articles.php

7. Lewis Hyde, *The Gift: Creativity and the Artist in the Modern World* (New York: Vintage Books, 2007), 189.

8. Teresa of Avila, qtd. in Bruce A. Demarest, *Satisfy Your Soul: Restoring the Heart of Christian Spirituality* (Colorado Springs: Navpress, 1999), 286. See also Teresa of Avila, *Let Nothing Disturb You*, compiled by John Kirvan (Notre Dame: Ave Maria, 1996), 180–81.

9. C. S. Lewis, Till We Have Faces: A Myth Retold (San Diego, New York, London: A Harvest Book, Harcourt Brace & Company, 2012), 75.

10. C. S. Lewis, "No Beauty We Could Desire," in *Poems* (New York: Harcourt Brace Jovanovich, 1977), 124.

11. C. S. Lewis, *Letters to Malcolm, Chiefly on Prayer* (San Francisco: HarperOne, 2017), 123.

12. I love how Frederick Buechner talks about keeping kairos time in life. By kairos time, he means the quality of time, not the quantity of time. He describes how art and music measure space and time in this world. And he encourages us to stop, look, and listen to these beautiful moments in time. For more on this, see his book, *The Remarkable Ordinary.*

13. 1 John 2:15–17.

14. This idea of rebuking the culture I discovered in G. K. Chesterton's work *St. Francis of Assisi*. Chesterton does not mince his words. He observes how every generation needs a band of revolutionaries who will bear witness to the truth of God and rebuke the world as St. Francis did during his life. He calls the Christian an incongruent person; a counter-cultural member of heaven. I love Chesterton's language, and how it charges me to not be afraid to walk my own path and live as a child of heaven.

15. Roland Delattre, *Beauty and Sensibility in the Thought of Jonathan Edwards: An Essay in Aesthetics and Theological Ethics* (New Haven: Yale University Press, 1968), 3–5.

A New Beginning: Recapturing Our Wonder

1. I am borrowing Lewis's now ubiquitous phrase from *The Last Battle*. C. S. Lewis, *The Last Battle* (New York: Macmillan, 1970), 158–84.